UGINF #40

PRINCIPAL DIMENSIONS

LENGTH OVER ALL	261' 0"
LENGTH BET. PERPS.	251' 0"
BEAM, MOULDED	43' 6"
DEPTH, MOULDED	28' 2"

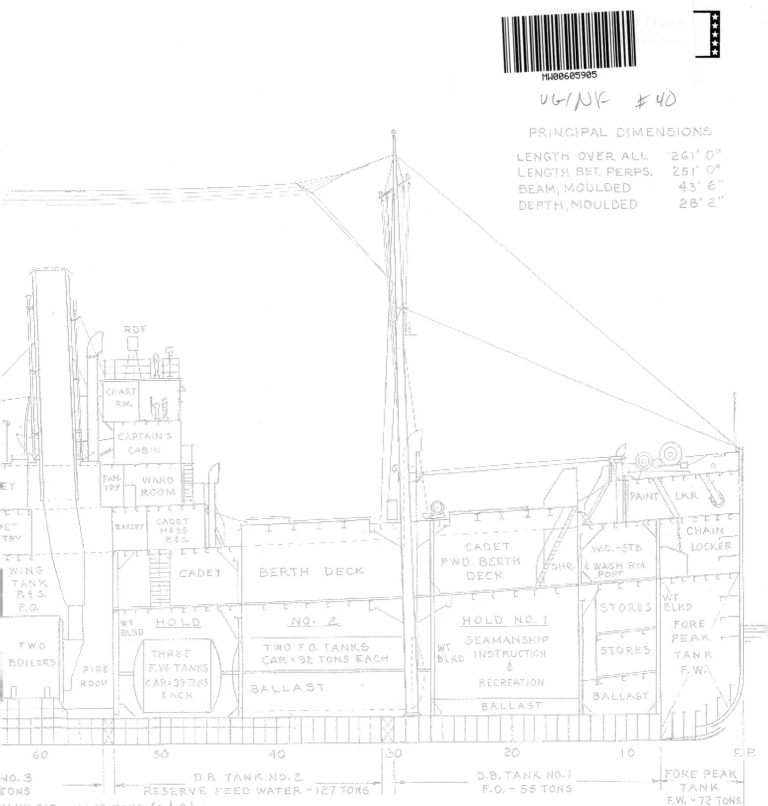

RDF

CHART RM

CAPTAIN'S CABIN

PAN-TRY

WARD ROOM

BAKERY

CADET M&SS P.&S.

CADET

BERTH DECK

CADET FWD BERTH DECK

PAINT LKR

CHAIN LOCKER

WC-STB SHR. & WASH RM PORT

STORES

WT BLKD

WING TANK P.&S. F.O.

TWO BOILERS

FIRE ROOM

WT BLKD

HOLD

THREE F.W. TANKS CAP.= 39 TONS EACH

NO. 2

TWO F.O. TANKS CAP.= 92 TONS EACH

BALLAST

HOLD NO. 1

WT BLKD

SEAMANSHIP INSTRUCTION & RECREATION

BALLAST

STORES

BALLAST

FORE PEAK TANK F.W.

60   50   40   30   20   10   F.P.

NO. 3
TONS

D.B. TANK NO. 2
RESERVE FEED WATER - 127 TONS

D.B. TANK NO. 1
F.O. - 55 TONS

FORE PEAK TANK
F.W. - 72 TONS

TANK CAP - 111.65 TONS (P.& S.)

51'

D PROFILE

<u>U.S.S. CALIFORNIA STATE</u>

R. Aker 1-12-96

To Bob Flynn:

Many thanks for
giving us today. Best of
luck.

Walt Kuffler
San Francisco

THE TRACK of the GOLDEN BEAR

THE CALIFORNIA MARITIME ACADEMY SCHOOLSHIPS

CAPT. WALTER W. JAFFEE

Copyright © 1996 by Walter W. Jaffee
Published by The Glencannon Press
P.O. Box 341, Palo Alto, CA 94302

First Edition

Library of Congress Catalog Card Number:
96-77093

ISBN 0-9637586-8-3

The photo on the front dustjacket is by George Bonawit.

The photos on the back dustjacket are from:
Jamestown — U.S. Naval Historical Center
California State, Golden State — California
                              Maritime Academy
Golden Bear I — Ralph Swany
Golden Bear II — California Maritime
                              Academy
Golden Bear III — California Maritime
                              Academy

Art director: S.L. Hecht

Dedication

To the alumni who keep alive the spirit of the ships,
To the midshipmen who infuse each ship with new life,
To the parents, whose hopes and dreams rest with the midshipmen,
To the faculty and staff who make it all work.

By the same author:

The Last Mission Tanker
The Last Victory, the story of the *SS Lane Victory*
The Last Liberty, the biography of the *SS Jeremiah O'Brien*
Appointment in Normandy

Of sea-captains, young or old, and the
    mates, and of all intrepid sailors,
Of the few, very choice, taciturn, whom
    fate can never surprise nor death
    dismay . . .
                Walt Whitman

ACKNOWLEDGEMENTS

Thanks to all of you who were kind enough to grant an interview and share your memories of cadet life aboard the *California State*, the *Golden State* and the *Golden Bears*. You are too numerous to mention, but you'll find your names throughout the text.

A special thanks to those who were willing to trust me with their memorabilia and photographs: Raymond Aker, John Athanson, Alvin Gregory, Harold Huycke, Rod Marshall and Ralph Swany. And to Charlie L. Bonham, Vice President, External Affairs, California Maritime Academy, for helping gather some of the history and data.

I'm also grateful to Ray Aker, Alan Dougall, Harold Huycke and Roger Putnam for reading and editing portions of the manuscript.

Last, but not least, a heartfelt thanks to my publisher for giving so unstintingly of her time and seeing the book through to its finished form.

Contents

INTRODUCTION

This book began with a conversation between Mark Goldberg (author of *The Hog Islanders, Caviar and Cargo* and others) and myself a few years ago. I was teaching at CMA and Mark said, "You know, one of us should write a book about the Cal Maritime schoolships. Something quick and simple, do a couple of weeks of research, put it together and publish it."

Mark went on with his *magnum opus,* chronicling the history of every ship built in the United States since the beginning of the twentieth century. I think he's on volume five or six now. But the idea settled in the back of my mind. I wanted to work on a novel, there was a history of the steam schooners to be written, and there was, at the time, a possibility of going on the *Jeremiah O'Brien* to Normandy for the 50th Anniversary of the D-Day landings and a book about that. But every time I started something my subconscious would say, "What about the schoolships?"

Came the day when the subconscious pushed the idea up to the front, a title suggested itself and the next thing I knew I was at the CMA library going through old yearbooks, photographs and records. The more I read, the greater the fascination. But "Something quick and simple? . . . a couple of weeks of research?" Hah! That was three years ago. It hasn't been quick, it's not simple, but it finally is published.

In telling the history of the schoolships I've tried to let those who lived the story tell it as much as possible. They were there. Their words convey what happened far more effectively than anyone else ever could. You'll find the viewpoints of deck and engine students, men and women, captains and instructors, the full spectrum of the Cal Maritime experience. There may not be some of everything in each chapter but I hope the book, taken as a whole, will provide a panorama of the complete experience, something like the old photographs of Gold Rush San Francisco which, when placed side-by-side, presented a great vista of the city and its abandoned sailing ships.

A few words of explanation: 1) This is not a yearbook. You won't find the name of every graduate of every class in these pages. There have been some 3,000 of them, far too many to mention. Those whose names are here were chosen because they were the most articulate or willing to talk or available. They spoke for their own experiences, but also as a voice of their class or era. To read their reminiscences is to share experiences common to most who went through the training. 2) There is a certain beauty and honesty in the spoken language; in the cadence and manner in which people converse. I believe in the importance of the spoken word. The way people put their words together, the idioms they use, their expressions, are as unique as their photographs. The searches for an appropriate word and the inevitable repetitions natural to an unscripted interview have been deleted, of course, but the basic syntax, even the occasional grammatical lapse, provide the "flavor" and "color" that make language delightful to hear. It would be a real loss to dilute the variegated voices into an undistinctive and uniform beige tone. Spoken errors of fact, if significant, are footnoted. Otherwise the language is preserved "as spoken." 3) This story is about the training ships. For that reason the history of the school, the administrations and the campuses are touched on briefly and only in the context of the ships. Perhaps some future author will tell the story of the school. My goal is to bring you aboard so that you can remember or share what it was like to be a cadet-midshipman on the California Nautical School/Maritime Academy schoolships.

It started in the 1870s with a man-of-war, a sloop named *Jamestown*. Part of the daily routine was drilling with cutlasses and manning 32-pounders . . .

Walter W. Jaffee
Menlo Park, California
June 1996

PART I

THE NINETEENTH CENTURY

CHAPTER 1

THE FIRST CALIFORNIA NAUTICAL SCHOOL

San Francisco in 1870 was only a few years removed from her notorious history, suddenly gone from being merely a lawless transit stop on the way to the gold fields to a major seaport and burgeoning city. But in her citizens' eyes she had become the dazzling metropolis of the Pacific Coast. "The Paris of the West," they called her, ignoring the less-than-Parisian realities of muddy roads climbing shack-lined hills. Nevertheless, settling into an era of law, order and concern for the well-being of its newly-respectable citizens, San Francisco was quickly replacing old values. From the wild, wicked boomtown of the Barbary Coast and vigilante law, the city now aspired to dignity with substantial buildings, the beginnings of a cultural life and the development of an educational system. In the eyes of the rest of the West, San Francisco was a seat of social progress.

But under her fragile veneer of pretensions and aspirations, San Francisco was only a step away from her raffish past. As the primary seaport of the West Coast, her streets were filled with immigrants, get-rich-quick artists and sailors of a score of nations. These seafarers lurched onto shore, working their way along streets whose foundations were made of the hulls of ships abandoned a decade earlier, and fell back into newer vessels bound for the distant reaches of the globe. The city fathers began to consider the necessity of having professionally-trained seafarers available to the merchant marine. Shanghaied drunks from the saloons of Pacific Street were not in keeping with the city's new-found image.

Another of the myriad problems and responsibilities facing San Francisco's citizens was its youth. Among them were many orphans and children coming from impoverished backgrounds. The equivalent of modern delinquents, they were a concern to those laying the foundations of the new city.

The *Daily Alta California*, November 28, 1875:

Our city is now the abode of not less than a thousand desperate boys,

3

who are constantly engaged in perpetrating every species of crime from petit larceny to murder. A record of the last month presents a catalogue of terrible crimes, causing the nerves to thrill and the blood to run cold. No person is safe after nightfall, particularly in more secluded portions of the city. Our Police Department furnishes very little security or protection against these constant outrages.

One of the more vocal groups interested in the welfare of the underprivileged youth of the city was the Mechanics' Deliberative Assembly. Consisting of 100 artisans, artists, teachers, lawyers, ministers, professors, physicians, merchants, editors and mechanics, the organization loudly decried earlier attempts at reform. First among their targets was the "Industrial School."

> ## The truth is, that the Industrial School ... has been a nursery of vice and crime from the beginning.

The *Daily Alta California*, November 28, 1875:

This institution was established May 17th, 1859. Since its establishment 1504 boys and 366 girls have been sent there. The whole cost of sustaining the institution, exclusive of the products from every source, has been $524,146.67, being an average of about $33,000 per annum or $280 per year for each inmate of the institution. During the sixteen years the institution has been in operation, there is recorded evidence of only nine persons having been thoroughly reformed, and no evidence whatever of any other positive benefit having been conferred upon any of them by the use of trades or otherwise.

In the last report for 1875, the Superintendent, D. C. Woods, makes the statement that "It is to be regretted that, from time to time, boys are committed to the School who seem to have made up their minds deliberately to lead a life of dishonesty, and who may be classed as criminals in every sense of the word, with whom the mild discipline of the School is not vigorous enough to contend successfully, and whose reformation must be left for other methods. . . ."

The truth is, that the Industrial School, as organized and managed, has been a nursery of vice and crime from the beginning. The adepts in vice and crime were there to educate those who were comparatively innocent in the mysteries of their craft.

An apprenticeship of six months or more under such tuition would qualify all to enter upon the career of crime with a zest, and such is the record which the Industrial School exhibits.

A secondary target of the Mechanics' Deliberative Assembly was the House of Correction, a reform school. The article continues:

This will be necessarily a second edition of the Industrial School. Its inmates are obtained in the same way. They are criminals or quasi criminals before they reach the institution. They are demoralized, debauched and degraded before they enter. Before they can make any progress toward the plane of virtue, *they must unlearn all they have learned in vicious habits.*

It occurred to the Mechanics' Assembly that both goals, eliminating the ineffective "corrective" institutions and creating a source of professional merchant marine officers, might be accomplished at the same time, through the use of a nautical school with a training ship. There were precedents. The nautical schoolship concept had existed in England for many years. On the East Coast, the training ship *St. Mary's,* operated jointly by the Board of Education of the State of New York and the New York City Chamber of Commerce, had for years successfully supplied seamen, officers and engineers to the Navy and the merchant marine. If New York could do it, certainly San Francisco could.

The idea was first suggested in a meeting of the Mechanics' Deliberative Assembly by General A. M. Winn in late 1873. It generated enough enthusiasm to carry the idea to the State Legislature where, on March 16, 1874, the Legislature "authorized the Board of Supervisors of the City and County of San Francisco to establish and maintain a training ship." The purpose of the schoolship was to "instruct in Nautical Science, boys under the age of eighteen years who had been sentenced for punishment by the Municipal Court and the Police Court for committing a misdemeanor."[1]

From the California Legislature, the concept worked its way eastward to the United States Congress. There, the establishment of State Nautical Schools was authorized with the California Nautical School specifically being created on July 20, 1874. Included in the federal legislation was the instruction that the "Secretary of the Navy [is] to furnish to several states a suitable training ship with equipment for the benefit of a nautical school for the instruction of youths in navigation, seamanship, marine engineering, ship construction, etc."

It seemed California could have a training ship merely for the asking. A committee from the Mechanics' Deliberative Assembly appeared before the San Francisco Board of Supervisors to propose that the city get a training ship from the federal government and establish a nautical training school. A full-rigged ship, the *Jamestown*, was located.[2] Her captain, Commander Glass, was in favor of the idea and willing to stay on as captain of the training ship. The Board of Supervisors asked the Governor to approach the Secretary of the Navy to designate the *Jamestown* as California's training ship.

The purpose of the schoolship was to "instruct in Nautical Science. . ."

Then, on November 22, 1875 it suddenly appeared that everything was lost. The original legislation written by Congress specifically stated that government vessels could not be used by "persons sentenced to or received at, such schools as a punishment or commutation of punishment for crime."[3] The San Francisco Board of Supervisors reversed itself and recommended to the State that they not ask for a training ship.

This caused consternation on the part of the Mechanics' Assembly and other

---

[1] *Daily Alta California*, March 16, 1874.
[2] By definition a full-rigged ship is a square-rigged ship of three or more masts, square-rigged on all masts.
[3] The Supreme Court later declared this in conflict with the law of Congress. *Daily Alta California* April 16, 1877.

interested citizens. The *Daily Alta California* of November 28, 1875 responded with its usual flowery prose:

> Such extraordinary inconsistency and self stultification is rarely to be met with in individual action alone, but that respectable representatives of the interests of a great city, after having repeatedly and solemnly pledged themselves by formal legislation in favor of an important public measure, which had repeatedly received the indorsement of

"The training ship will remove 250 boys at once from the influence of 'hoodlumism.'"

> their constituents, in every available form, should thus repudiate their own action and the wishes of their constituents, is quite surprising.
>
> The training ship will remove 250 boys at once from the influence of "hoodlumism," and not only preserve them from its contaminating and destroying influences, but will educate them properly, and thus qualify them for useful, virtuous and intelligent citizenship. Prevention is the only effective remedy.

It was an inspired tactic. Shifting the emphasis of the project from punishment to prevention won over the Chamber of Commerce which went on record in support of the issue and offered to take part in the management of the ship.

> . . . the Chamber of Commerce of San Francisco, after due consideration of the whole subject, is impressed with the importance of establishing a training ship, and believes that in this way great benefit can be secured for the city and her commerce at slight cost, therefore
>
> Resolved, That the members of the Legislature from San Francisco are hereby requested to introduce and urge the passage by the Legislature of an amendatory Act, which has been prepared by the Judiciary Committee of the Board of Supervisors, and which will, it is believed, remove all obstacles in the way of establishing and managing successfully the Training Ship.
>
> Resolved, That the Legislature as a body is hereby requested to take action on this subject with as much promptness as is consistent with legislative requirements, in order to permit the establishment of the Training Ship with as little delay as possible.
>
> Resolved, That his Excellency the Governor of the State is respectfully requested to take such action as may be necessary on his part, to secure for the city the United States Navy ship Jamestown and the services of the officers detailed for duty on board that vessel.

That carried the day.

Daily Alta California, February 11, 1876:

> The bill authorizing the city and county of San Francisco to accept a training ship from the Federal Government and providing for its management, having passed both Houses

of the Legislature, only needs the Governor's approval to become a law. Governor Irwin will not hesitate to approve such a commendable and beneficial measure. It now remains for the Mayor and Board of Supervisors to lose no time in having the Jamestown afloat in the harbor of San Francisco and to have her forecastle filled with boys, thereby putting the plan into practical effect.

The legislative stumbling blocks overcome, plans were made for the actual operation of the ship. A Training Ship Committee was created on the San Francisco Board of Supervisors. The Committee set salaries for the ship's crew at the following monthly rates:

Commanding Officer	$165
Executive Officer	$65
Navigating Officer	$45
Instructor in Seamanship	$35
Surgeon	$40
General Storekeeper	$50
Steward	$30
Master-at-Arms	$50
Ship's Corporal	$25
Ship's Cook	$35
Boatswain's Mate	$30
Gunner's Mate	$30
Carpenter's Mate	$35
Quartermaster (2) @ $30	$60
Coxswain	$30
Seamen (4) @ $25	$100
Total	$825

Lieutenant Commander Glass, USN, was appointed by the Secretary of the Navy to act as commanding officer. All officers and crew were required to act as instructors.

Requirements for admission were set. Boys had to be between the ages of fourteen and eighteen and have an aptitude for sea life. Application had to be made in writing by the student's parents or guardian. Before entering each boy was subjected to a thorough physical examination and any boy showing signs of disease or physical unfitness for life at sea would be rejected.

An entrance fee of $25 was charged to cover the cost of uniforms, hammock, bedding and text books. In addition there was a monthly charge of $15, payable in advance. The Board of Supervisors agreed to waive the fees in the event of poverty but the fees would remain as

An entrance fee of $25 was charged to cover the cost of uniforms, hammock, bedding and text books.

a charge against the student to be paid out of advance wages after going to sea. Enrollment was for a period of two years. In addition to studies and drills, all students were required to keep the ship and her rigging in good order.

Given the students' background, discipline was a primary concern. Commander Glass was authorized to order a summary Court-martial when "necessary for the trial of offenses deserving a more serious punishment than he is empowered to inflict." Otherwise, punishment would consist of reduction in rank, confinement with or without irons or solitary confinement on bread and water. The Training Ship Committee would hear appeals of anyone considering himself unjustly treated. Milder punishments included extra police duties, extra drills or duties aloft, deprivation of liberty on shore and confinement for a few

The "great guns" on the Jamestown *included eighteen 32-pounders. The drawing depicts such a gun with its equipment. Illustration by Gordon Grant from* The Book of Old Ships.

hours at a time. Cases of misconduct would be treated by discharge with more serious cases referred to the Board of Supervisors.

Visitors to the ship were prohibited unless they had a permit from the Training Ship Committee or the commanding officer. Boys would be allowed shore liberty once every two weeks providing they did not stay out overnight.

As to the studies, they included "all branches of seamanship," including knotting and splicing ropes, fitting, rigging, cutting and repairing sails, reefing, furling and bending sails, handling boats under sail or oars, boxing the compass, steering a ship and heaving the lead and log. Instruction in gunnery included handling and working "great guns," cutlass exercise, and drills with small arms. Thorough instruction in practical navigation was considered essential. This included finding a ship's position on a chart, plotting courses and ordinary "day's work."[4]

Instruction in English was to include reading, writing, elementary geography and arithmetic. Advanced classes included history, grammar and composition, higher mathematics and other studies "appertaining to a sound English education." Sundays were set aside for reading and moral instruction.

Examinations were to be held semiannually. Boys would then be transferred to the merchant service or men-of-war to finish their training. Those who showed a high degree of intelligence and aptitude for sea life would be retained on board the *Jamestown* as members of an advanced class and trained in the higher branches of seamanship and navigation. In other words, the ship had two curricula: training some boys to send to sea for further training as cadets and others to continue studies on board until they were fit to serve as officers on merchant vessels.

Part of the program included ensuring that the ship itself was well-manned with graduates. Whenever boys were found qualified to do the duties required on the training ship they were to be given employment and pay in preference to others.

And, very much like modern training, the students were sent to operating merchant ships as part of their education. The masters of such vessels had to agree to exercise all proper care over the morals and conduct of the boys and to afford them opportunities of continuing the studies commenced aboard the training ship. At the end of each voyage the masters filled out a form reporting the conduct of the boys while afloat, their attention to their studies and their proficiency in nautical matters.

With wages set, a curriculum laid out, and a large pool of potential students available, all that was needed was the arrival of the *Jamestown*. And that was just about to happen.

---

[4] "Day's work" is the daily routine of the navigation of a vessel at sea, usually consisting principally of dead reckoning from noon to noon, evening and morning twilight observations, a morning sun observation for a line of position and checking the compass, and a sun observation at or near noon for a running fix.

CHAPTER 2

THE *JAMESTOWN*

The *Jamestown* had a long and colorful career touching on much of the fabric of American history. Named after the earliest permanent settlement established by Englishmen in North America, she was built in 1844 as a sloop of war for the United States Navy and launched at the Navy Yard, Gosport, Virginia. Her first assignment was as the flagship of Commodore Charles W. Skinner who was in command of United States Naval vessels operating off the western coast of Africa to suppress the slave trade. Sailing from Hampton Roads on June 25, 1845 she patrolled the African Coast until August, 1846 when she returned to Boston.

While the ship was moored at the Boston Navy Yard, word reached the United States that for the second consecutive year blight had ruined the Irish potato crop depriving the people of the basis of their diet. A joint resolution of Congress authorized the Secretary of the Navy to place the *Jamestown* and the frigate *Macedonian* into service to provide relief to the Irish people. Commanded by Robert B. Forbes and George C. DeKay, respectively, the ships sailed from Boston on March 28, 1847 with full cargoes of flour, the *Jamestown* additionally carrying goods donated by the people of Boston. The *Jamestown* arrived in Cork, Ireland on April 12 (achieving the fastest time ever sailed up to that time between Boston and Cork), unloaded her cargo and returned to Boston on May 17.[1]

Then it was back to the African patrol. Now the flagship of Commodore W. C. Bolton,

---

[1] According to the *Daily Alta California*, April 9, 1876, Mr. John D. Farwell was third officer on this record voyage outbound and ". . . being charmed with the success of the ship, upon his return to this country carefully examined the plans used in her construction, and improving upon them to a slight extent, caused the first American clipper ships to be placed on the seas." In one sentence the *Alta* swept aside David McKay, the *Oriental*, the *Sea Witch*, the Baltimore Clipper and hundreds of well-researched books regarding the development of the clipper ship. Ed.
Literature from the Boston Marine Society has member J.D. <u>Farrell</u> as <u>second</u> mate on this voyage.

The Jamestown *underway in light winds, somewhere along one of the coasts of the United States (note what appears to be a lighthouse in the distance under her bowsprit). Credit U.S. Naval Historical Center.*

the *Jamestown* sailed from Boston on July 22 and spent the ensuing year on the west coast of Africa chasing slavers. In 1848 she was transferred to the Mediterranean Squadron to aid in protecting American citizens and interests during the revolutions that raged throughout Europe that year. As the political situation stabilized, the ship departed, returning to Norfolk on May 4, 1850.

Following a year on the Atlantic Coast, the ship was assigned to the Brazil Squadron and departed Norfolk on June 1, 1851. The *Jamestown* patrolled the east coast of South America until 1854 when she returned to the Philadelphia Navy Yard where she arrived on May 2 and was decommissioned nine days later. Idleness ill-suited the ship and she was recommissioned the following year for service once more in the African Squadron. This time she sailed from Key West as flagship of Commodore Crabbe, returning to Philadelphia on June 2, 1857 whereupon she was once again decommissioned.

Recommissioned yet again on December 16, 1857, she cruised the West Indies as part of the Home Squadron until decommissioning at Philadelphia on February 14, 1860.

With the outbreak of the Civil War, the *Jamestown* was once more recommissioned, June 5, 1861, and assigned to the Atlantic Blockading Squadron, where she created a record for efficiency and ability. Chasing the bark *Alvorado* ashore off Fernandina, Florida, the *Jamestown* set her on fire on August 5, then captured the schooner *Aigburth* off the coast of Florida on August 31, 1861. Four days later she captured, dismantled and scuttled the schooner *Col. Long*. Then, on December 15, the schooner *Havelock* was taken. She finished her patrol with the capture of the brig *Intended*, taken off Wilmington on May 1, 1862.

With the need for protection in the West, the *Jamestown* was transferred to the Pacific, departing October 12, 1862 on the voyage around the Horn, bound for San Francisco. She pursued her task of protecting American commerce in the Pacific from Confederate privateers until the end of the war. With postwar downsizing, the sloop was decommissioned and laid up at Mare Island on September 17, 1865. She was then converted to a transport and store ship and as such was recommissioned on September 3, 1866 and assigned the task of serving as a store and hospital ship at Panama. Because of an outbreak of fever on board, the ship was ordered back north and disinfected at San Francisco on April 2, 1867.

She then joined the North Pacific Squadron, serving as guard and storeship at Sitka, Alaska. She was at Sitka from September 11, 1867 to May 30, 1868 and was present on October 18, 1867 for the hoisting of the American flag after the purchase of Alaska from Russia.

Arriving back at Mare Island on July 23, 1868, she was decommissioned August 13 and recommissioned on January 25, 1869. For the next three years she provided an American presence on the Pacific Coasts of North and South America and as far away as Tahiti and the Fiji and Hawaiian Islands. Decommissioned on October 7, 1871 the *Jamestown* remained idle at Mare Island until March 16,

The Jamestown had a long and colorful career touching on much of the fabric of American history.

1876 when she was recommissioned as a State Public Marine School.

~~~

Prior to her new duty the ship was given a thorough going over. From the *Daily Alta California*:

> The Jamestown has recently been thoroughly overhauled, has been placed on the dry dock, and is now equal in point of strength to any wooden ship owned by the United States. Her timbers, which are of live oak, thoroughly seasoned, are as sound today as when they were first placed in position.

By April 9, 1876 the ship was anchored off the foot of Third Street in San Francisco, ready to receive the first students. Applicants had their height, chest measurement, color of eyes and hair and state of health recorded and were given their outfit. This consisted of a hammock, a mattress, a sailor's bag, one suit of clothes, two changes of underclothing, one pair of shoes, two pairs of socks and one cap.

The *Daily Alta*:

The youthful aspirant for nautical experience is then put in his "mess," and shown the particular hooks on which he is to swing his hammock. He is then considered as belonging to the Training Ship.

"The Jamestown is now equal to any wooden ship owned by the United States."

Because the initial concern was with the Industrial School, special dispensation was allowed applicants from that establishment. Any applicant from the Industrial School or whose parents could not afford the fees would become a ward of the city and have his expenses paid by the city. For others the charges were $25 for the outfit and $10 per month for residents of San Francisco, payable three or four months in advance. Those from outside the city were charged $25 for the outfit and $15 per month tuition.

The *Daily Alta California* continued following the school's progress.

A visit to the "Jamestown" was paid by an Alta reporter yesterday. Commander Glass met him at the foot of Third Street, and both taking the ship's gig, which was manned by six of the crew, were speedily pulled to the side of the Jamestown. Lieutenant Houston, Executive Officer, received the party.

The representative of the Alta found everything in excellent condition, and was courteously shown all over the vessel, from stem to stern. The only boys now on board are Wm. Mortimer Harrison and Harvey Kincaid Glidden. These were found busily engaged in making cords with which to swing their hammocks. This is the sailor's initiatory step — that is, our reporter believes it to be such. Never having had any practical experience in the nautical line, he is somewhat at sea on the subject. (No joke meant.)

From two hundred and fifty to three hundred boys can be accommodated. Their hammocks will be swung on the lower deck, and they will mess in the same part of the ship.

As yet the routine of studies has not been fully decided upon. On Tuesday next, the Training Ship Committee, Lieut. Houston and the ship's surgeon will pay a visit to the Industrial School, and there make selections from fifty boys who have applied to be transferred. Irrespective of these, the Training Ship Committee have received applications from the parents and guardians of some forty others who are desirous of having their charges instructed on board the Jamestown.

Commander Glass had this to say: "I am satisfied that the boys will take to this kind of life. There is no opening for an independent, wide-awake boy in San Francisco. All the mechanical avenues are closed against him, so to speak. Ship carpenters, caulkers, sailmakers, and others connected with shipbuilding will not take apprentices. Other mechanics say the same. They get all the educated help they need from the East, and say they don't want any apprentices around, for they will always be in the way. I hardly blame the great majority of the boys of San Francisco for being what they are, because they have no opportunity for being any better.

"The Training Ship must not be considered as a place where boys will be confined as a punishment. I intend to give any boy who behaves himself and takes an interest in his studies the fullest opportunity of becoming an officer in the merchant naval service. I believe that with a two-years' course of study any intelligent boy who comes on board will be fitted to act as first or second mate on a merchantman. After six or eight months study of and attention to the duties of a seaman, any boy can be transferred and go out in the world independent and fully capable of earning his own living."

The first training cruise sailed for the Sandwich Islands [Hawaii], arriving in Honolulu in early August, 1876. It was the first of many future calls at this port by California training ships.

Commander Glass wrote to Col. J. C. Zabriskie, one of the ship's early proponents, reporting on the voyage:

I am glad to inform you of my arrival in this port some days ago, after an exceedingly pleasant and interesting passage from San Francisco of nineteen days.

We were fortunate in our entire passage as regards weather, and I had every opportunity to carry on the instruction of my boys in the practical work of a ship at sea and at the same time to maintain the system of school instruction commenced before we left San Francisco.

We have not had a single case of sickness of any kind, and

In addition to indicating the Jamestown *"swinging" at various stages of the tide, the log shows several "boys" being shipped who were immediately put to work making clews for hammocks. Credit National Archives.*

fortunately no accidents have occurred in working aloft. The boys are contented and generally take an active interest in their duties. There are some exceptions, of course, but they are fewer than I anticipated in considering the material I have to work on.

While refitting the ship here I am giving the boys liberty on shore, and every one speaks in the highest terms of their conduct and appearance. The discipline on board is all that I could wish and I have to resort to punishment very rarely, and then use only the slightest.

You were right, sir, when you originated the idea of a Training Ship in San Francisco, and worked for it against the short sighted opposition which the scheme called up, and it gives me very great pleasure to report on the perfect success, for so I may term it, of the first attempt at practical work.

Commander Glass also reported, by letter, to the Board of Supervisors:

The ship encountered light winds for the entire voyage which gave good opportunity for instruction in all the phases of practical seamanship. Daily hands-on lessons were given in making and taking sail, working ship, trimming yards, steering, heaving the log, knotting and splicing ropes, fitting rigging and general duties. English instruction continued and some of the more advanced students took up practical navigation and the use of nautical instruments.

The ship returned to San Francisco, arriving in mid-September 1876. Tragedy struck on the return voyage. Commander Glass reported the accident, which occurred at sea on September 2nd, to the Board of Supervisors:

It becomes my painful duty to report the loss by drowning of Andres Perritt, one of the boys placed on board this vessel for instruction. While exercising at making sail, Perritt fell from the misen topsail yardarm into the water, striking one of the boat davits in his fall. Lieutenant Houston, the Executive Officer, was on duty at the time and made every effort to rescue him. The life-buoy was dropped near Perritt. The ship was hove to at once and the life-boat lowered and sent in charge of an experienced petty officer to recover him. A thorough search was made for Perritt, but after half an hour the boat returned to the ship with the life-buoy and reported that no trace of him could be found. At the time the accident occurred there was a moderate breeze and sea, and from the fact that A. Perritt was seen in the water a few feet from the life-buoy, but making no effort to reach it, I conclude that he was seriously injured or stunned, since he was known to be an expert swimmer.

The loss of Perritt is much to be regretted, as he was attentive to duty and gave promise of becoming a valuable seaman. He was transferred to this vessel from the Industrial School, at his own request, on June 23d, 1876.

The cruise at sea and the visit to Honolulu have had the happiest effect on the discipline on board and the great improvement made by the boys in their studies fully proves the wisdom of that section of the law which requires the Training Ship to cruise actively.

The health of the entire crew has been perfect and with the exception of the unfortunate accident reported in my letter the 2nd instant, no casualties have occurred.

This photo of the Jamestown *in San Francisco Bay was taken sometime between 1870 and 1880 and may well have captured the vessel while she was operating as a training ship. Credit San Francisco Maritime National Historical Park.*

After less than a year in operation, the training ship was considered a success. With its usual enthusiastic prose, Northern California's leading newspaper extolled the virtues of the experiment in an editorial datelined February 15, 1877. *Daily Alta California*:

It ought to be a source of satisfaction to every citizen of San Francisco to be able to point to one institution of the city, supported by its contributions, that can be contemplated with pleasure and satisfaction, and of which we can say, it has exceeded in good results more than even our anticipations. That institution is the Training Ship Jamestown, under command of Captain Glass . . .[2] A goodly number of the boys of San Francisco were enlisted and received on board, and their education for seamen commenced. It was not merely a manual education, the routine of ship duty, how to "hand-reef and steer," to scrub decks, and simply do the drudgery of a sailor's

---

[2] Although Commander Glass had not achieved the rank of Captain in the Navy, he was frequently referred to by that title. Tradition in the Navy and maritime service dictates that the commanding officer be referred to as "Captain" whether or not he technically holds that rank.

life at sea; but they commenced to study and be instructed in the branches which it is necessary for officers of ships to understand, by which they are able to guide the ships they sail in, to any point on the great oceans, with accuracy.

The ship has several times run over the ocean to the Sandwich Islands, and they have had excellent opportunities for learning seamanship and also the science of navigation. No one of them needs to remain in ignorance; and it is a pleasure to be able to say, from the testimony borne by their officers and the history of the ship, that the experiment has proved a grand success. The Training Ship is almost the only city institution which has not exceeded the appropriation allowed. Since the ship went into service, in May, 1876, two hundred and fifty-five boys have been trained on board the ship, and about one hundred and sixty have passed good examination and been discharged. This is a greater percentage than is shown of the Cadets at West Point and the "Middies" at Annapolis. One half of the discharged number are now on sea-going vessels, of whom several are officers. Of the whole, after discharge from the ship, one boy only has fallen into bad habits and been arrested by the police. This fact is as remarkable as satisfactory. More than one hundred have been taken from the Industrial School and put in way of making an honorable living.

"The ship has several times run over . . . to the Sandwich Islands."

Although there was no graduation, as such, and boys were sent on to merchant ships as soon as they were deemed fit, there was an annual examination and ceremonies awarding prizes. The first took place on April 10, 1877. Attended by Commander Glass, Supervisors MacDonald, Boyce and Hayes, naval officers, city officials and private citizens, it was held aboard the *Jamestown* at her anchorage off San Francisco's Third Street Pier.

The ceremony commenced with the students going through the manual of arms with rifles. They then went aloft, loosened, clewed and took in sails in eleven minutes, to the applause of the spectators. This was followed by a fire drill at which the boys had water spewing out the fire hoses within a minute and a half of the first alarm of fire.

The guests dined in the officers' quarters, after which they were treated to a parade on deck. Then came the awards ceremony. Henry Weatherbee was awarded a silver cup for his efforts in seamanship. A. Motzenbecker received a silver cup for his attention to duty. S. B. Moulton was given a silver cup for studies and E. S. Burke received a gold medal for exemplary conduct for jumping overboard at Honolulu and rescuing one of his comrades from drowning. Several boys were recommended for graduation to men-of-war or merchant ships.

The second cruise, in the summer of 1877, expanded the itinerary to include Hilo and Lahaina as well as Honolulu. On November 10 that same year another awards ceremony was held. This one was attended by both the incoming and outgoing Boards of Supervisors of the City of San Francisco, members of the State Senate and Assembly, the Board of Fire Commissioners and City and County officers in addition to "a number of gentlemen in private life and others who have officers for the merchant marine and the Navy — the demand for such officers simply wasn't there. It was a grand idea at the wrong time. For one thing, shipping was making the transition from sail to steam. For another, there wasn't enough funding to keep the school going. Despite the success of the Training Ship, the project was dropped and in February 1879 the first California Nautical School was abolished. Governor William Irwin wrote to the Navy department requesting that they withdraw the training ship from its use by the San Francisco Board of Supervisors. The record is silent regarding the official reason.

The end of the first nautical school training ship was described in a letter from Commander Glass:

August 8, 1877 and the Jamestown *has just arrived off Hilo, in the Sandwich Islands. Note the distance logged from San Francisco (center), the pilot already on board (lower left, sideways) and the record of sail (lower left). Credit National Archives.*

been anxious to get out of it." Everyone seemed interested in the newly-successful school. Ninety-one boys demonstrated their skills in the manual of arms, making sail, reefing the topsail and performing other feats of seamanship which were considered "remarkable."

Ironically, although the school did everything it was supposed to do — taking potential delinquents off the streets of San Francisco, training highly-skilled and professional

Mare Island Naval Yard, Cal.
Feb. 28, 1879

Hon. Board of Supervisors:
Gentlemen:
    I have the honor to inform you that having handed the battery and equipments of the Jamestown as required by Naval Regulations, and disposed of all

the property on board belonging to the city of San Francisco, under instructions from his honor the Mayor and the Training Ship Committee, I have today formally transferred the vessel to Commodore E. R. Calhoun, U. S. Navy, commandant of Mare Island Navy Yard.

All officers and employees have been discharged from this date, with the exception of Mr. F. J. Warren, Storekeeper, who will report to your committee for duties, in connection with making a final return of bills and expenditures.

The money accruing from the sale of city property has been turned into the Treasury and accounts of sale furnished your Committee.

In taking leave of your honorable body, as I now do, I wish to express my high appreciation of the uniform courtesy with which I have been treated by the members of the Board, and the city officials with whom I have been associated on duty.

I am, with great respect, your very obedient servant,

Henry Glass,
Lieut. Commander,
U. S. Navy

PART II

THE TWENTIETH CENTURY

CHAPTER 3

THE *CALIFORNIA STATE*

The second California Nautical School was chartered in 1929. The C.C. Thomas Navy Post #244 of the American Legion in San Francisco rediscovered the 1874 Federal Law that permitted the Navy to loan vessels to state nautical schools and lobbied the California Legislature to create a nautical school. Assembly Bill 253 passed and was signed by Governor C. C. Young on June 3, 1929.

A representative of the Pacific American Steamship Association then went to Washington to lobby the U.S. Shipping Board, the U.S. Navy and other government agencies for loan of a schoolship. The Shipping Board agreed to turn a ship over to the Navy for commissioning so the Navy could loan it to the State of California. Permission was granted to choose a vessel from the Chesapeake Bay Reserve Fleet. Eagerly inspecting the available vessels, the representative quickly chose a "Laker" class ship, the *Henry County.*

Built for Northern European service by the American Ship Building Company of Lorain, Ohio in response to the World War I needs of the United States Shipping Board, she was laid down as the *Lake Fellowship*[1] but by the date of her launching, October 18, 1919, her name had changed to *Henry County.*[2] The name change was the result of a regional Liberty Loan drive contest.

The launching party for the Henry County. *Credit The Great Lakes Historical Society.*

---

[1] Institute for Great Lakes Research.

[2] There are ten Henry Counties in the United States in: Alabama, Georgia, Illinois, Indiana, Iowa, Kentucky, Missouri, Ohio, Tennessee and Virginia. The record is unclear as to which of them the ship was named after.

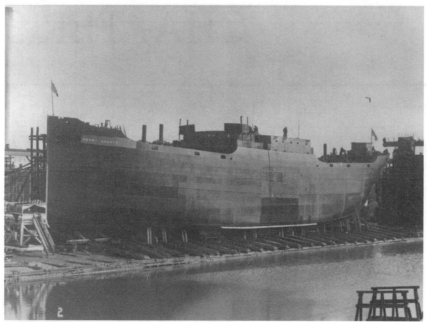

The Henry County *just prior to launching. She was launched sideways, a method common to narrow inland waters lacking the broad bays found in coastal regions. Credit Institute for Great Lakes Research, Bowling Green State University.*

chosen as the California Nautical School ship.

In early May of 1930 the U.S. Shipping Board pulled the *Henry County* from the Chesapeake fleet and placed her in a shipyard. Workers swarmed aboard chipping rust, cleaning, painting, overhauling machinery; in short, ensuring that everything was operable. Seventeen thousand dollars were spent overhauling the boilers, steam lines and auxiliary machinery to prepare the ship for her new life. The State of California paid for the

Dick Brannon '38: "They were a traditional design, a well-deck design, with a raised forecastle head, well deck, forward two hatches, then a raised midship house and then two hatches aft and a raised poop deck. There were hundreds of that Laker class built."

The *Henry County* made two voyages to Europe under the Potter Transportation Company, delivering cargo to Genoa and Dunkirk. The war ended the following month, however, while more than half the war-contracted tonnage was abuilding, and with the resulting surplus tonnage the *Henry County* was eventually laid up in Norfolk, Virginia, at the Shipping Board's Chesapeake Bay Reserve Fleet. There she languished until

installation of a 'tween deck with heating and lighting, converting the dark, empty cargo holds into classrooms, berthing spaces and a machine shop. On May 21 the ship was delivered to the Norfolk Navy Yard; ownership and title were officially transferred to the Navy, and the ship was commissioned on May 27.

Taking advantage of the ship's westbound voyage, the Navy loaded her with

Taken in 1924 in Philadelphia, this photo probably depicts the ship in an inactive status before being taken into the Chesapeake Bay Reserve Fleet. Credit Institute for Great Lakes Research, Bowling Green State University.

supplies to be delivered to two of its California bases, at San Pedro and Mare Island. She was also loaded with surplus material for the final conversion to a schoolship, including bunks, boats, emergency gear, compasses and other items. Sailing on July 12, 1930 under Cdr. B. V. McCandlish, the *Henry County* departed Norfolk, transited the Panama Canal and, after discharging at San Pedro, arrived at Mare Island on August 18, 1930. After decommissioning on August 22, the Navy "loaned" the ship to the State of California for use as a schoolship.[3]

Modifications, including fuel and water tanks and watertight bulkheads, were necessary to complete the conversion and the funding request to accomplish them, $244,360, was passed on to Washington.

The timing was bad. The country was in the Great Depression and President Hoover had just asked the Navy to return $30 million of its appropriations to the Treasury. No more money was available for the schoolship that year. But those who wanted the ship persisted.

Ralph Swany '33: "Emile Topp was the superintendent. He was the first one and he also had his master's license in steam and sail."

Captain Topp and the Chairman of the school's board of governors, J.C. Rohlfs (of

the Standard Oil Company), rushed to Washington to lobby for the funds.

Among those they talked to were Chester W. Nimitz, Chief of Naval Operations. Still interested in the project, the Navy had requested $240,000 to fund the schoolship the following fiscal year, but this was almost immediately slashed by the Budget Bureau to

Taken in August of 1930, this photo shows the Henry County *transiting the Panama Canal, on her way to a new life as a training ship. Credit San Francisco Maritime National Historical Park.*

$45,000. Conversion would have to wait. Nevertheless, notices went out for applicants to the new school.

The trip to Washington was not in vain, however. Captain Topp and Mr. Rohlfs also lobbied for use of the Navy's coaling station at California City, on San Francisco Bay, as a base

---

[3] The Navy retained technical possession of the ship and provided financial and material support until 1940 when it was transferred to the United States Maritime Commission.

for the nautical school. This was approved and on February 10, 1931 a "revocable license" was granted the California Nautical School to use the Naval Fuel Depot as a shore base for the school and the ship, which had been renamed *USS California State* (because the ship still belonged to the Navy it retained the "USS" prefix).

The base was ideally situated in the protected waters of the north part of San Francisco Bay. Equipped with a large machine shop, forge shop, sail loft, recreation building, academic building, boat basin and a pier suitable for the ship, it was a ready-made campus for the new school.

Ralph Swany: "I had been interested in mainly going to the military academy while I was in high school and was workin' towards that end. It came up that they had an ad in the paper where they were going to have entrance examinations which were going to be similar to the ones that they had for the students going into the military academies so I went down and took it, just to sort of get the feel of it, and it came up they notified me that I passed. So that's what got the ball rolling."

Cy Hansen '33: "In January, notices of impending written examinations for admission to the California Nautical School appeared in California newspapers throughout the state. We were informed that examinations would be held in February for admission in early March, 1931. Shortly after, we were notified that we had passed and were directed to appear at the office of the California Nautical School at 215 Market Street, San Francisco. We were informed that we should bring $125 in fees for admission and uniforms, black sox, a black tie, pocket handkerchiefs, white dress shirts, toilet articles and personal effects and that all non-

THE COALING STATION AT CALIFORNIA CITY

The Navy Fuel Depot was located in a small cove that was once the home of a tribe of Miwok Indians known as the Coon Tribe, because of the raccoon skin caps they wore. When Mission San Rafael was established in 1817, the Indians tended livestock and cultivated gardens for the mission in exchange for food, clothing and protection. Eventually the property became part of the Rancho Corte de Madera del Presidio land grant which encompassed the entire Tiburon Peninsula. The area was operated as a cattle

ranch, then dairy ranches, and finally sold off in parcels. In 1877 the codfish firm of Lunde and Hough bought the cove property and established one of the largest cod-drying, curing, and packing plants on the West Coast. The company built the first wharf and a two-story warehouse to receive shipments of fish. In 1904 the Federal Government bought the property from Lunde and Hough for $80,000 to use as a Navy coaling station. An L-shaped wharf-trestle, coal hoisting tower, storage bunkers, cable railway and power plant were constructed and the facility began operation in 1908. The station was closed down in 1930 when oil replaced coal as ship fuel.

The coaling station much as it looked when the second California Nautical School began. Credit Belvedere Tiburon Landmarks Society, courtesy Alvin Gregory.

uniform clothing would have to be sent home after admission."

In 1981 Cy Hansen (the oldest living alumnus at this writing in 1996) wrote a series of articles for *The Binnacle*, the student publication of the California Maritime Academy, titled "In The Beginning." In them he recalled his first view of the school.

As we passed Angel Island our attention was directed to the base, a short distance ahead of us; our first impression was a group of buff colored buildings perched on a steep hillside, an L-shaped double decked pier, a large water tower, all dominated by large piles of black material (coal) and a huge gantry crane straddling the coal piles. As we neared the spot we noticed cranes and metal coal cars on the upper deck of the pier and spotted a number of buildings on the lower level near the crane and the dock. This was the California Nautical School campus.

In the same series of articles, Harold E. Liden '33 recalled that first day.

On our first full day on the base some 10 shots [15 fathoms or ninety feet each] of battleship chain had to be moved 150' across a concrete apron by hand. Each link weighed about 160 pounds. One cadet quit [the school] before the noon hour.

Dick Brannon '38: "The school was at Tiburon, the old Navy coaling station, called California City. It was still exactly the same as it had been in 1906 when Teddy Roosevelt sent the Great White Fleet around the world, wave the big stick, all that sort of heroic stuff. He had the battleships all painted white. The Great White Fleet was coal-burning. California City, as they called it, still had 56,000 tons of beautiful, beautiful, boiler-steaming-quality fuel. All piled up there. Pocahontas was the name brand, Pocahontas coal shipped all the way out from Virginia. All the gantry cranes, the loading equipment was all still there, intact."

Ray Aker '42: "We drilled between the coal pits. It was the only level concreted surface in the place and the upper classmen sometimes made us charge up the coal piles during our Saturday drill [laugh]. Out there for close order drills and charge up the coal pile in your whites. Most of the time we were in dungarees, but on drill days we were in whites.

"A coal car ran between these piles. We sometimes had to push that thing with upper class cadets in it, back and forth. [laugh]."

The first log of the second California Nautical School began on March 2, 1931 at the base at California City. Most of the entries were routine, similar to those in ships' logs everywhere — periodic notations of weather and routine changes of the watch.

On March 5, 1931 the first students, fifteen in all, reported at Tiburon for duty but found no ship. It was still at Mare Island awaiting conversion funds. But by March 23 there were 38 students "aboard" the new campus of the California Nautical School.[4]

With the students aboard, the school could begin training. The log for a typical week records cadet routine at the California Nautical School.

Sunday, 29th March, 1931
Day comes fine and clear.
7.00 A.M. Reveille

---

[4] Although there was no ship the base was treated as if it were a ship. Students and faculty were referred to as being "aboard" or "ashore" when on or off campus and a ship's log of activities was maintained.

7.30 A.M. Breakfast

8.30 to 9.00. Cadets execute morn-
ing orders. Police barracks —
air bedding. This being the Sab-
bath, no unnecessary work is
performed. All cadets not on
watch have free gangway. Vari-
ous visitors are about the base,
visiting and inspecting.

9.00 P.M. — Tattoo.

9.15 P.M. Taps

Lights are out. Everything is
silent and this day ends.

  (signed) W. R. Bethel
  O.O.D.

Monday — 30 March 1931

 Day comes in fine and clear.

6.00 AM Reveille

6.15 AM Cadets muster. Execute
morning orders.

7.00 AM Recall from morning
work.

7.30 AM Cadets breakfast. Week-
end liberty party returns. All
present except Cadet Allen on
sick leave.

8.00 AM Crew turn to. Sick call.
Cadet Liden reports boil.

8.15 AM Assembly and inspection.

8.30 AM Cadets to first study.

12.00 M⁵ Crew to dinner.

12.15 PM Cadets recalled from
study.

12.30 PM Cadets to dinner.

1.00 PM Crew Turn to — various
details.

1.30 PM Cadets muster and turn to,
practical work.

4.00 PM Cadets recall from duty.

5.00 PM Crew cease work for night.

4.00 PM USS Algorma moored
navy target rafts #28 & 31 to
outside of outer wharf.

5.00 PM Cadets to supper.

6.30 PM M/S Mary E lands 7 sacks
rice and 2 ctns bread.

7.00 PM Cadets assembly and
study.

8.30 PM Cadets recall from study.

9.00 PM Tattoo and muster.

9.15 PM Taps.

Day ends fine and clear. Fog
over bay.

  (signed) Respectfully,
  G. Barkley
  O.O.D.

REMARKS:

Afternoon Practical Work: —
Rowing, Semaphore signalling, Canvas
serving (making ditty bags) Practical
work in machine shop. Cutting grass
and general upkeep work on reserva-
tion.

 Approved
  M.E. Crossman
  Executive Officer

Tuesday — 31 March, 1931

 Day comes in overcast. Thick
fog.

6:00 Reveille.

6:15 Muster: All present except
(Allen) Sick Leave. Execute
morning orders.

7:00 Recall.

7:30 Breakfast.

8:15 Assembly & inspection.

8:30 Assembly for study.

12:15 Recall from study.

12:30 Lunch formation.

---

⁵ Because AM means ante-meridian and PM post meridian, M is used to indicate noon or the exact time at the meridian.

The main gate on Paradise Drive in Tiburon. Credit California Maritime Academy, courtesy Alvin Gregory.

1:30   Formation for practical work.
  1st Sec. Nos. 1-10 to M.A.A. [Master at Arms] for work about grounds.
  2nd Sec. Nos. 31-40 ditto
  1st Sec. 11-30 in Machine & Electric Shop for practical instruction.
  2nd Sec. 41-50 with Bos'n on boats
  "   "   51-60 " Mr. Bethel & Cadet Gregory for boat practice (rowing).
4:00   Recall from practical work.
5:00   Crew cease work. Supper formation.
7:00   Mary E. landed stores as per Day Book.
7:00   Formation for lecture. Given by Mr. L. Marshall, Dist. Eng. Pac. Tel. Tel. Co. San Rafael.
8:30   Recall from lecture.
9:00   Tattoo: Muster.

9:15   Taps.
  Day ends fine and clear.
      (signed) Respectfully,
        E. T. Jaeger
        O.O.D.
REMARKS:
  Cadet Allen's resignation accepted this day.
      Approved
      M.E. Crossman
      Executive Officer

Wednesday 1st April 1931
  Day comes in overcast.
  6.00 AM Reveille.
  6.15   Cadets muster — All present. Perform setting up exercises.
  6.30   Execute morning orders.
  7.00   Recall from morning work.
  7.30   Assembly — Breakfast.
  8.00   Crew turns to. Sick Call. Morning Colors.
  8.15   Assembly — Inspection.
  8.30   Cadets to first classes. Study.
  10.15   Navy Tug Algorma came alongside dock for targets.

Cadets marching next to the coaling station trestle at California City. Credit California Maritime Academy.

11.15   Cast off lines on targets. Algorma underway with targets in tow.

12.00 M Crew to dinner.

12.15 PM Recall from study.

12.30   Assembly — Dinner.

1.30   Assembly — Fresh linen issued.

2.30   Locker inspection.

3.00   Fire drill — Box seven pulled.

3.05   Water on two hose lines.

3.10   Recall from fire drill — gear replaced.

3.15 to 4.00 Practical work — policing station.

4.00   Recall from work.

5.00   Assembly — Supper — Crew cease work.

7.00   Assembly — Study. Mary E arrived with freight.

8.30   Recall from study.

9.00   Tattoo — Muster — All cadets present

9.15   Taps. Silence.
This day ends, fine and clear.
          (signed) W. R. Bethel
                    O.O.D.
          Approved
            M. E. Crossman

Thursday — 2 April 1931
   Day comes in fine and clear.

6.00 AM Reveille.

6.15 AM Assembly. Cadets muster. Physical drill. Execute morning orders.

7.00 AM Recall from morning work.

7.30 AM Cadets breakfast.

8.00 AM Crew turns to.

8.15 AM Cadets assemble. Inspection.

8.30 AM to 12.15 PM Cadets at study and classes.

Semaphore practice on one of the hillsides at the coaling station. Courtesy Ralph Swany

12.00 M to 1.00 PM Crew cease work for lunch.

1.20 PM Cadets turn to — Practical Instruction.
   Details to:
      Boatswain — making ditty bags.
      Master-at-Arms — cleaning grounds.
      Machinist — for machine and electrical shops, practical instruction.

3.00 PM Fire drill. Sounded Alarm. Box 4.

3.03 PM Water on scene of fire-drill. All cadets present and equipment checked. Recall.

3.40   Recall from practical instruction.

5.00   Crews cease work for day. Cadets assemble. Supper formation.

7.00   Study formation.

7.30   M/S Mary E. lands stores.

8.30   Recall from evening studies.

9.00   Tattoo and muster. All cadets present.

9.15   Taps

          (signed) G. Barkley
            Officer-of-Day

Approved —
   M.E. Crossman.

Friday April 3, 1931
Day begins bright and clear.
6:00   Reveille.
6:15   Assembly; Muster, Physical Drill, Air Bedding, Execute morning orders.
7:00   Recall from morning work.
7:30   Breakfast formation.
8:00   Crew turn to.
8:15   Assembly. Inspection.
8:30   — 12:15 Studies.
12:00 — 1:00 Crew at lunch.
12:30 Lunch formation.
1:30   Turn to as follows.
     1st Sec. Engineers
     5th crew — sand & canvas whaleboat
     6th crew — to M.A.A. work on walk.
     7th crew — to M.A.A. Scrub float, Brightwork.
     5 men on 7th crew with Mr. Bethel for soundings.
4:00   Retreat from practical work.
4:00   Swimming call for 2nd Sec. 18 men.
5:00   Crew cease work for day.
5:00   Supper assembly.
7:00   Study formation.
7:00   Mary E. alongside with stores as per Day Book.
8:30   Retreat from studies.
9:15   Taps.
     Day ends clear.
     (signed) E. T. Jaeger
     O.O.D.

Saturday 4 April 1931
Day comes partly overcast.
6.00 AM Reveille.
6.15   Assembly — muster — physical drill.

6.30   Execute morning orders.
7.00   Recall from morning work.
7.30   Assembly — Breakfast.
8.00   Crew turn to.
8.15   Assembly — in dungarees. General field day.
10.30 Recall from work. Shift into uniform of the day.
11.00 Assembly. Commanding Officer's inspection. Cadets — personnel — quarters — All buildings.
11.30 Recall — Cadets dismissed. Inspection of buildings.
12.00 to 1.00 PM Crew to lunch.
12.30 PM Assembly — Cadets to lunch.
1.10   Assembly — Liberty Party mustered.
1.15   Liberty party shoves off in a shore boat. 33 cadets have weekend shore leave. 17 cadets go ashore for new uniforms. Men on watch and sick remain on board.
5.00   Assembly — supper.
5.20   Mary E. alongside with freight as per Day Book.

The yacht Velero II served as "training ship" until the California State could be brought into service. Courtesy Ralph Swany.

9.00 Tattoo. Muster. All present
except those having liberty as per
liberty book.
9.15 Taps. Silence.
Day ends clear and cold.
(signed) W.R. Bethel
O.O.D.

Ralph Swany: "We had seamanship
and navigation, then we had engineering
courses. We had physics and chemistry originally going in there, that was in the morning,
and then in the afternoon we had practical

"Velero II had an observation car rear deckhouse with 12' horseshoe settee complete with stereo. Yes, in 1931, Stereo!"

work. We worked around, cleaned, painting
up, paint and work in the station."

Pending the *Henry County* coming into
service, the students learned their trade on small
craft, including the private yacht *Velero II*.

Cy Hansen: "*Velero II* was the yacht.
Belonged to G. Allen Hancock. Hancock
College in Santa Maria is named after him. He
was an independent oil man. He brought that
up there basically to get around the state law
that said we were supposed to have a
schoolship in 1931."

Writing in 1983 Malcolm E. Crossman,
then Executive Officer of the school, recalled:

After the entrance of the first class in
1931, who had to sleep on cots in the
rat-infested shack on the dock because

we did not yet have a ship, some legis-
lators in Sacramento who were origi-
nally against the establishment of the
school, initiated a bill to abolish the
California Nautical School because, not
having a "proper vessel", the school was
maintained in violation of the law . . .
Mr. G. Allen Hancock, a wealthy South-
ern California resident and a member of
the Board of Governors of the Nautical
School, came to the rescue by loaning
us his 125 foot diesel yacht "Velero II"
to the school. By taking his craft for
"cruises" in the Bay with cadets on
board, we were considered technically
within the law and the bill to abolish
the school was defeated.

Harold Liden fondly recalled the *Velero
II* in "In the Beginning," although he remem-
bers it as being a bit shorter than Malcom
Crossman did.

Velero II was 110 feet of Honduras
mahogany and teak. She had a semi-
circular bridge house ending in a
homebreaker of an observation car rear
deckhouse complete with 12' horseshoe
settee complete with stereo. Yes, in 1931,
Stereo! She was moored in the middle
of the old battleship slip. One March
day we raised our ensign at 8:00 a.m.
in a force 3 wind — by 9:30 a.m. wind
force was 6 or 7 throwing spray across
our dock from a strong norther with a
San Pablo Bay fetch. Most officers were
away on a seminar. We tried to snub
our silly rolling Velero II down with 6"
and 8" manila with no luck. It was a
wonder we did not pull the bitts out of
her. Finally we bridled her longi-
tudinally and let her roll with breast
lines slack to the water. Another good
seamanship lesson! Two Marin ferry
boats almost broached-to on Alcatraz
island that day. We completely

refinished the "piano woodwork" on Velero II. I remember she had a flush turtle deck bow, which rounded into the scuppers. It was covered with more than 1" of hard carnuba wax to keep water out of lockers below. On a warm day footprints would show in the wax. We scraped it all off and tried to build it up but with dozens of coats, it was only 1/16". Capt. Hancock laughed and said we did a beautiful job . . . but it had taken 10 years of very hard work to build up and was the only thing that kept water out of the lockers.

Even in the 1930s sailing ships were yet active on the world's oceans. Part of the students' training included learning the then-still-traditional art of handling a sailing ship. From the deck log for July 17, 1931: "1st, 2nd, 3rd and 4th crews boarded launch to go to Alameda for practical demonstration of use of running and standing rigging of square-rigged vessels under direction of Executive and Third Officers."

It was probably with some degree of envy that the student body saw the New York State training ship pass on August 11, 1931. From the log: "*USS Empire State*, outbound, passed close off outer wharf. Cadets called to quarters and salutes exchanged between New York and California schools."

Cy Hansen: "The Navy agreed to turn over a Navy ship, much larger than the *California State*, to the New York Nautical School. It was put into condition in the Mare Island Naval Shipyard. Some of the cadets and crew came out from New York and operated it on its way back. The day it came down from Mare Island it came by the base and we were all standing out on the dock, waving and telling them 'Happy voyage,' and all the rest of it."

~~~

Funding for conversion of the *California State* finally materialized and in the fall of 1931 the vessel was taken from Mare Island to Bethlehem Shipyards in San Francisco for the long-awaited remodeling into a school ship.

Cy Hansen: "The ship had not been delivered. It was delivered to the Navy during that summer, probably in May or June and as far as I know it was towed down to Bethlehem Shipyard in the middle of the year for overhaul and conversion to a school ship. Richard Dwyer, the chief engineer, was up there quite a bit. He worked with the naval architects to get the ship ready. We went to Bethlehem in December of 1931 and that's where it received its final set of stores and touch-up and work was completed."

The worst football game had the CNS behind West Coast Army 100 to 0 at half time.

Meanwhile, there were the beginnings of a social life. The first formal dance for the nautical school was held at the Fairmont Hotel, atop Nob Hill in San Francisco on October 23, 1931. This was — and is — one of the most elegant hotels in the city with a grand lobby replete with marble pillars, sparkling chandeliers and high ceilings. According to the log it was attended by, "The Superintendent, the staff of officers, and cadet corps, with their ladies. . ." all of whom reveled in the contrast to their coaling station campus and the "hot dog and beans" dances held there.

In the early years there was a football team. One of the first games on record was against Tamalpais High School on September

The training ship was finally put into service. Here the California State *is at her permanent berth at the coaling station at Tiburon. Credit San Francisco Maritime National Historical Park.*

8, which they defeated 13 to 0. They didn't fare so well against Marin Junior College, losing 21 to 0 two weeks later. There were also games against West Coast Army, San Francisco State, Antioch American Legion and Petaluma

Inspection was a part of the routine. This one, in dress blues, was probably on Saturday morning just before liberty. Credit The State of California Department of Education, courtesy Ray Aker.

High School. The worst game had the California Nautical School behind West Coast Army 100 to 0 at half time.

Cy Hansen: "We didn't have time enough to practice. We didn't have a regular field either, just a plowed field up above one of the gantry cranes."

On Wednesday, December 9, 1931 the California Nautical School finally took possession of the *USS California State*. The students and staff went to San Francisco to bring her "home" to Tiburon for the first time. Her hull gleamed with fresh white paint. Her decks were clean, her masts straight, the rigging was bright and unblemished and the interior looked and smelled new. The first night aboard for the new students was December 11, 1931.

Three days later a new class of 31 cadets reported aboard.

Deck cadets adjust a compass during navigation class ashore. Credit The State of California Department of Education, courtesy Ray Aker.

Ralph Swany: "Our tuition was $150 for three years. For books and tools. When they got the ship they had classes on board. When we were at the base, though, we lived on the ship and the mess hall was at the top of the hill. We ate up there and they had the offices, the school and the classroom buildings there and then we had practical work on the ship."

With arrival of the *California State*, the daily routine was altered. Berthing and practical work were shifted on board. Meals were cooked in the galley and served on the mess deck.

Ray Aker: "It was a very rigid routine. We had reveille at five forty-five, a god-awful hour, and we swabs had to get out of the bunk right away. Boy, instantly! Jump out. Didn't take time to wake up. Just jump and hit the deck. You got a chance to get a cup of hot chocolate before you mustered on the dock for calisthenics and then went to work stations. Might be scrub down of white work, "soogee" we called it, polishing brass, cleaning up. The decks had to be swept and washed down every morning, whitework scrubbed and brass shined. When we were alongside at Tiburon it might include some duty ashore as well, such as chopping weeds and clean the base and classrooms. At seven o'clock we broke off from that, got a chance then to clean up, take a shower and change into the uniform of the day which was a navy blue uniform, with a wool serge shirt having three-quarter length sleeves so you weren't wearing holes in your elbows. Then we went to breakfast at seven-thirty. Eight o'clock, we mustered for inspection. See that your hair was cut, uniform clean and shoes shined.

"Saturday was the same thing, except we had military drills for Naval Reserve requirements, mainly close-order marching with rifles and bayonets. We had a half day off on Saturday, and all day off Sunday, unless you had watchstanding duties.

"Eight o'clock we went up to morning inspection. And if you didn't pass that you might get a couple of demerits and extra duty. Then we went off to classes. In the afternoon we had what they called practical work. Rowing drill was also conducted in the whaleboats. Seemed like lots of it."

Cy Hansen: "Afternoons was practical work. It seems like we did a lot of hoeing weeds and did a lot of painting. All the buildings were that beige color the Navy used on everything. We repainted all the buildings white with green trim and that included the water tower."

Ray Aker: "I can't remember what time we knocked off, now, but it was in enough time to get cleaned up and get ready for dinner in the mess deck. Then we would go to evening study sessions. That was in the classrooms up on the hill. We studied together as a class and did homework. Soogee, our mascot [a malamute], attended study sessions. Sometimes George Barkley [the ship's executive officer] would check up. He was referred to as "the beard" because he wore one. The gangway

George Barkley, executive officer of the California State, *also known as "the beard." Courtesy Ray Aker.*

watch would call ahead with a warning, 'The beard is about.' That cut short any horseplay in the classroom."

Roger Swain '42: "During those evening study periods ashore, we were pretty well removed from surveillance of ship's officers aboard ship. The third classmen, instead of studies, would have to put on an entertainment smoker for the upper classmen."

Ray Aker: "Ten o'clock was taps. Everyone except the watch had to turn in. Lights went off in the berth deck. If you wanted to study some more, you might have to sneak off someplace in number one hold, find a hide-away somewhere. But that was it, nobody except the watch was up and around on deck."

Ralph Swany: "After we got the ship, we worked the afternoons on practical applications of seamanship and the engineers, they worked down in the engine room on the ship."

Cy Hansen: "Engineer cadets started the boiler up at four in morning and we had cadets on duty all during the day and cut it off around nine in the evening. That was routine. And deck cadets stood regular watches on board."

Dick Brannon: "We lived on the ship the whole time. We were the crew of the ship. So we had a tremendous pride in the ship itself. Every morning we got up at maybe seven o'clock and had a field day. Actually, when we got up we went out and did exercises,

Checking the gauges at the main operating platform of the California State *was but one of the engine cadets' many duties. Credit San Francisco Maritime National Historical Park.*

An engine cadet fires off the ship's boiler under the watchful eye of an instructor. Credit San Francisco Maritime National Historical Park.

aerobic physical exercises, then we'd go on board the ship and had a half hour or forty-five minutes of clean sweep-down fore and aft. Then breakfast, then all morning in the classroom. We marched ashore to the classrooms, the old Navy buildings and all that were fully operational. We had a superb campus, really, a magnificent campus.

"Then, in afternoon, back to the ship, all our eating and everything was done on the ship. There were no facilities for living ashore. So, back aboard the ship, noon meal, turn to in the afternoon. The afternoon was practical seamanship. I've slid up and down the stays, the standing rigging of the ship, slushing the wires. I've been through all of that. When the ship was off the dock and to sea I was down in the chain locker stowing the chain, all the basics. I went through the whole thing, got my hands dirty."

Ralph Swany: "We had a sailmaker 'cause we did all our own canvas. We did three tarps for every hatch, all the boat covers, all the ventilators, all the awnings. They were all handwork. And the thing is, if you didn't put nine stitches to the needle length and you tried to stitch in seven, you'd have to rip it out and do it again."

Ray Aker: "On deck it was painting and soogeeing and chipping paint. There might be some wire splicing or re-reeving some rigging. Then boats. We had a lot of boat work. In the afternoon, we took those whale boats out and rowed, sailed, spent the afternoon in things like that, practical seamanship."

Dick Brannon: "We all went through that, engine, deck, absolutely. We all had to do everything. We had a basic training that was fantastic. Three years of that with basic hands-on work was really concentrated on steamship working, living, handling, doing things. It was all basic steamship operation, deck and engine. Every one of us was down inside those scotch boilers scraping and

Learning to sail small boats was an important part of the deck cadets' training. Credit California Maritime Academy.

cleaning, every one of us was doing everything for three solid years. It was really a fantastic training period."

~~~

As with military and nautical schools everywhere, the new cadets were subject to disciplined hazing to help "build their character." This included memorizing the answers to nonsense questions, being ordered to do push-ups at any time, being called out in the middle of the night to answer to upper classmen, learning to say "Sir," and, in general, being respectful toward anyone not in your own class. It began with assignment to a temporary group known as the "swab division."

Cy Hansen: "Since we were the first class there were no upper classmen. We got the hazing from the officers. Barkley and Crossman were graduates of the Mass. Nautical School and one of the engineers was a graduate of the Pennsylvania school ship.

"Basically we came into it as pioneers. There were no ifs, ands or buts. We were treated like Naval Academy cadets. That brought us closer together. We did a lot of things together that later classes didn't do. We were out at Tiburon, isolated and we made strong friendships."

Charles Audet '39: "It paid to have a good sense of humor because life was tough. We had no money, no time to ourselves, no privacy, the only food was on the ship. In

Tiburon we were totally isolated. There was no transportation. I had a car, against the rules. I kept it hidden in the weeds off the grounds."

Ray Aker: "We were swabs. We were used like swabs. Any dirty job that came along, get a swab. The best way to avoid getting caught for some onerous duty was to look like

A mess table on the California State *with upper classmen in the foreground, third classmen in the background against the bulkhead. Credit U.S. Naval Institute, courtesy Ray Aker.*

you were busy. If you had to walk from one place to the other, look like you had some purpose.

"We sat ten men to a table, the big mess tables. The upper classmen were up at the head of the table and the second classmen were in the middle and the swabs were down at the end. The food was brought out in big metal trays. The first classmen got their pick; they would off-load that tray right away. We'd be down there looking. So out comes another tray, and if there was anything more the first classmen wanted they'd pick it off. Then it gets to the second classmen and they'd clean it up. By the time we'd get that tray it was picked over. There might be another tray coming down but that would get a little bit of picking over too."

Charles Audet: "Hazing was fairly minor. It supposedly lasted the whole year and after the end of the year we were all friends. The direst punishment was if you were

BASIC TRANSPORTATION

Although against the rules in later years, apparently cars were allowed earlier. John McCreary '34 wrote about his experiences with a car in an alumni publication:

When I returned from the first cruise my Mother had given me to use an old Marmon. When I returned from our first leave I drove up [from Southern California] in it, bringing some of the cadets with me to help pay the cost. It was a gas-and-oil eater from 'way back, and on a later trip over the 4th of July, on the way South, the main bearing gave out and eventually the clutch went out completely, leaving us stranded in Ventura. We hitched a ride to L.A. and there I bought a Model A roadster. Except for its initial cost it cost me nothing to operate it, for the cadets were always glad to pay reasonable fare to L.A., or San Diego, or up the coast to Eureka and vicinity, and for shorter trips around the Bay Area. Occasionally when I was restricted to the base I rented it out to other cadets at so much a mile, so it was a great advantage at no cost.

sentenced for something to captain's mast and you were sentenced to work shoveling coal on the coal pile. You'd just shovel it from one pile to another."

~~~

Because many of the cadets came to the school without a maritime background or any knowledge of shipboard life, they were allowed several months before committing to either deck or engine. In this way they learned both types of work and could choose their seagoing future based on experience.

Ralph Swany: "The first cruise, the first half of the cruise, I spent with engine room watches, then the second half of the cruise I took deck watches."

Cy Hansen, "In The Beginning":

The Cadet Corps was divided into two watches; the Port and the Starboard watch for routine tasks and classroom instruction as well as for liberty. The watches were further divided into two groups, those standing sea watches and those working about the ship. Because the upper classmen were without sea experience, each was required to stand sea watches on both deck and in the engine room so that he would get enough experience to make a decision as to specialty later during the cruise. The writer remembers being on watch in the boiler room when leaving San Francisco, and being at the helm when the ship crossed the Equator on the twentieth of January 1932. In addition, other cadets were assigned to duties as cadet officer of the deck, master at arms, sweepers, and messmen, work which related to internal discipline and internal operation of the areas assigned to the Cadet Corps.

Ray Aker: "If you had six months in the engine room, you worked down there and did other things pertaining to the engineering. There was always a lot to do in the engine room. Cleaning up, swabbing up, painting and taking things apart and putting them together again. That would include some instruction and a bit of machine shop instruction. The third classmen, the lower classmen, didn't get very much of that machine shop instruction, but we got a little. The upper classmen were learning

to use the lathes and the planers and things of that sort.

"A lot of the kids didn't really know what they wanted to get into. I was pretty much set on going on deck. My interest was in seafaring and in the ship itself. I'd rather be on top of things, so to speak, rather than being an engineering specialist down in the engine room. I was interested in the operation of the ship and the navigation and the operation as a whole, even though I liked machinery and would probably have enjoyed being an engineer, too. The school required that in the

"The first year you had to spend six months on deck and six months in the engine room."

first year you take six months in the engine room and six months on deck. And I think it was a very good thing because if you're going to think about the ship as a whole, you've got to know how it works. You're dealing with a lot of mechanical stuff. I thought it was a very good training and I valued that."

Dick Brannon: "You signed up for a three-year course. The first year you had to spend six months on deck and six months in the engine room. That was compulsory. They would not let you make a decision as to whether you want to be an engineer or deckie. So you spent six months each way and after my six months in each department I made the fatal decision or fateful decision to stay in the engine room."

Ray Aker: "We had a twenty day vacation each year. Holidays off if you weren't standing watch and weekends off. Except on

Saturday mornings we had to do the Naval Reserve requirements for drilling. I think that another requirement of the Navy, too, was that you have experience in the engine room as well as on deck. There was a merchant marine classification in the Navy. Now it is line officer. You'd have to be capable of taking charge of any part of the ship. Engine room or gunnery or navigation or whatever."

Dick Brannon: "My first assignment was on deck. I didn't even know what made a ship go, actually, when I went aboard. I had no idea what made a ship move through the water. I was determined to be deck, but then my six months in the engine room opened up another spectrum. I made the decision to stay in the engine department and the *Henry County* [*California State*] proved to be a very, very fine training ship because she had scotch boilers and an up-and-down triple-expansion engine. The instructors at that time were old-time professional marine engineers from World War I. We had two Scotsmen, Dave Warwick and Walter Lewin, both typical old-time Glencannon-type Scots tinkerer-engineers, but with a little bit more polish than Colin Glencannon.[6] They gave us our basic training and they were basic full-time engineers.

> *Dwyer was the engineer who took over the Leviathan from the Germans in World War I.*

Then we had a guy named Walter Clark who was a professional modern steam engineer. I don't know what ships he was on but he introduced us into modern water tube boiler steam turbine-type engineering.

"The head of the engineering department was Dwyer. He was the engineer who took over the *Leviathan* when the Americans took the *Imperator* or *Vaterland*, whichever one she was, from the Germans in World War I.[7] She was a coal burner. When the Americans took her over as war reparations, they converted to oil and Dwyer was the engineer that was assigned to convert her from coal to oil. So we had absolutely top-quality old-time engineers who had made the gap from scotch boilers and coal to turbines and oil, watertube boilers. We were right at the transition period in the middle thirties, absolutely magnificent training.

"Our superb engineering instructors took us through all the basics of basic engineering. We did casting and foundry work. If we wanted to make a spare part, they made us do it in the foundry at the old Navy coaling station. By extension, the deck cadets were thoroughly schooled by really professional navigation people. We had ex-Navy people, the executive officer was George Barkley who was a graduate of the Massachusetts schoolship. We had a very, very fine, fine group of instructors who doubled as the ship's officers on the ship."

Ralph Swany: "Everybody was a merchantman. The executive officer came out of Standard Oil, and the chief came off the waterfront, Grant came off the waterfront, Barkley, he came off the waterfront. And

---

[6] Colin Glencannon, a fictional creation of Guy Gilpatric, was a Scots Chief Engineer on a British merchant ship. The Glencannon stories appeared in *The Saturday Evening Post* in the 1930s, 40s and 50s and had a world-wide following among mariners and others.

[7] Great Britain got the *Imperator* as a war prize and renamed it *Berengaria*. The United States seized the *Vaterland* in New York and renamed it *Leviathan*.

Dwyer, he was the chief engineer, he was off the waterfront but he had been chief engineer on the *Leviathan* and he was the head of the department of engineering. Real good guy."

Charles Audet: "Safety was, of course, hammered into people all the time and I think it just became second nature with me. It was one of the bonuses of that training, the old saying 'One hand for yourself and one for the ship.' It registered. People were very, very, safety-conscious."

~~~

On December 29, 1931 the ship was alongside the dock at Union Iron Works in San Francisco, preparing for its first training cruise. Sailing two days later, the cadets began an enviable five-month odyssey — down the West Coast of South America, through the Straits of Magellan, up the East Coast of South America, into the Caribbean, up the United States East Coast, down through the Panama Canal and back to Tiburon.

But first the ship had to get away from the dock . . .

Cy Hansen, "In the Beginning":

. . . the bridge signaled for the engine to go astern to back out of the slip. The engine would not turn because the condenser was plugged with mud and the ship was hard and fast aground. Seems she had come over to the Yard from Tiburon and after arrival had been filled with fuel, water, provisions, cadets and crew, and the water was not deep enough, so she sat in the mud, immobilized, unable to move. Fortunately, Captain Langren, father of one of the first classmen, who had come over on the Standard Oil tug he commanded, was able to get a line aboard, and in short time had us backed off the mud bank. The condenser was cleared

of mud and we were off on the first leg of our first cruise, around South America.

Cy Hansen: "We had a full crew. It was the only cruise in which we had a full crew, three engineers and three mates on watch. The cadets soon learned how to run the ship and we didn't do that afterward."

John McCreary '34 described the effects of a storm early in the voyage in a letter home:

THE CRUISE OF 1931		
Port	**Arrival**	**Departure**
San Francisco		12/31/31
Balboa, Canal Zone	1/15/32	1/17/32
St. Elmo's Bay, Panama	1/17/32	1/18/32
Callao, Peru	1/24/32	1/26/32
Valparaiso, Chile	2/2/32	2/8/32
Straits of Magellan	2/12/32	2/16/32
Buenos Aires, Argentina	2/22/32	2/27/32
Montevideo, Uruguay	2/27/32	3/1/32
Rio de Janeiro, Brazil	3/6/32	3/13/32
Port of Spain, Trinidad	3/26/32	3/27/32
Hampton Roads, Virginia	4/4/32	4/5/32
Washington, D.C.	4/6/32	4/12/32
New York City	4/14/32	4/20/32
Cristobal, Canal Zone	4/29/32	
Balboa, Canal Zone		4/30/32
San Diego, California	5/13/32	5/16/32
Los Angeles	5/16/32	5/22/32
Santa Barbara	5/23/32	5/24/32
Tiburon	5/28/32	

Boy! We hit the Gulf of Tehuantepec the other day. Some were sick early in the morning and by night most of the rest were or had been. About midnight the waves were breaking over the bridge and the boat was standing on one end and then the other, but always a clear sky with lots of stars. We cut our engines down to 4 1/2 knots and at times we didn't gain a foot for minutes . . . Most of the food is phooey, but the desserts and cereals are always good . . .

Everyone has it all planned what they will get to eat when we get ashore.

The first of many Crossing-the-Line ceremonies was held aboard the schoolship. This centuries-old rite-of-passage indoctrinates novices (pollywogs) into the realm of King Neptune by making them "shellbacks" as they cross the equator.

Cy Hansen, "In the Beginning":

On the night before we crossed the Line an advance party boarded the ship and all the Ship's company who were not "shellbacks" were served with sum-

On April 7, 1932 the cadets were guests of President Hoover at the White House.

monses to appear before the court of Neptunus Rex on January 20, 1932 for trial and punishment for having the audacity to enter the Royal Domain.

Cy Hansen: "We crossed the equator going south. Of course, all of us were land-lubbers and some of the ship's officers, too. We all went through the ceremony. George Barkley was the navigator. He was sent up on the bow the day before with telescope and dress blues and bridge coat to look for the Neptune party."

The *USS California State* became almost an instant celebrity. In each port the ship and her complement were given preferential treatment.

In Callao, Peru, the American Ambassador came aboard to tour the ship. Whale boat races were held with crews from nearby Peruvian Navy Warships.

In Valparaiso, Chile, the cadet corps visited the *HMS Dauntless*.

Cy Hansen: "We went through the inside passage of Chile. A couple of times the ship appeared to be heading straight for the mountains, then a slight change in course and a narrow passage would appear. We went through English Narrows, so narrow that it looked like we could pick leaves from the trees on each side. In the lower parts of the Straits we saw icebergs, glaciers and volcanos. We stopped at Punta Arenas, then went up to Buenos Aires."

In Buenos Aires, Argentina, the Seaman's Institute held a dance for the cadet corps and in Rio de Janeiro, the American Foreign Society held a dance for them at the Country Club. The cadets found themselves acting as unofficial ambassadors for the State of California and, to some degree, the United States.

Cy Hansen: "In Buenos Aires we went to a meat packing plant that was one of the largest in the world and saw the process of preparing the beef. One or two of our cadets even participated in killing the animals. Then across the river to Montevideo, to another packing plant, the Swift Company plant, then Rio de Janeiro. My class celebrated its first anniversary there."

The ship continued up the east coasts of South, then North, America.

Cy Hanson: "At Hampton Roads we cleaned up the ship and proceeded up the Potomac River to the Washington Navy Yard. We stopped the engines on the ship and coasted past Mount Vernon. We lowered the flag and brought it back up again with all hands in formation."

The cadets visited the White House on April 7, 1932 where they were guests of

President Hoover. After the usual picture-taking ceremonies he graciously told the students, "If there is anything you want or any place you want to see, and they won't let you in, come to me."

Ralph Swany: "When we were in Washington, D.C. we were tied up at the Navy docks and they had an open house. I was showing two ladies around and got to the point where they looked down at the main engine, the top of the cylinders. 'Oh! What is that, your sewing machine?' Cut me to the quick."

Cy Hansen: "The ship was open to visitors. We had thousands aboard. One of the interesting things was some looked down at the engine room and said, 'My, what an interesting washing machine you have.'

"They wanted to know if we stopped every night at sea. They seemed surprised when we told them we didn't."

New York City rolled out the welcome mat for the ship and the students. The New York State Maritime Academy sponsored a circle tour of Manhattan for the cadets and they visited the famed Roxy theater as guests of the management. A special tour of the great trans-Atlantic liner *SS Leviathan* was arranged on April 16 and on April 18 they toured the Sperry gyroscope factory. On April 19 they paraded at City Hall for Mayor Walker and toured what many considered the eighth wonder of the world, the Empire State Building.

Cy Hansen: "We went downtown with the New York Nautical School to see Mayor Jimmy Walker and City Hall, then went to the top of the Empire State Building which had been built the year before. There we visited with Al Smith [who lost the 1928 presidential election to Herbert Hoover]. That was one of his projects."

Transiting the Panama Canal, then up the West Coast, the ship put in at Los Angeles and the cadets toured Universal City and Hollywood picture studios. In Santa Barbara, the City feted the corps and officers at a luncheon.

Interest in the new schoolship was high. After their return, 130 members of the San Francisco Propeller Club visited the ship, arriving in water taxis provided by Crowley Maritime.[8]

~~~

Crew a ship with a corps of healthy young men, add the well-known effect of sea air on the appetite, stir in a vigorous schedule of class work and ship work, and you can expect an interest in food. Meals were served on board, whether the ship was on cruise or tied up to the Tiburon coaling station.

Ray Aker: "[The pamphlet they gave us] says the food served is 'simple and substantial but abundant.' It might have been abundant, but we didn't think it was very good. It was like institutional food. We used to joke about some of the food that came aboard in cases. They used surplus food, state surplus, wherever they could get that, and they had kind of a stock food. The case would say, 'Not approved by USDA standard, but fit for consumption.' Well that was all right. But you were getting the same thing over and over."

BELOW U. S. STANDARD
LOW QUALITY BUT NOT ILLEGAL

Courtesy Ralph Swany.

---

[8] Crowley Maritime began on San Francisco Bay in the 19th century ferrying crew and supplies to anchored ships with Whitehall boats. By 1932 it was one of San Francisco's leading tugboat and launch companies. Today it has expanded to international shipping and barge traffic, but in early 1996 announced it was ending its tugboat operations in San Francisco.

THE SHIP'S ROUTINE AT SEA

While the ship was on cruise it was operated 24 hours a day 7 days a week and it was necessary for those on duty roster to stand watch on a 24 hour basis: 12 midnight to 4 AM, 4 AM to 8 AM, 8 AM to 12 noon, 12 to 4PM, 4PM to 6PM, 6PM to 8 PM (second dog watch) and 8 PM to midnight. Deck watches were Cadet officer of the watch and helmsman, both first classmen, and messenger, bow lookout and lifebuoy watch, second classmen. The Cadet officer of the watch was in charge of the watch and performed duties of a ship's mate on watch at sea. The helmsman sometimes attempted to sign his name on the vast Pacific but rarely ever returned to dot the "i". The messenger and lookouts spent hours looking into the void ahead or behind the ship and/or running errands and fetching coffee for the Cadet officer of the watch and the helmsman. The messenger also acted as "alarm clock" for night watchstanders and for Cadet master at arms each morning. Engine room watches (black gang) were platformsman (Cadet watch engineer), oilers, water tender and firemen. The platformsman was in charge of Cadets in the engine room, read gauges and thermometers and entered hourly information in the engine room log. There were three oilers: upper oiler, lower oiler and auxiliary oiler. The upper oiler squirted oil into the oil cups on the engine crossheads to keep the cranks lubricated and tended to the generators, evaporator and forced draft blower which were located on the middle grate level; the lower oiler oiled the main journal bearings, eccentrics, adjust bearing and the bearings in the propeller shaft tunnel; the auxiliary oiler oiled the pumps and air compressors in the lower engine room as well as the ice machines and steering engine aft. The water tender kept an eye on water level in the boilers and in the hot well. Firemen manipulated fuel oil pressure, temperatures and burners to maintain constant steam pressure and make squiggly marks on the recording "tell tale" in the Chief Engineer's office as well as send out smoke signals even if there were no Indians in the area. Duties included cleaning burners once a watch and helping blow tubes when required, a hot dirty job. Occasionally a burner was pulled without shutting off the oil and the hapless fireman would then have an opportunity to wipe up the spilled oil as well as get an opportunity to appear at Captain's mast and get some extra duty and/or liberty restrictions.

Communication to the Bridge and to the Chief Engineer's room was by voice tube. A whistle was attached to the terminals of the tubes which was sounded by blowing air from the mouth of the caller to actuate the whistle. Surprisingly the tubes conveyed the voices very well. Engine operating signals were sent from the Bridge by means of a mechanical engine room telegraph provided with a dial to indicate engine speeds "ahead" or "astern" and a large bell to alert the engine room crew. Bell signals were recorded by deck and engine personnel in a "Bell Book" used only for the purpose of recording such information.

The bridge, small and somewhat crowded, was typical of the bridges on merchant ships of the day. The bridge consisted of the wheelhouse, two bridge wings and the chart room. A multispoked wooden wheel located in the wheelhouse was the object by which the helmsman steered the ship by following the course set by the officer of the watch. The helmsman had to watch a magnetic compass installed in the binnacle directly in front of the wheel, although they usually steered by a gyro compass repeater mounted alongside of the binnacle. The Officer of the watch was usually stationed on one of the wings of the bridge to observe the condition of the sea ahead and to be alert for ships or objects near the ship. There was no radar (it hadn't even been invented) or Loran. The only aid to navigation was a primitive radio compass device. Lookouts fore and aft were stationed to watch for approaching vessels, land falls, etc. They reported any sighting by hailing the bridge and shouting the information to the Officer stationed there. No telephones were installed for communication between the bridge, the lookouts, or the engine room. A flying bridge, complete with wheel and compasses, was located directly above the bridge and an after steering station was located on the poop deck near the steering engine room. Means were also provided to operate the rudder from the steam winches aft in event of loss of the steering engine.

Cy Hansen, "In the Beginning."

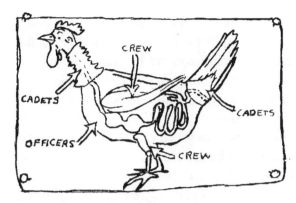

This drawing from the Hawse Pipe *shows the cadets' view of the way food was apportioned.*

Cy Hansen: "The food was so-so. We had problems with the type of people we got for the cruise. The cooks and the rest of it weren't the best. On the trip south, after Valparaiso, the food got so bad a lot of us got to eating bread and butter and when the butter got to tasting rancid then it was bread and mustard and sugar. We got better food again after Buenos Aires."

Being constantly hungry, the cadets weren't too fussy. They'd eat anything. Credit Hawse Pipe.

Ralph Swany: "The food was lousy. There's one sticker, 'Below U.S. standard but not illegal.' It was actually on the cans. That was the food we had. The baker was the head man on the ship, baking bread. I know I used to eat a lot of bread. They used to have these Tea Garden preserves. That was real fancy preserves. We got a lot of that. We had that and put it on the bread, or mustard. Bread and mustard. And I can still take bread and smear it with mustard, eat and relish it. We kept the baker busy. Otherwise we weren't happy with it [the food]."

Ray Aker: "We got pancakes in the morning which were really tough. They called them 'collision mats.' I used to like pancakes when I was a kid but these would really load you up. You felt like you were bloated. But they were nourishing. And eggs, God, we'd get fried eggs in the morning and they'd be half-done. Well, I guess it was a standard breakfast, you got some fruit, it might be canned apricots or pineapple or grapefruit. Not an awful lot of fresh stuff but you'd get some."

From one of the early yearbooks: "A subject of great mirth and constant grumblings among the ranks of the Cadet Corps is the 'Verse Padded Menus' that appear each day in the galley for cooking instructions to the culinary dept. To read one of these choice morsels is enough to make any outsider lick his chops with delight, but to those of us in the Cadet Corps 'PRIME BRAZED SHORT RIBS OF BEEF, AU JUS' are just plain old 'dog bones' with a fancy name."

But others had a different view. Dick Brannon: "In the middle '30s the United States was coming out of a horrendous economic depression. The standard cadets who came in were from all walks of life, the sons of people who had survived the economic depression, fellows like myself whose parents were just scraping along, WPA, Works Progress Administration, all that, just scraping by on welfare.

We all went aboard that ship on October 24, 1935. Still, we weren't in the clear yet, depression-wise. I, who'd grown up on oatmeal and peanut butter and the fruit we'd raised in our own garden, was alongside people from Hollywood and Santa Barbara, wealthy people who had steak and eggs.

"I thought, my God, the food was the most fabulous food I'd ever heard of in my life. My God, I'm eating for the first time in my life. The people from Hollywood, the upper echelon, 'Yeeuch, oh, my God what are they feeding us now?' How in the hell can they bitch about the food? I'm eating meat and good stuff for the first time in my life and I couldn't understand how people could bitch about the food.

"We had a dedicated galley crew from ashore and they did the best they could with the material on hand. We were adequately fed, nothing fancy, but the food was, in my humble opinion, coming from a depression home, very, very good."

The galley crew was part of the ship's hired crew. In addition, there were a doctor, radio operator, cooks, laundrymen, a machinist and two or three seamen.

Dick Brannon: "We had a professional laundry guy, he prepared all the ship's laundry. We had a laundry on the ship, so we didn't have to scrub clothes in a bucket or anything like that. We had a regular laundry and that was a big plus."

Charles Audet: "The laundry man, George Goetz, was nicknamed 'Suds' and he had an assistant nicknamed 'Soapy,' and we had a cook and a helper and a pantryman and they were more or less permanent."

Dick Brannon: "We had no room stewards, no help of any kind, just the galley staff, and the cooks. We did all of our own cleaning and housekeeping on the ship.

"Instructors in the classroom at sea were the ship's officers. In addition to the engineer instructors we had one professional machinist, an all-around machinist. He was a floating professional who took care of our refrigeration and our electricity, our machine shop work. He was a combination instructor and a hired hand but available at all times. You might call him deck engineer, machinist or combination. On deck we had a hired bosun, Paddy McCarthy. Now, <u>he</u> was a relic from the old sailing ship days. He hung out up on the fo'c'sle head. He had a carpenter shop, bosun's stores, the whole thing, traditional, on the starboard side of the machine shop in number four 'tween deck. He was a hired professional bosun. He was the deck instructor for basic seamanship. An old-time bosun. So we had absolutely professional help. We learned it right on the ship."

Paddy McCarthy was a true sailor, having been on the Downeaster *Jabez Howes* at the turn of the century.

Cy Hansen: "Paddy McCarthy was an old sailor on the ship. He was a typical Irishman. He had a little bit of an Irish brogue, white, white, hair, large nose, Just a great story teller, always had stories to tell about this and that. We used to like to sit around and listen to him. He was a great instructor, taught marlinspike seamanship. He taught us how to mix our own paint with white lead, turpentine and linseed oil. The carpenter was Kenny Cameron, a Scotsman."

~~~

In November 1932, the ship was towed to Mare Island for repairs and further outfitting in preparation for her next cruise — around the world. She was placed alongside the *USS Ramapo*, then at Berth "B" Mare Island, into Drydock #1, then alongside the *USS Altair* and, finally, at Berth "H".

Two views of the California State in drydock at Mare Island before her around-the-world cruise. Courtesy Ralph Swany.

THE CRUISE OF 1932

Port	Arrival	Departure
Tiburon/San Francisco		12/31/32
Honolulu, Territory of Hawaii	1/9/33	1/11/33
Apra, Guam	1/26/33	1/27/33
Manila, Philippines	2/1/33	2/6/33
Singapore, Malaysia	2/11/33	2/14/33
Colombo, Ceylon	2/20/33	2/23/33
Suez, Egypt	3/9/33	
Alexandria, Egypt		3/17/33
Naples, Italy	3/22/33	4/1/33
Villefranche, France	4/2/33	4/14/33
Barcelona, Spain	4/16/33	4/24/33
Gibraltar	4/26/33	4/27/33
Funchel, Madeira	4/30/33	4/30/33
Curaçao, Dutch West Indies	5/14/33	5/15/33
Cristobal, Canal Zone	5/18/33	
Balboa, Canal Zone		5/19/33
San Diego	6/1/33	6/3/33
San Pedro	6/3/33	6/9/33
Santa Barbara	6/9/33	6/10/33
Tiburon/San Francisco	6/12/33	

While the ship was in Cairo, the cadets visited the pyramids; half the student body visited one day, the other half, the second. Courtesy Ralph Swany.

Cy Hansen: "Prior to the cruise we took the ship up to Mare Island and we then worked with the crew at Mare Island, opening valves in the engine room, grinding valves, re-packing, adding a new forced draft fan. The ship was in good condition when we sailed."

In late December there were various tests and trial runs around San Francisco Bay just prior to departure. Commanded by Capt. Emile Topp, the ship performed splendidly.

Some highlights of the 1932 cruise:

— Singapore, Malaysia. The cadets challenged the American Association to a base-ball game and beat them 11-4.

— Colombo, Ceylon. It was necessary to chase off the bumboats by turning fire hoses on them.[9]

Cy Hansen: "In Colombo, one of the great points was we went up to the city of Kandy. We were guests of the school there and they put on some native dances. Then they asked us to sing some California songs but all we could come up with was 'Clementine.' So we sang that and they liked it."

— Suez and Alexandria. Ralph Swany: "We came up into Alexandria, Port Said, and the French Government wanted excess funds for our transit of the Suez Canal because President Roosevelt had just devalued the dollar, took it off the market. It cost us a lot of extra dollars to make the canal transit through Suez, so with that we went from Port Said up to Alexandria, then from Alexandria we went to Naples and Villefranche de Mer.

---

[9] Bumboats are small boats which congregate around ships in foreign ports offering all manner of goods and services.

The California State *at Naples during her 1932 cruise. The stern is moored to the dock with the bow held in place by either a buoy or the ship's anchor. Courtesy Ralph Swany.*

We were supposed to go to Piraeus but the curtailment of funds had taken our fuel money so we cut Piraeus and went right to Villefranche."

Malcom E. Crossman, the first executive officer, wrote in 1983:

> *For a while, on the round-the-world cruise, it was doubtful that we would be able to transit the Suez Canal. The "Bank Holiday of 1933" caused all banks and savings and loan associations to close. The French firm of De Lesseps that controlled the Suez Canal, believed that the U.S. was broke and that our money was worthless. So, we stayed at anchor for 2 or 3 days until the U.S. Consul-General, who was named Emillard, arranged with a friend of his in the Egyptian Bank, for us to transfer our dollars into Egyptian Pounds, and from Egyptian Pounds into French gold francs. De Lesseps accepted the francs*

for the toll and we were allowed to transit the Canal and continue our round-the-world cruise.

John McCreary described the Suez transit in his writings to alumni in the 1980s:

> *Suez is a funny place, from the sea, small, two and three story houses, level desert nearly all around the horizon; but on one side high cliffs where mining operations were in progress. As we went full ahead up the canal, close to the houses on one side (yelling kids, men on bicycles, veiled women) and desert on the other (camels, low huts similar to Mongolian desert homes) the light grew dimmer, the moon came up from the east, Mars shone as the Eastern Star and the setting was perfect; the sun left beautiful shades on the hills and in the sky. On the focsle it was quite cold, but such a thrill resulted from the peace, quiet, beauty, made us all forget the*

cold. . . . At midnight we passed a ship tied up in one of the tie-up places (for passing), a Maru boat, and some Englishers on the after deck waved hallos. The Suez Canal is even more thrilling than the Panama. At four all around was desert, and buoys in the Canal. At five. . . we were in Port Said about <u>sixty</u> <u>feet</u> from shore. Across the other side they are coaling ship by hand. . .

After transiting the Suez Canal, the ship tied up in Alexandria for several days, allowing the cadets to tour Cairo and take an unforgettable trip to the Pyramids.

— Naples, Italy. Visits were exchanged with the Naples Nautical School. The ship later shifted to Capri.

Cy Hansen: "Almost the whole ship's company went to Rome. The highlight was an audience with Pope Pius XI and that afternoon we were taken to the Pallazzo Venetia and were guests at a private audience with Benito Mussolini. This was followed by a party at the American Embassy and then we were the guests of the Italian Navy."

— Villefranche, France. Cy Hansen: "We were there ten days. The cadets traveled all over Europe. We didn't have very much money between us, either. I went to Paris. The round trip to Paris was seven dollars and that practically broke me."

— Barcelona, Spain. The cadets played a baseball game with Liga Baseball Barcelona and basketball with the Second Army Corps of the Spanish Army.

Cy Hansen: "I got the flu in Barcelona, so I couldn't go ashore. I caught it and the chief cook had something similar and had problems with his stomach. He had been a dope user and this flu upset him. He died and we buried him at sea. It was a very impressive ceremony. We stood in formation and we had two sailors and a bosun and carpenter who were old time sailors that sailed on sailing ships. It was very impressive, very moving. The ship was stopped, the captain read the burial ceremony and we dropped him over the side."

— Gibraltar. Word was received that the California Nautical School might close.

Cy Hansen, "In the Beginning":

Captain Topp had all hands mustered on the foredeck and made a very dramatic and impassioned announcement that the State of California had not allocated funds to continue operation of the school and that it was doubtful that there would be enough money available to finish out the school year and graduate members of all three classes. On this somber note we sailed from Gibraltar . . .

A Lesson In Getting Tattooed

From the *Hawse Pipe*: "Colombo was dead as far as entertainment for the cadet corps was concerned. They spent their leisure time getting tattooed. Harry Sweetser, future side-show-man, had several more works of art added to his collection. A few third classmen had their virgin skins marred by an anchor or a sweetheart's name.

"'The fall guy,' was McTussel. This gallant martyr had not one amorous epistle from his amorata since the start of the cruise. In Colombo her name, Bernice, was artistically inscribed in the center of a large heart upon his noble biceps. Later while at sea our hero became down-hearted, melancholy, and forlorn. The lady had not written! "Sharper than the serpent's tooth, is a love that is scorned." Shaking his blond curls with determination, McTussel burned the inscription off his arm with a red-hot iron. 'Love's labor lost.' The very next port he received a number of letters from the object of his agonies."

Capt. Emile Topp, left, and Chief Engineer Richard Dwyer. Los Angeles Times, *1932, courtesy Ralph Swany.*

The cruise was a wonderful, horizon-broadening, culturally-enriching experience for the cadets, many of whom had never been out of the State of California. They sailed the sea lanes of Caribbean pirates. They saw first-hand the mysterious cultures of the East, the languid lagoons of tropical islands, the grandeur of Egypt and Rome, the vitality of centuries-old civilizations. But realizing romantic dreams of world travel was not all.

Cy Hansen: "The second cruise was around the world, which was very ambitious. One of the things we learned, which we all got, was we learned an awful lot about commerce. Those of us that wanted learned a lot about what was going on in the world."

~~~

Cy Hansen, "In the Beginning":

The years 1934-1935 were a period of uncertainty and concern for the continuing operation of the California Nautical School. It was a time of the great worldwide Depression and the State of California Legislature was very reluctant to appropriate monies for the continued operation of the school. . .

After the graduation of the 1934 class in February, 1934, the remaining students and officers readied the California State for shutdown and all cadets were granted an indefinite leave

until additional funds for operating the school were appropriated.

In August of 1934 the vacationing cadets were informed by letter that school would be resumed, that there might be enough money available for them to complete their training and graduate and that they should return to California City to resume training. The Board of Governors decided that the school should make a short cruise to as many California cities as possible to publicize the school and let as many people as possible see what type of training was being provided for California youngsters and if possible recruit new students for future classes. The cruise started on November 23 and ended on January 3, 1935 . . . As a result of the cruise a number of interested boosters were able to convince the Legislature to appropriate $25,000 to be matched by Federal funds and thus ensure the continued operation of the school, graduation of the class of 1935 and provide for a new class of 1938 to be admitted in the fall of 1935.

The West Coast "show the flag" cruise of 1934 included the ports of: Crescent City, Eureka, Monterey, Port San Luis, San Pedro, San Diego and Tiburon.

Cy Hansen continues the saga of the school's financial woes in "In the Beginning":

The final cruise [before the school was temporarily shut down for a second time], a trip to the Hawaiian Islands, was made between April 3 and May 20, 1935 with stops at Hilo, Lahaina and Honolulu. Because of the lack of funds the cadets were required to do most of the shipboard work, except food preparation, including mess cook duty and assisting in the laundry. They stood all watches at sea including Officer of the Deck and Officer in charge of the engine room. As a result they came out of the school well qualified to perform the functions of a watch officer in the Merchant Marine with confidence in their ability. However, due to an interpretation by the Steamboat Inspection Service relative to actual length of time spent at sea they were unable to obtain certification as able seamen and were forced to sail as ordinary seamen or wipers until they had completed the required twelve months of sea time. Thus they were in possession of a ticket certifying them to be a

"The state just didn't have money for the school."

third mate or third engineer, but they were not certified to be qualified as a petty officer.

Upon return to the base, members of the class were sent to take their license examinations in groups of seven, however, after about a week, those still waiting to sit for their examinations were told there was no more money available to feed and house them and they were forced to find accommodations elsewhere.

. . . another class, 1938, was admitted later that year and the school [resumed operation].

With the license exams began a tradition that continues to this day. John McCreary '34 recalled in the 1980s:

The tests take a day or two, and due to the large number in the class it was split in two. Almost immediately we began to gather the questions that were asked them, as they came back to the ship and repeated as much of the examination as they could recall. This gave us hints on which subjects and portions of subjects to concentrate.

The cruise of 1935 included the ports of: Oakland; Hilo, Territory of Hawaii; Lahaina, T.H.; Honolulu, T.H.; San Diego, Long Beach, Santa Barbara and Stockton.

Then, according to Cy Hansen: "The ship was laid up. The class of '35 was going to be cut. Then one of the Santa Barbara cadets [through family connections] got the money together to make the cruise. The ship was laid up after the cruise and the school started up again after the first of January 1936.

"The state just didn't have money for the school. We were always in a sweat around there for oil and water and food."

Although the school may not have technically reopened until January 1, 1936, the *Hawse Pipe* records new cadets coming aboard in October. "The first half of our present class of cadets entered the school on October 15, 1935. Until we went to Mare Island for our annual overhaul, much time was devoted to cleaning the ship up, as very little work had been done on it since the last class graduated in June.

"On November the fourth we made our first trip, of about four hours, to Mare Island Navy Yard where the cement ballast was restowed in number one and four holds, the engine was overhauled, the boilers tested, settling tanks cleaned, the boat deck recaulked, and numerous small jobs were done by the yard workmen. We helped with those jobs as best we could, but most of our time was spent chipping and painting the decks. There was plenty of work for everyone . . .

"The last half of our class entered on January the eighth, and for the first two weeks

DECK VS. ENGINE

Traditional rivalry between deck and engine was no stranger to the *California State.* From the *Hawse Pipe*:

A FRIENDLY WARNING

Blessings on thee, little man
    Who wants to be a mate,
Think of all your wasted life
    And the years you'll have to wait

Think of all your loved ones
    Their heads all bowed in shame
Thinking of their errant son
    Besmirching the family name,

Now if I were you, I'd think again
    And discuss it o'er your beer,
The very best thing for you to do
    Is to be an engineer.
           —A Knight of the Oil Can

SOME GOOD ADVICE

To heck with him, that little man,
That so-called knight of the oil can,
Who always wears his greasy shoes
On any clean deck that he should choose.

He thinks a lot of a reduction gear
And shouts it for all the world to hear.
He fools around with boiler compound,
And with a smoke screen, he's a hound.

Now me, I'd rather be on deck
Then go below into that heck.
I have no yen for pressures on steam
Or any broken valve to ream.

I'd rather stand up on the bridge
And pitch and roll from ridge to ridge
And chip and paint the whole day long
And sing some Black Ball chanty song.

I'd rather be deck-hand, number six
On a ferry on the River Styx
Than be a wiper the whole long day
On the "Queen Mary" or the "Normandie."

Now take my advice, you class coming in,
You may have plenty of vigor and vim,
And if you have any sense at all
You sure won't answer the engineer call.

If you sign for the deck, you can't go wrong,
And you'll never hear that well-known gong,
And a captain you'll be and then you'll rejoice,
And you'll never regret you made this choice.
           —King of the Kingposts.

THE BLACK GANG

Ahoy, you swabs, what's this I hear
Are you trying to libel an engineer?
It may be so, these things you say
About our greasy shoes,
About your nice clean paintwork,
And about our dirty blues,
About our easy classes,
About your hard ones, too,
I know you wouldn't lie to me
But I can't agree with you.

Then here's to the engineers
A goodly bunch are they
Sliding around in the heat below,
Keeping the engine from going too slow.
You say you'd rather be on deck
And watch the deep blue ocean.
The leeward rail will be holding you up,
Inspired by that rolling motion.

So come with me to the engine room
Down to the heat and the din.
When the going is tough and the seas are rough
It's the black gang that brings you in.
           —A Knight of the Oil Can.

they had a christening of rain. With all the Class of 1938 present, much time was spent in soogeeing, painting, and taking on stores . . . in preparation for our first big cruise."

One of the early traditions that no longer exists was that of the "Swab Smoker." Shortly before their first cruise the third classmen were assembled for boxing matches. This was long before the oriental forms of self-defense such as *judo* and *tai kwan do* were popular. Some knowledge of boxing was considered an essential part of any young man's well-rounded education.

Cy Hansen: "When we first went up there we built a beautiful boxing ring in the warehouses. We had boxing matches between the deck and the engine group and between the classes. Boxing was something you did even going to college. It was something everyone did."

The *Hawse Pipe* of 1936 describes one such event:

> We had our first bit of entertainment — a smoker of which movies were taken — aboard ship the evening of January twenty-fourth. The purpose of this smoker was to raise money for a coffee pot in order that the night watches could have something hot to drink. The evening was a success; we got the coffee pot, and several of us got battered up.

Charles Audet: "We held a smoker for every incoming class which included boxing. And it really wasn't much and then we had something like that on the cruise, too. We used to blindfold a couple of guys and let them go at it. That was real fun [rueful laugh]. Entertainment was part of the smoker. We had a guy named Nagle and he used to do a stand-up comedy routine. Had a guy played the piano, other music. It was pretty amateurish

and didn't amount to much but it was something to do. Those were the days before TV or VCRs or anything like that."

Dick Brannon: "[When] I graduated from high school, my sole ambition was to join the Navy, take the competitive exam and go to Annapolis. I went to the Navy recruiting depot in Southern California. And the guy gave me a very nice reception, he said, however — this, mind you, was during depression years — and he said, 'If you pass all the entrance qualifications, if you get into the Navy as an apprentice seaman that will take you at least six months just to get into the Navy because times are extremely tight.' OK. So I went home, and thought it over. At that time California Maritime Academy was in its fourth year of existence and was recruiting cadets. I took the statewide competitive examination and squeaked through and was able to go to California Maritime Academy. So the die was cast."

Cy Hansen: "I came back in the middle of 1936 as an engineering instructor. I came aboard with the new class and stayed until December 31, 1940.

"Brannon was one of the better students we had there."

The school's financial difficulties were temporarily overcome and the cruise of 1936 offered an itinerary that was still restrained but more in keeping with earlier tradition: Tiburon, San Pedro, Balboa, Las Perlas Islands; Cartagena, Colombia; Vera Cruz, Mexico; Houston, Balboa, San Diego, Long Beach, Santa Barbara, Tiburon.

Tragedy struck on this cruise enroute from San Pedro to Balboa. Cadet Willard Moore was stricken with spinal meningitis. He died on February 9 and was buried at sea. A call was put out for assistance. The United States Navy responded with doctors, nurses

Medical Aid on Way

DESTROYER NEARS S. F. PLAGUE SHIP

1 DEAD, 1 STRICKEN

Liner Gives Training Ship Small Supply of Serum

SCHOOL SHIP VISITS PORT
Feb 3 — 1936
New Cadets Get Storm Training
A. At Times California State Departing Today on Cruise to Last Eighty-eight Days

Doctors Rushed to California State Training Vessel
Feb 13
BALBOA, Canal Zone, Feb. 13

Meningitis Serum Sped To State Training Ship

ONE CADET IS DEAD, SECOND IS STRICKEN

The San Francisco papers sensationalized the incident. The headline in the San Francisco Chronicle *(not shown) read "Serum Reaches Death Ship." Courtesy Alvin Gregory.*

and serum. Placed aboard the destroyer *Tatnall*, they raced from Balboa, Panama, to meet the ship. On board was "all the serum available" at Balboa with the promise of a supplemental air drop. On February 10 a second case was reported. The Grace Line ship *Santa Paula* reached the *California State* first, in the early morning of February 12. She put aboard a small quantity of serum and a medical attendant. The Navy destroyer arrived shortly after. The *California State* arrived in Balboa on the evening of the 15th without further outbreaks. The cadets and crew were quarantined for six days and finally granted shore leave.

Dick Brannon: "The first trip I made was direct from San Francisco down through the Panama Canal to Cartegena, Colombia and Vera Cruz, Mexico. In Vera Cruz the Mexican government hosted us on a trip up to Mexico City by train, put us up at the Mexican Military Academy, the equivalent of West Point. The American ambassador, Josephus Daniels, received us at the ambassador's residence. They give us the red carpet treatment. From Vera Cruz we went up to Galveston, Texas. Howard Hughes, he was Mr. Big already at that time, entertained us royally at the Hughes Industrial Complex. Then back down through

the canal and home. We stopped at Mazatlan, had a very nice port stay, then we went across the Gulf of California into Magdalena Bay where we anchored and painted the ship top to bottom. We cleaned and painted the ship ready for our triumphal return to California."

By the mid-1930s the shipboard routine was well-established and had become tradition.

Dick Brannon: "It was open berthing in number one and two holds forward of the house. We only had two holds with tier bunks. All open bunks, and forward in number one were the latrines, one side was showers and wash basins, the other side was the trough type

Inspection on the main deck in white uniforms. Credit U. S. Naval Institute, *courtesy Ray Aker.*

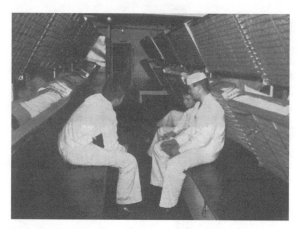 

Left, bunks triced up in the stowed position, while, right, they are down and clearly being put to good use. Left photo Our Navy, *right* U.S. Naval Institute, *both courtesy Ray Aker.*

gravity flow latrines. The messing was in the midship house."

Ray Aker '42: "Somehow we got fed but we had to wait on ourselves. We had a couple of professional cooks on the ship and a baker. The baker would bake bread and cakes and that kind of thing. The galley was on the deck above. The food would come down from the galley to us, where we'd put it out on the trays and have the dishes and so on. We'd take it out to the mess tables. One of the lower classmen was designated to wait on the tables."

Charles Audet: "Cadets did all the washing, cleaning, waiting on tables. We did everything except we had a month or two months up in Mare Island when they did overhaul. In those days it was pretty much a hands-on experience."

Ray Aker: "We'd have to do all the dishwashing and clean up the whole messroom after every meal and scrub down. Saturdays we had inspection, so Fridays we really had to work over that messroom. These were oak tables and we had to scrub them down with sand and canvas and some bleach we put on there to disinfect them. Saturday, you had Saturday inspection and, gosh, the Old Man and George Barkley, the executive officer, and a couple of other officers come on through the ship, through the whole works. They'd be checking the overhead pipes to see if there's any dust up there."

Cy Hansen: "On Saturday mornings we'd have holystone parties on the boat deck. We used chlorinated lime to scrub the decks. It was basically antiseptic and bleach and sand. Then we used the same techniques to clean bulkheads with sand and canvas."

Al Gallant '40: "The reason that the kids did so well who graduated from that school was that all the work done on the school or ship was hands-on training. As I recall, nobody ever did any maintenance on the ship except the students. I can recall doing things such as chipping rust in the bilges."

~~~

By the mid-'30s the economy was stabilizing. President Roosevelt's policies and resolute, upbeat persona infused confidence into the nation. As the Great Depression waned, there was a sense of better times in the offing. Ambitious plans unfolded and construction began on both the Golden Gate and Bay Bridges. From Tiburon, the California Nautical School students watched the bridges go up and saw the creation of Treasure Island at the mid-point anchorage for the double-spanned Bay Bridge. Filled with civic pride over the great accomplishment, San Francisco

General W. E. Gillmore presents Capt. Dwyer with his commission as "Envoy Extraordinary." Oakland Tribune, *courtesy Alvin Gregory.*

announced the Golden Gate International Exposition would be held in 1939, celebrating the opening of the bridges. An atmosphere of positive anticipation was everywhere and extended to the Nautical School.

In October 1936, the *California State* went to Mare Island for annual overhaul. After the "local cruises" of the preceding years the next would be a major trip.

Richard Dwyer had replaced Emile Topp as master. Capt. Dwyer was made "Envoy Extraordinary" and asked to invite Pacific countries the ship visited to attend the 1939 Exposition.

The ship departed Tiburon on November 21, 1936. The ports of call were: Tiburon; Papeete, Tahiti; Auckland, New Zealand; Melbourne, Australia; Sydney, Australia; Suva, Fiji Islands; Pago Pago, Samoa Islands; Honolulu, T.H.; San Diego, Long Beach, Santa Barbara and Tiburon.

Charles Audet: "That was one of the longest cruises the Academy ever made. It was a five months' cruise. Half of my first year was on cruise."

Of course, to reach Australia, the ship had to cross the equator, again invoking the "Crossing the Line" ceremony.

From the 1937 *Hawse Pipe*:

On any ship, when she crosses the Equator, an old custom is dragged out and aired. To wit: that any sailor, passenger or what have you, up until the time he or she actually crosses over the Equator, is in King Neptune's court, regarded as scum, vermin, pollywogs, lousy landsman not fit to grace the table with their presence at any ship's mess. However, once safely across all these sins are forgiven and the much-chastened victim becomes a shellback, deep sea blue-water sailor with a soul as guileless and pure as the proverbial snow.

This miraculous transformation is accomplished under the watchful eye of King Neptune himself, who comes aboard the ship and holds court. Victims are allowed to plead their cause and a defense attorney (Mr. Cadwell) is in attendance for that purpose. His plea in all cases is however some thing like this — "I think he is guilty myself, King. Give him the works!!!!" Across his long flowing shirt tail is a sign reading, "I never win." The prosecuting attorney (Mr. Clark), his running mate, has, "I never lose" on his judicial robes. Neptune (Mr. Warwick) himself, is seated with much pomp and fanfare with his entire court lounging at his feet. His wife sits at his right and the Royal Baby with the hula dancer at his left. The baby is generally some obnoxious looking person selected from the black gang to play the part, and wearing nothing but a dirty grin and a loin cloth sits with his foot smeared with foul smelling grease, which all pollywogs have to kiss with much Gusto.

The sickened swab is next sent to the Royal Doctor for internal treatment where he is given a liberal dosage of a

The Neptune ceremony is held by the Royal Court, above, with the defense attorney, right, and the hula dancer, left, helping to convert pollywogs to shellbacks, below. Bottom photo courtesy Ray Aker, all others courtesy Ralph Swany.

very unsavory liquid composed of castor oil, lubricating oil, fish oil, and any other foul tasting substance that can be found. The stench and sight are enough to nauseate any strong healthy soul. The Royal Doctor is generally some retired abortionist, or by this time the victim thinks so, and he takes great brushes of goo — and paints palpating tonsils with same.

The swab is by this time too groggy to care much what is to happen next. He merrily lies complacently stupified wondering mildly when death's sting will be felt. He cares so little by now that as through glazed eyes he meets those of Mr. Barkley dressed in undertaker black with a coffin under one arm and a large black cross on the other - he sneers - yea, he is that near to eternity, that in a final gesture, he sneers back into those leering eyes.

Up the thirteen stairs to the Royal Barber's chair where an old egg is

opened and (gently??) massaged into the skull, care being taken to get plenty in the ears and nose. From the trap chair the victim does a swan dive in reverse into a tank of sea water in which hardened shellbacks stand waiting to perform such experiments of great scientific value, as to how much salt water the human carcass will hold without becoming water logged. The body is lifted from the tank and left to dry in the sun. If, after a few minutes, it shows signs of life there is one more shellback.

We CNS boys went through it all, and came out better in spite of the rough treatment. Our only consolation being the thought that we perhaps might some day play the part of the royal court. Then will the hideous tortures of the ten cent thrillers seem as a Spring outing. Until then we have only to wait with our sadist ideas. God pity the next group of third classmen if we ever

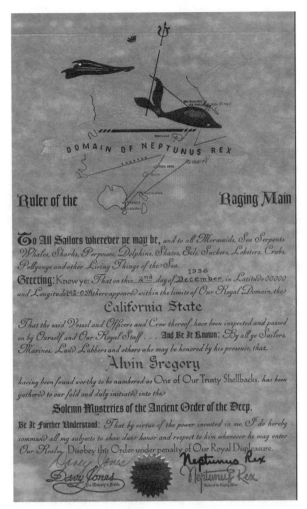

The Neptune Certificate, showing that the owner is now a shellback. Courtesy Alvin Gregory.

enter the domain of King Neptune's Rex again."

Ray Aker: "The upper classmen delighted in putting this on. It was mainly for the benefit of the new kids, swabs. The ceremony would be held on the forward deck. They had that all fixed up with a barber's chair, a throne for the king and the queen and a water tank which they made with dunnage materials and canvas. They got the lower classmen on the afterdeck and made us stay back there while they pulled you through, one or two at a time. You'd hear all that screaming forward. Then the king and the queen were up there on the forward part of the deck with the royal baby.

You'd have to kiss the king's foot and of course it would have all this emulsion stuff on it. Another thing, they had a big trough like a hog trough filled with slops and the daily garbage. You'd have to go through that with your face in that. And finally, at the very end, they put you in a trick barber chair where the royal barber lathered you with engine oil emulsion. He had a great big wooden razor and slashed you across your face a couple of times and then 'All through. Next,' pull the lever and down you'd go into the tank backwards. That was your initiation. Then you spent the rest of the day getting off the grease, red-lead and whatever else they slopped on to you, trying to get that off with saltwater soap and a saltwater shower. It was fun for those that were doing it, but not much fun for those who were going through that."

Charles Audet: "We crossed the equator and I got picked to head up the group that put others through. I had some interesting parts, did Princess whatever her name was, did a female impersonation. And I had a friend of mine act as photographer and he had a camera with a bulb that squirted water. Then we dunked everyone in a large tank."

Dick Brannon: "They pulled out all the stops, everything. The Santa Barbara group (Howard Mollenkopf and Lou Rossi and other guys were the Santa Barbara crowd) they had all this experience with sailing and some of them had been across the line. I was very young when I went there. I was seventeen but some of these guys were much older and [they] had some seagoing experience. There were enough of them who'd been over the line through yachting and the instructors, ship's officers and all who had been on the big cruise around the world, the first big trip for the ship, they had a hard core crew to conduct the pollywog ceremony out on number two hatch. They rigged a big tank and set up the traditional chair and they stripped you down and put crazy clothes on you and cut your hair and you were all blind-folded. They sat you in a chair and lathered you all and shaved you with soaps like emulsion we have in the main engine and made you swallow horrible yucky stuff. And while they're shaving you also they tipped the chair back and dumped you into the pool. And you didn't see any of this, of course, you were still blindfolded. Well, then they took the blind-fold off and they initiated you. They took you up forward and the new pollywogs came up from aft, so you didn't know anything that was going on. But it was the full ceremony, it re-

"They stripped you down and put crazy clothes on you and cut your hair."

ally was, they had a King Neptune and all that. It was one hundred percent, and then inasmuch as Matson was a very, very strong supporter of the whole shebang, they supplied all our certificates, international dateline and shellback and going across the equator and all.[10] So all our certificates are original Matson certificates."

~~~

Cy Hanson: "When we made the cruise in 1936, '37, to Australia, we carried some of the early developments in shortwave radio that enabled all radio people to communicate by shortwave telephone. That was quite an interesting thing because that was put on specifically for the purposes of experimentation and discovering what could be done with short-wave radio. They were quite impressed with the idea that they could actually communicate

from New Zealand and Australia directly with the Coast Guard in San Francisco."

Arriving at Auckland at Christmas time, the ship was hospitably welcomed. Auckland girls and their families took many of the cadets on drives through the surrounding country, and to their homes for Christmas Dinner, English style. Those cadets who remained aboard for dinner were treated to delicious roast young pig, with all the trimmings.

Jack Summerill '38: "I met a gal in New Zealand that I later married. She came aboard with a couple of uncles to tour the ship and I had the duty at the entrance to the ship that evening. I just thought she was something else and I went up to the captain and asked if she could stand watch at the gangway. She did and was there four hours."

Dick Brannon: "We followed the Matson routing one hundred percent, out to Hawaii, down to New Zealand and Australia, back through Samoa and Fiji, Hawaiian Islands then back to San Francisco. That was a long, very interesting cruise and we had a fantastic reception by the New Zealanders and Aussies. There seems to be an affinity, a cultural affinity between New Zealanders and Australians [and us]. We were down there at their time of the abdication of King Edward, when he abdicated in favor of this three-time divorcee wife. New Zealand was practically in a state of mourning, black arm bands, 'How their King could even think . . . How he could possibly abdicate in favor of this . . . 'bimbo from Baltimore.' They were just shocked and horrified. A few days later we were in Australia and they were laughing, 'Oh, God, let's have another beer, mate, hey, that's great. So, the king, yeah, ha, ha,' a big laugh. They thought it was a huge joke. It was just a fantastic difference of opinion."

---

[10] Matson Navigation Company ran from San Francisco to Hawaii and the Pacific Islands beginning in 1882. It is one of the few American-flag steamship companies still in existence and currently operates between the West Coast of the United States and Hawaii.

The "Swab Smoker" of 1937 took place on January 22, while the ship was enroute from Melbourne to Sydney. The tradition had now evolved to include several boxing matches and a "Battle Royal." From the *Hawse Pipe* of 1936-1937:

French Warship and U.S.A. Training Ship Pay Friendly Calls

The Melbourne Sun-News Pictorial *caught an aerial view of the* California State *across the dock from the French sloop* Rigualt de Genouilly. *Courtesy Alvin Gregory.*

An improvised ring was set up in the classroom and a series of six bouts was run off with Doug McMurtry as announcer and Jack "Fagin" Dreyer handling the referee's job. [After the scheduled six bouts] All the swabs who had not participated were called into the ring; blindfolded; given one glove, and turned loose. At the stroke of the bell all hands went at it hammer and tongs, every man for himself. Most of the time they swung on emptiness but occasionally one of the boys would groan and slump to the deck in blissful slumber after meeting somebody's haymaker. Some say it was blind luck, others say it was skill, however the fact remains that Julienel carried away the blue ribbon.

Charles Audet: "When we got to Sydney we had no money and no fuel. The skipper telegraphed the legislature that we needed money. The State legislature went into emergency session and sent us $25,000 to get home on."

Upon completion of the cruise, a new problem developed. For reasons unknown, the Navy suddenly decided that since the

BASEBALL

A TEAM FROM THE VISITING UNITED STATES TRAINING SHIP

U.S.S. CALIFORNIA STATE

WILL PLAY

GOODYEAR

AT

Goodyear Sports Ground

CAMELLIA

Sunday 24th January, 1937

AT 3 P.M.

THE PUBLIC IS CORDIALLY INVITED TO SEE THIS GAME, WHICH WILL BE ONE OF THE FINEST EXHIBITIONS OF THE SEASON.

GOODYEAR BRASS BAND WILL FURNISH MUSIC

ADMISSION FREE

TRAIN TO CAMELLIA LEAVES CLYDE AT 2.32 P.M.

Argus Print, Parramatta.   UW 8804

The California State *baseball team played in Melbourne and Sydney. Courtesy Alvin Gregory.*

California State was technically theirs and only on loan to the school, they would provide the captain for the ship from retired Navy personnel. Capt. Dwyer was replaced as master of the ship by Capt. Niels Nichols of the Boston Navy Yard. This brought an outcry from the Masters, Mates and Pilots Union.

As merchant marine officers we most strenuously object to this appointment. Captain Nichols may be a first class Navy officer, but he has no training nor knowledge of the American Merchant Marine. Furthermore, why should a Navy Officer, retired on a pension, take a position which should rightfully go to a merchant marine officer, who, when he retires, gets no pension?

The California Schoolship was created to train merchant marine officers, and there are many members of the Masters, Mates and Pilots competent and experienced to fill this position.

We do not believe that officers, appointed through special privilege or financial circumstances, to take a bunch of privileged boys for yachting trips, are going to do very much towards building officer material for the American Merchant Marine.

The Navy replied that since they owned and supported the ship with an annual contribution of $25,000 and did all the drydocking and repairs at their base at Mare Island, they had the right to select the master.

The cruise of 1938 began in February. The ports of call were: Honolulu, T.H.; Hilo, T.H.; Acapulco, Mexico; Mazatlan, Mexico; San Diego, Long Beach, Santa Barbara, and Tiburon.

When the ship departed Honolulu, Cappy, a dog belonging to navigation officer Bennett E. Dodson, was left behind. Somehow it was discovered who he belonged to and Matson shipped the pet home on the *SS Matsonia*. He was waiting on the dock when the *California State* arrived in Tiburon.

Unfortunately, the trip was cut short because the engine, known to many of the cadets as the "coffee grinder," broke down. Originally the *California State* was to sail for Callao from Hilo.

Courtesy Alvin Gregory.

This photo of the California State *at Hilo might be better suited to a travel brochure. Credit U.S. Naval Institute, courtesy Ray Aker.*

As the ship came alongside, Cappy, foreground, and Soogee were reunited. Credit San Francisco Chronicle, courtesy Alvin Gregory.

Dick Brannon: "Our port of departure on our last cruise was Hilo, Hawaii to Panama and we were going to go down to South America. On the way between Hilo and Panama, geographically in, I think, the most remote spot of ocean of any place in the world, the piston ring broke in the HP piston and fractured and jammed the piston in its stroke at full speed. The engine came to a screaming, clattering, banging halt and the shock bent the piston rod, wrecked the packing and we

STATE AT AUCKLAND NEW ZEALAND DEC. 23. 1936

literally came to a screaming halt right in the middle of the ocean two thousand miles from the nearest land."

Cy Hansen: "I was supposed to be on watch in '38 when that thing busted. I was down in the engine room in about thirteen seconds."

Dick Brannon: "The old-time engineers, they just took a look at it, 'Yeah, OK.' They said we'd just have to go two-legged: IP, LP. And this engine is so remarkable that in just a very few short hours, with cadets doing all the work under these old-time instructors, we disconnected all the mechanical components on the HP piston and we came in on two cylinders."

Cy Hansen: "We tried to make repairs. We had a spare rod so we got that out and dressed it and tried to repair the damage. But the cylinder was too badly beat up."

Al Gallant: "We spent three days fixing that thing. We took the cylinder head off and down there we could see all the damage done in the cylinder."

Dick Brannon: "They aborted Panama, they said, 'Well, two cylinders, if something else happens we might be in trouble.' We diverted from the Hilo route to Panama, to Acapulco. We put into Acapulco and looked everything over, decided there was nothing we could do there, so we came back direct. They cut out the rest of the cruise.

"But we had a nice stay in Acapulco, went up to Mexico City, this time by bus, a twelve-hour trip up the river beds while they were building the highways. Really an interesting, long, long, bumpy twelve-hour ride. I guess now, on a superhighway, you can make it in three or four hours."

Cy Hansen: "I was the 'water king.' And we were low on water. We got some water in Acapulco in our lifeboats, and they sent out a couple of leaky old water barges that didn't help any. And our evaporator wouldn't make

enough. By the time we got into San Diego we were down to three or four inches of water. Now, Soogee was normally the first one down the gangway when we got in port, but I went off with water hoses on my shoulders and hooked them up and started pumping. And I beat the dog down the gangway."

Dick Brannon: "Our engineers, they went up to Mare Island. Mare Island was very supportive of the ship, they loaned us all the equipment we needed.

"We came back and Dwyer went to Mare Island and found out there was $25,000 available and that the yard could do certain work and that included new casting for the piston, rings, follower plate, new rods. They poured some new rods for us. What we did was line the engine up, the engine was out of line a little bit. We removed the old broken cylinder liner and they cast and machined a new liner for us. And this stuff was all brought to the base and we had a beautiful machine shop on the base, a huge lathe with a forty-two inch throw. The cadets did all the pistons and liners and new rods, machined them and cut the taper and threads on them."

Al Gallant: "We took out the old cylinder liner. Lot of work. Cleaned up the inside, measured the diameter of the hole, then we had a machine shop up on the hill that had belonged to the Navy. There was a lathe up there that could handle eighty inches in diameter. We put this liner up there and machined it on the inside and the outside. To make it fit we had to put the cylinder liner into the icebox and lower the temperature down to minus twenty degrees. That shrunk the diameter of the liner. We brought it around to the engine room door. Above the engine was a crane and we rigged that and because it [the liner] was shrunk in size we lowered it in place and as the temperature got warmer it got tight."

Dick Brannon: "We rebored and rebuilt the HP cylinder, all cadet labor, and parts were no problem in those days. We rebuilt the engine right there at Tiburon. That was an extremely valuable lesson in hands-on marine engineering, repairing one of these engines. Learning how to deal with the problem when it happens at sea, learning how to correct it after we get alongside. We never called in any shoreside help of any kind. It was done right on the ship."

Al Gallant recalled on another occasion his first lesson in common sense seamanship: "Several of us were in the shaft alley near the stern tube, where the packing is. The ship was a riveted hull, it was not a welded hull. We were chipping in the bilges and I was chipping on a rivet and all of a sudden, whamo! The rivet let loose and I had chipped a hole right in the hull. So right away we had to go get a piece of wood and cut a plug and we plugged the hole and that stopped the water. We got word to one of the deck officers, and we told him what happened. He said, 'Get a broomhandle and tie a string on it and push it through the hole. Get a bolt the same size as the hole, get some gasket material and put it around the bolt. Pull the string back through the hole with the bolt on it.'

"On the bolt, the side that came through the hole, we filed that square. Then we put a washer on the bolt and nut and by putting a wrench on the square end, tightened it that way. Next time they put the ship in drydock they put a rivet in there. And so that was the end of that problem."

~~~

The "Swab Smoker" had evolved to include entertainment as well as the earlier "murder and mayhem." From the 1938 *Hawse Pipe*:

After having several months to get acquainted with itself, the swab class was able and willing to organize its own smoker complete with music, drama, and boxing. Such an affair was presented for the edification of all upper classmen and officers one day short of

ABOUT THE ENGINE

The ship was propelled by a steam power plant consisting of two Scotch boilers each fitted with three oil fired furnaces with Howden system of forced draft. Fuel was Bunker "C" residual oil heated to temperatures about 180°-208° F. and at pressures of 125-150 pounds per square inch. Steam at 180 psi was used in the engine, engine room auxiliaries and for deck machinery, winches and anchor winch, steering engine and ice machines. The engine was a triple-expansion double-acting steam engine with three cylinders, the high pressure about 30 inches in diameter, the intermediate pressure about 50 inches in diameter and the low pressure about 80 inches in diameter. Steam entered the engine through the throttle valve at 150-psi and was exhausted to a shell and tube condenser at 25-28 inches of mercury. Condensate and non-condensible vapors were removed from the condenser by an air pump driven from the low pressure crosshead by a walking beam. Valve gear was Stephenson link type with two eccentrics for each cylinder. Reversing was accomplished by means of a steam ram which moved the links and put the backing eccentric into service. The main circulating pump was a steam engine-driven centrifugal pump. All other pumps, feed, bilge and ballast, fuel oil transfer, fire, fuel oil service and domestic water were steam-driven reciprocating pumps.

The evaporator was a multicoil type. The thrust bearing was a horseshoe type mounted directly astern of the engine. A small steam-driven jacking engine was located near the thrust bearing. The shaft extended aft to the propeller through the shaft alley and through the stern of the ship to a single propeller. Ice machines located in the upper engine room on the main deck were steam engine-driven ammonia compressors. Temperature in chill and freeze boxes was maintained by manual adjustment of expansion valves. Domestic hot water was generated by water heaters located in the upper engine room.

Cy Hanson, "In the Beginning"

Acapulco. Following a few more-or-less musical numbers, the third class Thespian Society performed in some slapstick burlesque, featured by a descent to the class room, via a ventilator, by Hero Severence bent on saving little Nell from a fate worse than death.

A series of boxing matches followed, in which Snyder and Reading proved themselves capable glove men. The "Piece de resistance" was a titanic battle between Palmerson, the baby faced killer, and Hall, the terror of Inglewood. The fight, billed as a struggle between the two toughest men in the third class, was fought with unprecedented fury. At crucial stages, Hall's countenance became so frightening that many spectators blanched in terror. This nerve wracking affair safely over, first classman J. "Pile it high" Coker invited all participants in the beard growing contest, under way since departure from Honolulu, to step up and be judged.

Captain Nichols selected Spike Secrest, who bore a strong resemblance to Gen. U.S. Grant, as the man with the heaviest growth of foliage. Other prize winners: Best trimmed beard, Huber; Reddest beard, R. B. Simpson; Longest blond beard, Butts; Complete lack of beard, Davis; Best all around beard, Mr. Barkley.

~~~

The 1939 *Hawse Pipe* lists the board of governors of the California Nautical School as being five men, four with backgrounds in shipping, and the State Superintendent of Education.

Qualifications for entrance were: male citizen of good repute, not under seventeen or over twenty-three, able to pass a physical examination comparable to that required by the U.S. Navy. Competitive examination held annually throughout the state.

THE CNS PRAYER

Now I lay me down to sleep,
    I pray the Lord my soul to keep,
Grant that no lousy swab shall take,
    my shoes and pants before I wake.

Dear Lord grant me in my slumber,
    that no one tear my bunk asunder,
And may no gripe or lashing break,
    and smash my dome before I wake.

Keep me safely in thy sight,
    and grant there be no drills tonight,
And in the morning let me wake,
    mid wondrous smells of pie and steak.

Lord protect me in my dreams,
    and make things better than they seem,
Grant three years may quickly fly,
    and all report masts pass me by.

Guard me through the long dark night,
    and grant me more of wonderous sights,
And then do this poor sailor bless,
    with no more tricks of serving mess.

Then take me back to solid land,
    where they scrub the decks with soap not sand,
Where there's shelter from the rain and blows,
    and the WOMEN wash the dirty cloths.

K. Dett.

The course of instruction was three years, each divided into five months ashore and five months on cruise with the remainder taken up in annual overhaul at Mare Island Navy Yard and shore leave periods.

The school term began around the first of October, at which time the training ship moved from its base at California City to the Navy Yard for a period of six weeks for annual overhaul. Then the ship was provisioned and made ready for the cruise.

The purpose of the cruise, of course, was to put the classroom knowledge into practice. Cadets served in their respective departments, either in the engine room or on deck. On his first cruise, a cadet had duty in both departments. This dual instruction was valuable training, giving cadets knowledge of ship management. After the first cruise, the individuals could decide which department they wished to join.

After their final cruise, the first class cadets took their examinations before the Steamboat Inspectors.[11] Graduates were licensed as either third assistant engineers or third mates on any ocean-going vessel of unlimited tonnage.

Events moved rapidly in pre-war San Francisco. The Golden Gate Bridge and the San Francisco-Oakland Bay Bridge linked all sides of the Bay Area and it grew into a major metropolitan region. The great celebration, a sort of "coming out" party, was the 1939 Exposition at Treasure Island. No effort or expense was spared to make this one to rival the great Chicago Exposition of fifty years earlier. It was to be a memorable event, unforgettable even a half-century later.

Charles Audet: "In '39 we were invited to come over to Treasure Island there in San Francisco and become part of the 'Greatest Show On Earth.' We were there, on display, most of the summer. And right in front of us was a ferry boat they used as dormitories for workers. Gypsy Rose Lee had a bunch of G-string dancers that may have lived on one of those."

Ray Aker: "Ships and going to sea was something that I always wanted to do, from an early age. I had several ambitions, one was to get into naval architecture. I was also very interested in maritime history and artwork and historical things. However I realized these were indulgences and you really have to do

something to make a living. So it's going to have to be going to sea and getting into ship-building or naval architecture.

"So my Dad took me up to San Francisco while I was still in high school and we had a chat with a very well-known naval architect, who principally designed tankers. He said, 'Well, you know, if you want to get into this field, you really have to get the practical experience, and you should go to sea for a

SECOND CLASS LAMENT

When first they joined our loving flock
    Their heads were wreathed in flowing
    locks,
Blond and dark; short and long.
    But now a new day's come along.

Their noggins now must needs be neat
    Which means a haircut once a week,
We have our barbers to be sure
    But some are really amateur

Fair damsels take one look and say,
    "Why not buy a good toupee?"
At this our swab must never flinch
    A wig must also be one inch

So they wear their hair cut short
    just so we may have our sport.
They wore their hair cut short until
    One sorry day, and then the mill.

Here crisscross and there a square.
    denuding mister swab of Hair.
For this we paid in full, by gee
    By loss of half a liberty.

Our swabbies now look quite demure
    Because they choose their own coiffure
But it's over now and all is well
    So what the hell, boys, what the hell.

        "Barber"

---

[11] Until just before World War II license exams and licenses were given by the Steamboat Inspection Service. These duties were then taken over by the Coast Guard.

ON FIRST ARRIVING AT CNS

The following, which appeared in an early edition of the Hawse Pipe, *captures the confusion and bewilderment of a newly-accepted cadet to the schoolship.*

"Boy! I just received an appointment to the California Nautical School; just wait until I show the letter to the folks down at the General Store. Won't all the young fellows around Cornville be jealous of me when they see this. I guess Sally won't like it, but I can't help that. I want to go to sea on a big passenger liner and walk around in my uniform and have all the girls look at me.

Well, mother, I guess I have everything packed. I only have another hour before the train is due. Will you tell Pa to get the car out? Goodbye, mother, I'll write soon and tell you all about the school.

There's Cy out there flagging the train so I had better be going.

My arrival in San Francisco was nearly tragic. I was looking at big buildings when I started across the main street, so I didn't notice where I was walking and a big traffic jam resulted. I was rescued by an officer of the law who put me on a street car with directions on how to get a ferry. As I crossed the bay I was amazed at the big ships that were going in and out of the harbor.

I got on a bus that took me to Tiburon and was told that I had to walk three miles to the ship. I liked Tiburon because it reminded me of Cornville; only thing different was, that the streets were paved, in this quiet little town. I stopped in a little store called "Hooper's" and had an ice cream soda; this is a nice place to spend a Saturday nite sipping a milk shake, or something.

I started to walk the three miles to the school; it was a nice walk, reminded me of walking home from high school. After walking a mile or so, my new black shoes started to hurt my feet. I had to sit down for a while and let them cool off.

After walking two miles I finally saw the big white ship, as I turned a bend in the road. Smoke was coming out of the chimney, so I started to run, because I thought the ship was going to leave; I made it alright. I arrived breathless, but was able to walk up the steps. There was an important looking fellow at the desk so I went up to him and said,

"Hello." He just looked me up and down and then asked me my name. I answered, "Hammerslag." He looked in a book and then looked at me as though I was crazy. He asked me if I was one of the new cadets and I answered, Yes." He asked me for my letter telling me of my appointment. I showed it to him, after spending five minutes trying to find it. He looked at it and then in a disgusted voice asked me why I hadn't told him that my last name was Roe and that Hammerslag was my first name. Then he jumped on me for not using "Sir" when I spoke to him. He spoke to another fellow and said that my bunk was number B17. This second cadet took me down some steep steps and I just about broke my neck, and dropped all my bags. He showed me a bunk and said it was mine and then lifted up a door and told me 'that' was a locker to put all my stuff in. I was putting my new clothes in the locker when I heard someone yelling out my name. I went up to him and he told me that Mr. Barkley wanted to see me. I didn't know who Mr. Barkley was, but I went anyway. He took my tuition money; and I then thought how hard I had worked for some of it and how my three uncles and two spinster aunts had also helped get the money.

I went back to work putting away my clothes when someone was again calling my name. I felt rather important having my name called out so that everyone could hear it; so I answered in a loud voice, "here." Everybody around me looked at me with a disgusting manner. The fellow who called my name came up and said I was wanted in the classroom. I didn't know where that was so I just started wandering. I saw an opening in a wall so I walked in. It wasn't a classroom. This certainly is a big ship; I was lost and didn't know where to go. There was a man standing in the room so I asked him if that was the classroom. He gave me a queer look and said, "Hell no." He was very nice to me though and showed me where the classroom was.

I was met at the bottom of the steps by a rather chunky fellow. He asked me what my name was. I told him. He shoved me a pile of clothes and said that they were mine. He kept calling me, "lad" just like old "Tex" did, down on the farm. I had to count the clothes and sign a slip.

I had to take the clothes down to my lockers and put my name on them. They gave me a stencil that had my name on and by putting ink on it, my name, H. P. Roe appeared. Somebody told me that the "Rules and Regulations" showed where the clothes were to be marked, and also to be careful not to spill any ink on the deck or locker tops. I was getting along fairly well when a fellow in work clothes came up to me and asked me if I had bought any toilet paper as yet. I said, "No." He said that he could get me some very cheap and would sell it to me at half price. I told him that I had brought along my "Montgomery and Ward Catalogue," so I wouldn't do any business with him now, but might be able to, some time in the future.

I went back to my stenciling, and then found out that I had marked all my white hats on the outside instead of the inside, so my name was showing on the front. My next big worry was how I was to mark my mattress, my sheets, my blankets, and the pillow. Another fellow, who looked as though he knew something, told me to mark them on both ends and all sides.

A bugle was blown and just about scared me out of my wits, and then the big bed room was filled, like magic. The bells that were constantly ringing were annoying. All these other fellows around make it more difficult than ever to stencil my clothes. I was getting in everyone's way and was always on somebody's locker top and then having to move my clothes.

After about an hour of this constant moving and being in someone's way I was finally finished. I heard another bugle blow and wondered what it meant. A fellow came around blowing a little tin whistle and kept yelling "Clear the berth deck." I supposed he wanted us to get out of there, so I left and went up and looked at the water. Somebody come over and told me to get out of my civilian clothes and get into a uniform of the day. I didn't know what that meant but I went down in the big bed room again and opened my locker. I had a hard time opening my lock, because I had forgotten the combination. I noticed everyone was wearing the

same kind of blue uniform that was given to me so I tried to find it. I finally found it at the bottom of the locker. As I was putting on these clothes, the bugle blew again. I was beginning to wonder if it blew all the time. There went that darn bell again. I heard the clattering of feet over my head and it sounded as though something was happening. There was no-one around and I thought that I might be missing something. Just as I came up at the top of those steps again I heard someone saying, "Roe absent, Sir." I yelled out, "I'm here." I was again given a dirty look as the commanding cadet said, "March your men to mess." I walked into the room where everyone was sitting down to eat. I sat down at a vacant place but a fellow next to me told me to get the heck out of there and to sit at the outboard end of the table. I didn't know what that meant so I started to walk around. The fellow with the little tin whistle showed me a place to eat.

On my left was a sad looking fellow who looked as though he had come from a small town like I did. I started to talk to him and he told me he was from Hollywood. I became very interested and asked if he had seen any of the movie stars. Just as I was getting along beautifully, the fellow on my right told me to "Shut up." Then he started to fire questions at me. The questions were like, "What is a water hammer," and "why does the wildcat roar." I didn't know any of the answers.

After dinner, all of the new cadets were told to be in the classroom at 1800. I went down there and "they" asked me a lot more questions and then they told me the "law" of the school and how I should do everything. They also told me who was the boss.

Finally they let me go so I went back to the big bed room to go to bed. All the lights were out. I had a hard time finding my night gown in the dark, and also had to make my bed. I didn't know how so I just lay down on top of my mattress, completely exhausted; even more tired than if I had worked all day with the old team of horses.

couple of years at least and work in a shipyard, then go into it. And, of course, it's a very rigorous course with lots of math, it's almost all engineering.'

"Engineering was not my strong point, nor math, but you have to bite the bullet. Anyway, going to sea was certainly an important part of it because you have to know what a ship is all about and what people did aboard ship.

"In 1939 the school ship was at Treasure Island at the World's Fair. I went over there and had a look at the ship and their program and it looked pretty good to me, so I said, 'Well, what the heck, I can get a little education at the same time I'm going to sea with the academy.'"

The cruise of 1939 departed on January 17, 1939 with Capt. N. E. Nichols, Superintendent, as the ship's Commander. Ports of call were: San Francisco, San Diego; La Union, Salvador; Balboa, Panama; Callao, Peru; Valparaiso, Chile; Balboa, Panama; Manzanillo, Mexico; Long Beach, Santa Barbara and Tiburon.

Roger Swain '42: "George Barkley was Exec. He was commonly known as 'the beard.' After the war broke out, he was called in the Navy and got a fleet of purse seiners that became minesweepers."

Ray Aker: "We all had a fear of him. He was a strict disciplinarian. But he was fair."

Jack Summerill: "Barkley was a tough son-of-a-gun. He enjoyed his job. He kept us on our toes all the time, but we liked it. We were proud of it — the ship was clean, our clothes were clean, we were clean. And we

didn't act smart to the officers. Especially to Barkley."

OUTLAW

Mr. Barkley is the Jury
Mr. Barkley is the Judge
Mr. Barkley takes the case in hand
And settles out the grudge.

Attorney is the bearded man
And a lawyer for the state
He issues verdicts to the swabs
Then beckons for the mate.

Whether a man is guilty
Mr. Barkley has the say
Whether he is free to go at will
Or stay aboard to pay

He bats his eyes uneasy like
Maybe he has a scare
But after everything is proved
He's not afraid to blare.

One hundred demerits and stay aboard
To the landsmen may seem odd
But to the "Kay-Dett" on the "Old Cal State"
Mr. Barkley is our God.

Capt. N.E. Nichols relieved Capt. Dwyer as master of the ship. Courtesy Ray Aker.

The discipline, designed to make men of boys, was difficult for some. Others adjusted to it.

Ray Aker: "You had to work an hour for every two demerits. You could lose a weekend; oh yes, absolutely, you had to work those off on your own time. I remember getting a few and I had to work them off in Panama. We were going through the canal, it was on the first trip. And, of course, we stayed a few days in Balboa. Well, I had to work those demerits off on my shore time and I got the job of painting the top of the port boiler. It was shut down and somewhat cooler than usual, but in Panama, in that heat, boy, what extra duty that was. You'd get some real choice jobs, the engine room had plenty of them. Get down below the floor plates and swab the top of the tanktops . . .

"At the sound of the bugle and reveille, everybody hits the deck and our dog, the mascot, would be up there barking and howling into the open hatch. A big malamute. He lived on the ship. His name was Soogee. He went to sea like the rest of us. Managed to be the first one off when we got to port. He'd find some lady friend [laughter]. We had to hold him down, but, boy, he was ready to go. And he'd always get back to the ship on time. We had to be a little bit careful with him, in foreign ports. He would get picked up by the police. But he was nice to have. We'd go swimming, he'd be down there in the water with us."

Charles Audet: "Soogee was our doggy. He was primarily cared for by the laundry man. Soogee was a very well-behaved dog."

Cy Hansen: "Soogee made the second cruise, around the world. He was a nice dog.

"One cruise we had a coatimundi, a honey bear. It was kind of a pest, always running around dirtying things up. It loved eggs and would suck eggs dry and drop the shells on deck for cadets to clean up."

One of the highlights of the 1939 cruise was a visit to some of the old square-riggers that were tied up in the port of Callao, Peru. The *Hawse Pipe* described the visit:

> . . . several old square rigged vessels were anchored in the harbor. The sailing ships, comprising two, three-masted and one four-masted barks, were the remainder of a once-proud guano fleet. Irrespective of their cargo, these ships were clean and well kept up, considering the small crew that they carried. Several interesting friendships were made between the mascot of the California State and the mascots of these ships. Whereas ours is a dog, a

Soogee in his favorite place on the ship, the "chains" from which the lead was thrown when taking soundings by hand. Courtesy Ray Aker.

> pig is carried on each of the others; so the mutual attraction must have been their common plight of all living on ships.
>
> A thorough inspection below decks and on deck having been made, the temptation to climb the rigging was soon realized and everybody went aloft. It was a very pleasing sight to look down on a ship without a funnel and know that she had no engineers on board. Several cameras were taken up and a number of candid shots were taken of cadets climbing up and patting the "truck" and going out on the loftiest "yards."

Ray Aker: "These ships were in Callao, Peru, four of them anchored out there in the harbor, and we sacrificed some of our shore liberty to go aboard and climb aloft. Two other ships were German cargo/passenger ships that were interned in there during the war. We visited those also."[12]

---

[12] Three of the sailing ships were the three-masted barks *Maipo* and *Tellus* and the four-masted bark *Omega*.

The California State *arriving at Havana with Morro Castle in the background. Courtesy Ray Aker.*

The cadets receiving rifle practice at Guantanamo Bay, Cuba. Courtesy Ray Aker.

By 1940 the tuition was $100 for uniforms and textbooks with an additional $225 a year ($500 for non-California residents) to help pay for food, quarters and the annual cruise.

In that same year, under the terms of the Merchant Marine Act of 1936,[13] ownership and support of the vessel was transferred from the Navy to the United States Maritime Commission.

Ray Aker: "We were still at the coaling station [Tiburon]. The ship was the academy. We lived on it, we ate on it, but the coaling station was our campus. And we had classrooms in the old Navy barracks buildings on the station. One time we had to move into a converted chicken house for a classroom. It was all fixed up, it had lighting, and it was part of the caretaker's building, I guess. We had to take care of that station, too. It was a little disconcerting, I think, to some of the new kids coming into the school to have to go out and chop weeds and rake up the whole campus and clean it up and do the garbage detail and all of that. But that's how it was, that coaling station was our campus."

The cruise of 1940 included the following ports of call: Long Beach, San Diego, Acapulco, Mexico; Balboa, Canal Zone; Havana, Cuba; San Juan, Puerto Rico; Miami, Newport News, Washington, D.C.; Annapolis, Md.; Cristobal, Canal Zone; Magdalena Bay, Mexico; San Diego, Long Beach, Santa Barbara and Tiburon.

Ray Aker: "We went ashore at Guantanamo Bay in Cuba where they had regular rifle ranges and instructors." The cadets were invited to practice on the rifle range as part of their Naval Reserve training.

Roger Swain: "Magdalena Bay was usually to clean up or spruce up, interspersed with time off to fish from the ship's boat.

"There was whale-watching, of course. We caught tuna of one form or another: yellowtail, albacore, bonita, mackerel. Sometimes they'd cook it on the ship, and I believe we even brought some in the freezer back to the States."

There was no town at Magdalena Bay. The only diversions were those which nature and time allowed: relaxing on deck, fishing, swimming, sailing, rowing and, of course, painting the ship. In other ports, however, such as Acapulco, Mazatlan, Callao or Valparaiso there were opportunities for sightseeing,

---

13 The Merchant Marine Act of 1936 was the "Magna Carta" of the American merchant marine. It revitalized a dying industry, anticipated the needs of World War II and, among other things, replaced the antiquated Steamboat Inspection Service with the Maritime Commission.

sampling the local cuisine and admiring the local girls, who, in turn, were attracted to the young cadets in their good-looking uniforms. Although seldom mentioned, encounters were frequent and enthusiastic. That, too, is a part of going to sea.

~~~

Food was always of prime interest. At sea or on land, as part of the day's routine or sometimes simply as something to do, food and eating were always a priority. Ray Aker: "Well, this happened the day after Thanksgiving and, you know, cadets are always a hungry bunch of characters. Claude B. Mayo was captain. He was regular Navy and he lived on the base. He had a nice house, the commandant's house 'way up on the hill. And he had a Thanksgiving dinner for friends and family and they had a big turkey. His house didn't have enough room in the kitchen refrigerator for the leftover turkey so he brought it down to the ship to put in the freezer. Somehow the guys on watch down in the engine room had a key to the freezer. They would go up there in the night to see what was left over. They took some of the leftovers down to the engine room for the night lunch. But on the QT because we had kind of a night lunch on the messdeck, too, a little bread and cheese and coffee, cocoa, if you wanted it.

"But, anyway, they found this damn turkey and they didn't know it belonged to the skipper. So it went down into the fire room and they were having turkey sandwiches down there.

"Well, the next day, the day after Thanksgiving, Mayo wanted his turkey for dinner or lunch or something, leftover turkey. Gone. He was madder than heck. Nothing left. And who stole it? Holy smokes, you know, nobody was going to say anything. And we had to go through that same damn thing that they went through in the Caine Mutiny over the strawberries.[14] They searched the ship. Everybody was searched. Everybody was taken up, one man at a time, up to the wardroom and grilled, like being before a court martial. The officers and the old man, 'Do you know anybody who took that?' Oh, boy, well, some days later, I think somebody found a few bones in the bottom of the furnace of one of the boilers, a scotch boiler. So there were turkey bones in the bottom but nobody was talking. That was as far as Capt. Mayo got with it. But, boy, that was really something because if you got caught stealing that turkey there was going be no end to demerits and extra duty."

John McCreary recalled a similar incident during the ship's second cruise in 1932 enroute from Gibraltar to Funchal. From "In the Beginning":

The baker was short one large angel food cake out of a locked cupboard, and during attempts to find it (including a locker inspection) the First Assistant was prowling around number four hold and found two empty cases with one empty can in each, and in another place a can half full of plums, with three spoons. So he calls all the engineers together and asks who took 'em. And one guy says he took some of it and two others said they ate some. Then last night the Exec got all hands together and after the usual pep talk he asked who had anything to do with the theft and about six guys stood up, and later three others, and that was nowhere near even half of the fellows who were

---

[14] In *The Caine Mutiny,* by Herman Wouk, Capt. Queeg interviews each crew member on the ship over the theft of a small amount of frozen strawberries from the officers' pantry.

really involved, nor did it include those who had taken other things for he didn't ask about the nuts and raisins and citron and sandwich spread and several other cans of things taken at different times by the same and other cadets. If he said "How many have taken or eaten stolen ("pilfered") food during the cruise?" the cadet corps en masse would have stood up . . . The vast majority of the thieves (!) were engineers, and was the First griped!

By late 1940 the second World War had engulfed Europe and was spreading to Africa and the Middle East. In the Far East, Japan had embarked on her war of conquest. German and Japanese submarines were constant threats in the Atlantic and Far Pacific. The United States Congress was still resolutely "neutral," but secret agreements between President Roosevelt and Prime Minister Churchill provided support to shore up the British war effort.

During the months of January through April of 1941, the *California State* made its last prewar training cruise. It was a cautious itinerary which kept the ship and her crew close to the West Coasts of North and South America. Ports of call were: Long Beach, San Diego; Balboa, Panama; Callao, Peru; Stockton and Tiburon.

The United States was technically at peace, but even the most ardent believer in neutrality could see the war clouds growing larger. The *California State* and her cadets, like everyone, everywhere, would soon feel its impact.

Courtesy Alvin Gregory.

CHAPTER 4

WORLD WAR II

The first change was swift and decisive. In May 1941 the California Nautical School was summarily evicted from Tiburon. The Navy needed the site as an antisubmarine netting station for San Francisco Bay.

Roger Swain '42: "We went on a cruise in January of '41, when we came back from the cruise, war had occurred [in Europe and the Far East] and the Navy took over the base. First we floated around in the South Bay on the training ship, then we got use of Pier 54, then the Ferry Building.

"My first impression, I was pretty gung ho. I thought it was great. I thought being on board ship was the greatest thing. It didn't seem like a stinkin' little old Laker, then, it seemed like an immense big white ship.

"We got accelerated classes. Actually, there were three classes of '42, one graduated in January, mine was July and there was a class in December."

The school located a semipermanent home at the Ferry Building at the foot of Market Street in San Francisco and the *California State* was towed there on the morning of September 30, 1941. The ship's launch and motor whaler followed, each towing several whaleboats. The ship was given a berth at one of the adjacent piers (slip #2) and the school was allowed to hold classes in the Ferry Building itself.

~~~

December 7, 1941. Without warning, the Japanese Empire attacked the U.S. Pacific Fleet in Pearl Harbor. Eighteen ships were hit, among them the pride of the American fleet — the battleships. The *Arizona* was destroyed, the *West Virginia* and *California* sunk, the *Nevada* severely damaged. More than 2,400 Americans were killed. The nation was in shock. As the magnitude of the disaster became known, the old desire for isolation became anathema. Families gathered around their radios to hear President Roosevelt declare war on the Axis powers — Germany, Italy and Japan.

Evicted from the coaling station at Tiburon in 1941, the California State *tied up at various locations in San Francisco Bay until acquiring a semipermanent berth at the Ferry Building. Here the ship is tied up on the east side of Treasure Island with the San Francisco Bay Bridge in the background. Photo by Mike McGarvey.*

Until now, the California Nautical School seemed isolated from world events. Life for the students consisted of the ship, the annual cruise and the campus. Occasionally there was some anxiety about whether or not the State Legislature would fund the school for the coming year. Otherwise, the cadets and faculty lived a sheltered existence. All that changed, with a vengeance, on December 7, and the school was thrown into the cataclysm of world events that would alter everyone's lives forever.

In San Francisco there was a very real fear that the West Coast would be the next target of the Japanese juggernaut. Air defense of the Pacific seaboard was nonexistent — there was nothing to stop Japan from invading.[1]

Ray Aker '42: "When Pearl Harbor broke out we were down there at the Ferry Building. I was stuck with duty that day, a Sunday. There was only a handful of us aboard and we were shooting the breeze in the cabin of the cadet commander. We're in his cabin when we heard about Pearl Harbor, on the radio news broadcast. We could hardly believe our ears when we heard that. We were afraid that the Japs were going to make a raid on the San Francisco waterfront. So we had to batten down all the deadlights for the portholes and get the ship all battened down and get our fire equipment ready. And, sure enough, at dark there goes the air raid siren from the Ferry

---

[1] The only pursuit plane on the West Coast was the outdated P-40 but all the P-40s available had been disassembled for shipment overseas. The air defense of the Golden Gate on December 7 consisted of two AT-6s which had 30 caliber machine guns installed on them. The guns were not synchronized. Firing them meant that the plane's propeller would be the first casualty. *San Francisco Chronicle*, Dec. 5, 1981.

Building. Blackout of the city. It was not long before the waterfront and the city behind it went dark, except for one disturbing, very big electric sign nearby still flashing its message to San Francisco Bay commuters: 'Wellman Coffee.' It seemed to take an agonizingly long time to stop it from beckoning our location to enemy pilots.

"That was the first day of the war. 'Bye, 'bye vacations and Christmas leave and all that.

"On Monday morning, the skipper, Mayo, had us line up on the forward deck under the bridge. He was on the bridge house and we got up on the hatch. And I remember one thing he said, 'Gentlemen, you've all lost your boyhood. No more going home to your friends over the weekends.' That was the first sobering reality.

"Then he said, 'Those that are upper class will have to get out, take your license, go

Roger Putnam with rifle and bayonet, guarding the gate to the California State*'s berth. Photo by Harold Huycke.*

off to sea and those that are left will take an accelerated course.'"

Don Peterson '42: "I was on the way back to San Francisco from Auburn. I hitchhiked home but my folks were driving me back, and they were going to spend the day with me in the city. That morning we were on our way back when we heard about Pearl Harbor. They were all in favor of turning around and going back home again. I said, 'No, I gotta go, they're telling all military personnel to report to base and that kind of stuff.' I was going to hitchhike back if I had to."

Tom MacFadyen '42: "Home for me was Palo Alto. I heard it that morning and, of course, headed back to the ship. The interesting thing was as we came onto the parking at the north side of the Ferry Building, the ocean side, where we went in to board the ship, they already had some sentries out there. They were cadets and they had rifles with bayonets, but no ammunition . . ."

Don Peterson: "Swabs had to work sentry duty. We learned close order drill, you know. We could march and drill and do the manual of arms and that kind of stuff, but nobody ever fired a rifle, to say nothing of if you had it unloaded."

Harold Huycke '44: "The school ship was moored at the north end of the Ferry Building in the last slip. They had modified it in a way that there was a gangway to the dock and out to a gate, and there was a guard box where we stood gangway watch out there with a Springfield rifle and an ammunition belt. We stood regular watches marching up and down like a sentry. It was part of the training, but it served as a discouragement for the people that might want to casually walk in and see the big iron boat tied up down there."

Tom MacFadyen: "They had cadets standing watches because they had to guard the ship. And we were in the Sausalito slip, bow in, stern out, which is just about the end of the slip. They had a stern watch, with a cadet back there, and he had a forty-five on his hip which was obviously empty. We stood two-hour watches. I was out there one night a few weeks or months [after Pearl Harbor] and, of course, they would have air raid drills. On this midnight-to-two watch there was an alert and you could see all the lights all over the city going down, I mean all over the Bay the lights going off, even on the Bay Bridge. The only light that stayed on was the Wellman Coffee Company, right there about three hundred feet away. Of course, the Ferry Building siren was the biggest siren in the area. So when the drill was over with, they turned the juice on to the Bay Bridge lights and they were orange phosphor or some other damn thing. They came on individually, not as a string. And a light'd come on here and a light'd come on here, and a light, and then even around across the Oakland side, lights would start coming on and that was a phenomenal experience."

Don Peterson: "Some of the early blackouts were disasters, in that about half the lights didn't go out. As the war went on they got better at turning lights out."

Just after Pearl Harbor, while in the shipyard for its annual winter maintenance during December 1941 to January 1942 the *California State* was repainted gray for the war effort and renamed *Golden State* in keeping with the Maritime Commission's policy of naming training ships of state schools for their state nicknames. New York's training ship became the *Empire State*, Massachusetts', the *Bay State*, and so on.

Tom MacFadyen: "The name of the ship was the *California State*. For some reason they were going to change the name to the *Golden State*. There was the Golden State Dairy Company at that time, big in Northern California. And we were sort of pissed. They didn't consult us cadets. Not that it would

have made a damn bit of difference, but we could have expressed our feelings. We felt like painting a cow on the stack. But we never got around to doing that.

"For some reason, when we went into drydock they went down around all the seachests forming cast concrete around them. It was supposed to somehow or 'nother do some good in case we were in warfare. And the other thing they did, and I thought this was great, shows you how naive I was, they set up the destruction of the ship, in case we were about to be captured, I guess. Scuttle it. And because I had shown that I knew how to use this cutting torch, I got the assignment to be back in the shaft alley to cut the hole in the skin of the ship. I thought that's a pretty prestigious job — until I got to thinking, how the hell do you get out of there?"

Alan Dougall '42: "There was a lot of interest along the waterfront when the

The California State *in drydock where its name was changed to* Golden State. *Courtesy California Maritime Academy.*

battleships came in from Pearl Harbor for repairs. The engine cadets went in their engine rooms and learned quite a bit."

In 1942, the school, operated by the California State Department of Education, underwent its final name change, from "California Nautical School" to "California Maritime Academy."

The overall course of study was condensed from three years down to eighteen months and cadets were no longer allowed the luxury of spending six months on deck and six months in engineering before committing to one or the other.

Roger Putnam '44: "We didn't have time to choose deck or engine. We had to designate before we got there."

Harold Huycke: "The war was on, they needed men, they said. They needed ships in wholesale lots. They cut out a lot of the superfluous courses and they gave us only the essentials that would get us through our licenses, with very little extra thrown in. The training was good. The education was good. It was probably a little bit better than what the Maritime Commission was throwing out in the upgrade schools.[2]

"We were all very, very green peas. Very few guys had even been in a skiff before. And, in all candor, in all frankness, these guys were draft dodgers. They admitted it. They didn't want to go in the Army. They went to the maritime academy and got an extension and got an education and stayed in the school for eighteen months.

Dick Jenness '44: "As the war geared up the draft came into being. One of the first things was the big drawing that determined the sequence of when we were to be called up. My draft number gave me a bit of time. I didn't have the grades to make it into Cal Tech from high school so I was taking classes at Pasadena Junior College but time was running out. Dad said he didn't know what the best service was but he knew the Army was the worst — he slept in too many foxholes in World War I. A seagoing friend suggested CMA. Therefore, I entered the program, not from a love of the sea, but one who had been warned of the alternates! I probably should have chosen engineering but I had this mental view of a torpedo sticking its nose into the engine room. With that in mind, it seemed logical to be someplace else, so, I elected the deck department."

Harold Huycke: "I went in the deck department. We all made a choice at the beginning. I don't think anybody changed and everybody had to make a decision at the foot of the gangway, what were you going to take, engine or deck. Well, there were fifty-five in my class, probably a two-to-one ratio, deck to engine."

"The exam I took was in L.A. I had a physics book and read that on the Greyhound on the way down."

~~~

Wartime draft concerns aside, there were many reasons cadets became interested in the sea or why they came to the nautical school. But fairly common inspirations were

---

[2] During World War II the Maritime Commission operated upgrading schools, which trained experienced mariners to become officers, at Alameda, California and Fort Trumbull, Connecticut. In addition, it trained unlicensed seamen at Sheepshead Bay, New York, Catalina and Port Hueneme, California and St. Petersburg, Florida.

the writings of Howard Pease and Guy Gilpatric.[3] Another was having seen the training ship in one of the California ports during its annual cruises.

Roger Putnam: "Before I could even walk my Dad took me aboard the cutter, *Bear*, in Oakland. I can still remember the ship and the leather and the little rooms. That was one thing. Then my Dad took me on the old *Saratoga* and on 'Old Ironsides' in the '30s. I went on it a couple of times. I was born in Oakland and liked to ride the ferries. When I was in the sixth grade I started reading Howard Pease. On the bulletin board at high school they had a picture of the old white ship there. The dean said, 'Try the test.' The exam I took was in L.A. I had a physics book and read that on the Greyhound on the way down. I took the test and it was a bugger. My Dad opened the letter when it came. I was accepted. I went to San Francisco, reported January 6, 1943. I was kind of like a new puppy in a pound with all these upper classmen hanging around."

Don Peterson: "My background was about the same sort of a thing. I read Howard Pease's stuff which was just very fascinating. He wrote good stuff for boys. Boys ran away from home, ran away from school, went to sea which was the kind of life you could sort of identify with. And he didn't paint a rosy picture of it but it was still fascinating. And then the Glencannon stuff which was in the *Saturday Evening Post*. My dad was a mining engineer

> *"Pease's books sounded just great to be on a ship in the engine room as a wiper."*

in Wisconsin. His father came from Norway as a little boy, and since Norwegians are seafaring types . . ."

Tom MacFadyen: "I had read Pease's books about seagoing, sounded just great to be on a ship in the engine room as a wiper. I didn't have very good grades getting out of high school and the Academy choice came along and I managed to pass the exam so that was that."

But, looming over everything was the draft. The inevitability of the call-up was a paramount consideration for young men in their plans for the future.

Harold Huycke: "I first saw the school ship in Los Angeles in 1936 or '7. I was already showing interest in ships, wanting to go to sea. I liked fishing, I had my own little boat. I got interested in the waterfront, ships and the smell of fish and saltwater . . .

"The school ship came into Los Angeles on one of her cruises, all painted white, and I'd go down there. My dad occasionally would take me down and there was the school ship. I was only fourteen or fifteen when I first saw it. I used to hang around the Santa Monica pier, that's where I really got my feet wet. The fishing barges had been sailing ships and they were anchored off Santa Monica pier so I got interested in the history and in the romance of it and I got in almost anything that smacked of deep-sea ships. I used to fish off the pier and I got acquainted with an old seafaring man on the pier. Real, real deep-sea old characters in the business of bygone years.

"Well, I wanted to go to sea, but I didn't know how to do it, so I went to college. And I didn't do too well, but I got through the first year and the second year then I ruined my left knee playing football. It ruined an otherwise unillustrious career as a football player. But

---

[3] Howard Pease was the author of more than 20 books about seafaring. Many of them were written for young boys.

my knee was so badly injured that my dad was tired of paying miscellaneous doctor bills. He said, 'We're going to have to get that fixed.'

"So in June I went to Santa Monica hospital, got my knee operated on, came out on crutches and I spent the rest of the summer going to summer school, making up for my poor performance at college. I took mathematics, algebra, geometry, trigonometry. It was a break that was divinely inspired. I got back into school but I knew I wasn't going to be allowed to finish because of the draft. I was going to be twenty in November and as soon as I passed twenty somebody in the service was going to grab me and I had to jump before I got grabbed. I was taking a course in Spanish, and there was a guy in one of the dormitories that was in my class and we used to study together. His name was Wayne Harthorn. One day in the first week of November, 1942, I went down to his room, I said, 'Well, let's study Spanish.' There was no Spanish book in sight but he was studying chemistry, physics, algebra and geometry. I said, 'What are you doing?'

"He says, 'I'm going to take the test for the California Maritime Academy.' Suddenly the bells began to ring.

"I said, 'When is this test?'

"He says, 'November twenty-third.' Two weeks away.

"I says, 'Can I get my application in?'

"He says, 'I think they're closed.'

"I said, 'Where'd you get that?'

"He said, 'Oh, up at the CMA office up on Van Ness in San Francisco. A guy by the name of Culver.'

"This was Friday. The office closed on Saturday at noon. I went out of his room, back to my own dormitory. I packed up a change of socks and underwear and a shirt. I went out on the highway and I started hitchhiking that night. I hitchhiked all night, got up to Van Ness ten minutes before the office closed. I went in there to see this guy Culver, and I said, 'I want an application for the examination in Los Angeles for CMA..'

"He said, 'I'm sorry, we're closed. We're not taking any more applications.'

"I said, 'I came all the way from LA to get that application. I'm not leaving without it.'

"He says, 'Well, O.K., here, take this home and get it filled out but I've got to have it back right away. The examination's on the twenty-third and the exam is going to be in either your choice of physics or chemistry, whichever you feel proficient in. Algebra and geometry and that's all. If you pass that you'll either be accepted or you will be considered an alternate.'

"Went out of the door, started hitchhiking back to LA. I got back the next morning in time for breakfast, pulled out my old physics books and math books and went to work. I studied and studied and finally got a notice that the exam would be held. I was as ready as I would ever be and I ignored all my other classes knowing that this was a go-for-broke one-shot deal, because I was never going to finish the semester anyhow. The army was looking right down my throat. By the early part of December I got a notice that I had been selected as an alternate.

"I was ordered to report for pre-induction physical. We got punched and looked at and probed and given a card and he said, 'OK. You're alive, you're warm, you can walk, you're a subject to the Army. Unless you take

> *"I said, 'I came all the way from LA to get that application. I'm not leaving without it.'"*

advantage of pre-induction choice. Before you are drafted you have your choice of joining any of the armed forces.'

"I knew that on Monday, the second of January, my draft card would be in the mail and then I would be in the Army with no maneuvering room left. My dad said, 'Why don't you send a telegram up there, tell them that you want to get in, that you want to be accepted.'

"This was the day after Christmas. Five days left. So I sent a telegram to Culver. In the meantime, to open up two more options, I went over to the draft board in West Los Angeles and volunteered for induction in the Coast Guard. And if I didn't get that message by Saturday the thirtieth I was going to go over and join the Coast Guard so as not to join the Army.

"The mail came, a big fat thick envelope, 'You've been accepted in the primary class, get all these things — socks, underwear, and all these other paraphernalia — and be at

A new cadet reports aboard for the first time. Credit California Maritime Academy, courtesy Rod Marshall.

the gangway of the schoolship on Monday the second of January!'"

The new cadets reported aboard for eighteen months of training that would change their lives. To say they were bewildered is an understatement.

Paul Marin (Marincovich) '44: "I had my suitcase, the clothes I was supposed to bring. I had to be there about ten o'clock and I'm walking up to a guardhouse and there was a young fellow, a midshipman, in a sailor's uniform with a rifle. I reported in as a new midshipman. I was directed a few yards away to the gangway that led up to the ship. I walked up the gangway and there was the varnished oak desk with an upper classman at the gangway and there I reported in."

Harold Huycke: "All of this was a different life, a different atmosphere. Upper classmen herded us like sheep, go here, go there, line up, drop your gear. What's your name? And by nine o'clock or ten o'clock we were pretty well sorted out. We lined up to get our blue dungarees."

Paul Marin: "Up in number one hold there was a canteen, a storage area, and we all got in a single file and went past the men that were handing out our uniforms: dungarees and work shirts.

"We then were gathered together and were assigned bunks and lockers under the bunks and so forth."

Harold Huycke: "We were supposed to have brought black shoes. We were whipped into shape, we were given a box of matches and we were given the Swab Rules which we had to memorize [See Appendix A for Swab Rules]. We learned to say 'Sir.' It was 'Yes, Sir, no Sir.' That got in our blood stream. And we had to have matches that fast [snaps fingers] if an upper classman said, 'Swab, I want a match.' Hand him a match. 'Swab what are the Swab Rules?' And, boy, I tell you, within an hour, you memorized the Swab Rules."

Roger Putnam: "We studied over in the Ferry Building and we had to memorize the Swab Rules. We had to know them backwards. You had to tell them anything they wanted, you were never right. Then the second classmen would come in and just give us hell. But it didn't hurt me. I felt better because of the whole thing. They could have been twice as bad and I would have profited by it."

Paul Marin: "We were all young and awestruck by the military bearing of the upper classmen who had been there for a year or two. They had this military training, the way they hold their shoulders from marching and so forth. We were young guys and we had this feeling we're going into the service, because everything was military. We accepted it, we expected it. That was the way it was. We knew that we were midshipmen United States Naval Reserve, that we were going to be trained to be officers aboard ships in the merchant marine or in the Navy. So we were apprehensive, keeping our eyes wide open, our ears open, trying not to screw up, not knowing how to do right or wrong, but there in sort of wonderment and awe and apprehension."

Tom MacFadyen: "We were told a few days after we got there, we were supposed to come up with jokes. Everyone was supposed to have a joke for every meal. Now there's seven days and three meals, that's twenty-one jokes. Boy, when I went home, that's all I cared about, give me some jokes. The thing was if they'd already heard it, it didn't count. Then you'd have to use up another joke, and that went on for another two or three weeks."

Harold Huycke: "I hadn't been on that thing more than two hours before I was assigned to start washing dishes.

"The system on the dish washing was that at five o'clock you got up and you went up and cleaned up all the coffee cups that were left over from the night watch, and the mess that was left. We had to clean up, swab the decks, wash the dishes, run them through the sink and one of the [cadet] engineers, a guy name of Lee Marshall, washed the pots and pans. I washed the dishes. And I ran this wooden rack with all the dishes on it through this steam table, took them out and then put them in a drying table, hot air dried them, stacked them in racks and put them away. Six o'clock was reveille, everybody out. You had time to get dressed, you came up to the mess deck, and by that time, we had hot chocolate made. Not coffee, it was hot chocolate, and everybody got a mug of hot chocolate."

"In the morning, we really looked forward to the hot chocolate."

Roger Putnam: "In the morning, we really looked forward to the hot chocolate."

Tom MacFadyen: "The lower class, we did all the mess duties. In the morning they had a big coffee urn they made the chocolate in. One guy'd pour in about ten or fifteen cans of canned milk and stir it all up. Once, some guy happened to look inside the big urn, and there was a scrub brush in there that had been there for days."

Don Peterson: "Reveille blows, then you could have chocolate before you went out on the cold, foggy pier and have close order drill and that kind of stuff. That pretty well woke you up and then you came on board, you got warm, before you went to breakfast."

Roger Putnam: "Calisthenics at six in the morning out on the pier."

Don Peterson: "It was a revelation, wake up nine-tenths asleep and have to go out on that cold, foggy dock and do close order drill or something to wake you up. That was pretty interesting."

Tom MacFadyen: "You might get a little hazing as you went along, so you no more got your chocolate in your hand, and it was always hotter than hell, before you had to put it down. And then when you came back you couldn't return to your cup of chocolate. It was time to get cleaned up, get ready for breakfast and get the day going.

"... a whole curtain of tracers and smoke and flames all heading up that way ..."

"You learned to dress fast. But the thing was the lower classmen could not come up to number two hatch to the mess room. They had to go forward."

Harold Huycke: "There was a little bit of a hatch up forward, a booby hatch of some kind, which the third class had to use, third class only. We could not use the after one that led up to the main deck. Don't ever get caught using that thing while you're swabs. This was privileged.

"After the wash-down we went in, cleaned up. Meanwhile, the guys in the galley were cleaning up the coffee mugs and setting the tables. There were three or four guys, messmen that were assigned to the job, while two of us were washing dishes and washing pots. That's three or four other messmen under a second class supervisor or a first class supervisor, for the week. The mess boys had to set up the table, put everything on, silverware, stainless steel, plates.

"They gave us a fifteen minute coffee break. We had to clean up after that and again

In the CMA catalog, the caption on this photo says, "The reason a new midshipman is called a Swab." Credit California Maritime Academy, courtesy Rod Marshall.

we missed class while we cleaned up. Then we had to leave class early to come over and set up for lunch, then we had to clean up the dishes after lunch. So we were missing part of our class for a week. We had to make up for it.

"Then on Saturday morning, after breakfast, that's when the next gang came on and that's when I realized there was another life outside of the galley, because I'd been there a week. And I had done my duty and I had done my part in the galley. I was the first one assigned to washing dishes in my crew. I never got it again until months later."

"On Saturday mornings we had a field day or special cleanup. After the dishes were collected and washed, the swabs had to really scrub down the mess deck. We had to scrub down the pantry where we washed dishes and pans and pots. Somebody hooked up a live steam hose to a nozzle and turned on the valve. The hose had a long slender pipe-like nozzle with a half-inch opening and it was just big enough to stick in all the old rivet holes and cracks and corners. That live steam went everywhere and here came streams of cockroaches out of all the other cracks and overheads, everywhere! Six generations of them, all the way from back in 1919. Of course, they all ran down some other crack and into the hidden corners, so we'd give them another blast, kill a quarter of them, and then plan the attack for the following Saturday. Once they were out of sight and the corpses swept up, it was back to Saturday drill and Liberty."

Preparing for war on the homefront, the Navy put guns on the ship. Eventually the cadets were given some training in how to use them, although, as time passed, it became obvious that Japan was not planning to attack San Francisco.

Harold Huycke: "Guntubs were put on at the beginning of the war. We had a twenty millimeter gun on either side and it was a regular Navy style, with a trunk and then a round gun platform. We never went up in them but I think there was either a Lewis machine gun or a twenty millimeter up there. I don't know whether they ever intended sending the ship outside the Golden Gate. I think they must have thought about it, and then after the attacks by the submarines on this coast, where tankers and freighters were sunk, it was prudent to keep it inside."

Don Peterson: "They put some guntubs on the boat deck. That was the sole armament, a couple of guntubs where they put in a fifty caliber machine gun. We had to stand gunner's mate watches, too. None of us knew anything about machine guns, you know, but that was one of your watches, one of your duties. Nobody knew one end of a fifty caliber

Everything on the ship was kept spotless, including the stack. Here a cadet rides a boatswain's chair as he soogees. Credit California Maritime Academy, courtesy Rod Marshall.

machine gun from the other. I don't know what we could defend ourselves against in San Francisco Bay, but that was one of the watches you had to stand.

"Later, the military sent vehicles and we got to go down to Point Montara [20 miles south of San Francisco] for antiaircraft training. I think they provided thirty-eights, fifty caliber machine guns, on the bluff, overlooking the water. They had aircraft fly over from seaward to landward towing a sleeve target quite a bit behind the tow plane. There'd be a whistle or a siren or something and everybody opened fire at once, with everything. So we all got one crack at firing a fifty caliber machine gun at the target. You had a full belt of ammunition and then you'd stand there and blast away when this target went overhead. And when it was my turn just a whole curtain of tracers and smoke and flames all heading up that way. Nobody knew what anybody was doing. You couldn't even see your tracers at all.

"So I got on the thing and the plane went overhead and the main target was behind it and they blew the whistle or the siren. I opened up along with everybody else, blasting away up there, not knowing what was going on. And I got through the whole belt of ammunition and got to the end of it and I got out and stood away from the gun. Everybody's cheering and clapping and come up and shake my hand.

"Gee, what did I do? I'd been so far off target, there's a poor little sea gull over here flapping away, and he ran right into my stream of fire. Shot down a sea gull. Poor thing thought he was safe, you know, right before I started. Everybody congratulated me for shooting down a sea gull."

Alan Dougall: "When I was there we took the ship up into San Pablo Bay and fired the fifty calibers a couple of times, somewhere up around Skagg's Island where they couldn't do any harm."

In addition to gunnery practice there was off-site training for some of the ship's equipment.

Roger Putnam: "We went to Mare Island for fire-fighting school. We went to Sperry gyro school somewhere in San Francisco and it was a good program. Ultimately we had to be able to start that thing blindfolded. Then they took us ashore to teach us about barrage balloons. They taught us how to inflate them and tie them off."[4]

Dick Jenness: "Fighting an oil fire in an enclosed concrete blockhouse was a confidence-building experience. Those lessons have never been forgotten."

Cadets always wore some type of uniform on board. Later, they received working blues, white day uniforms (bell-bottoms and square collared tops) and dress blues, but at first they were issued dungarees. For the work they did that was all that was needed.

Harold Huycke: "We had no other uniform, only dungarees. Our dress blues and our ship board blues were ordered and fitted and that took another few weeks. Everybody was assigned a certain job to start cleaning up the ship and they washed down, fresh water, I think, with squeegees on the painted deck. The decks were all steel and they were all painted. So you got all the soot off of it and all the night dew off of it and just to go through the routine of cleaning you swabbed down the decks with squeegees and a hose. Of course, the swabs were on the end of the squeegee and

---

[4] Barrage balloons were large, blimp-shaped balloons filled with helium tethered to a ship with wire rope. They floated above the ship and discouraged enemy aircraft from getting too close lest they collide with the balloons or their wires.

Uniforms included, left to right, dress blues, two variations of undress blues, undress whites and dungarees. Credit California Maritime Academy, courtesy Rod Marshall.

we polished the brass and we washed this and we washed that and we emptied the waste baskets and we took the garbage out and we went through this drill of cleaning all the way from the boat deck on down. The boat deck was wooden caulked but the main deck was steel, fore and aft. All painted grey."

Roger Putnam: "The school ship was spotless. It was an old junker. It had nothing up-to-date or modern on it, but it was kind of a fairy-tale, in a way — a piece of history."

Jack Summerill: "Everything was clean, from our mode of dress to our bodies to the ship. We kept that ship immaculate. It was the cleanest ship on the coast."

Harold Huycke: "We went to Joe Harris, the uniform outfitter up on Sacramento or Clay. Everybody went over there and got fitted for a regular Navy blue uniform just like regular USN. Blue serge heavy duty wool,

hot as hell in the summer time, O.K. in the winter. They were all three-button, with the California Maritime Academy buttons. It had 'Eureka' on it, the state seal. Had regular high pressure hat with white hat covers. And we were allowed only a one-quarter inch gold braid chin strap. Don't get caught with anything more than a quarter inch. No gold braid on our sleeves, 'cause we were swabs. Over our left pocket was the Naval Reserve emblem that looked like wings, had 'USNR' on it. Somebody with a little imagination managed to weasel his way into a night club by saying with CMA up here [on the cap device] that we were from an international flying group of Central Mexican Airways. And that 'CMA' opened a lot of doors.

"When we became second classmen we were entitled to increase the width of our chin strap to three-eighths inch. We looked forward to that as much as anything, to get away from this little quarter-inch gold thread that you could hardly see. On weekends we could go to some outport and change the hatbands as long as nobody caught us, gain a little bit of prestige that way. But when you came back to the ship the quarter inch went back on your hat again.

"We went to these outfitting stores and we'd buy those chinstraps, they would be bright gold, bright, bright, bright. Everybody knew by looking at it you were a green pea. So they hung them out of the porthole at night, let the salt air get on them, darken them up a bit, take the luster off it a little bit. In no time at all, why, it had that seasoned, old-timer's, old seaman's look even though we were still just barely able to shave."

Dick Jenness: "On one of my first home leaves, my Mom saw the gold chin strap turning a fine, greenish gold. I awakened to find she had restored the glittering gold with gold paint!"

Harold Huycke: "When we were second classmen we got a hash mark, a little bit of a single quarter-inch gold hash mark sewed on your uniform, diagonal, probably about nine inches long, that meant you were second class. When you were first class, depending on whether you were a petty officer or not, you would have a complete stripe around each sleeve and if you were not a petty officer you were only allowed one stripe around your sleeve. It was in direct proportion to the Navy style but they were just a quarter of the size. You might have a full three-eighths stripe and one or two quarter-inch stripes."

The cadets at CMA had a strong sense of community spirit. This was especially true during World War II when there was a sense of purpose in the country toward winning the war. The student body's normal camaraderie was heightened by the patriotic fervor of the war effort. Of course, to the enterprising cadets, "patriotic fervor" could also have a self-serving component.

Tom MacFadyen: "We read about giving blood. I went up to Severin, the XO, with this idea if we could get the cadets to give blood, could they do something for them. They quickly agreed every cadet that gave blood could have a longer weekend. So, out of the cadet corps of 150, we got 120 signed up. We called the Red Cross, they brought station wagons down. We had to dress up in our dress blues. We went up and gave blood and then we were free to go. Can you imagine this young gang of spiffy cadets going up there and these nurses are taking blood out of 'em? We got written up in the paper and I think we got an extra day off on the weekend."

For everyone, a part of the ship's routine always remembered clearly even fifty years later was reveille at 0600. Weekday or weekend, everyone on board started his day with the sound of the bugle blown down the hatch. Then it was up <u>instantly</u>, especially for lower classmen, a quick shower, dungarees, a hot cup of chocolate, and before it was cool enough to drink properly, out on the dock for morning exercises.

Harold Huycke: "At the main deck was a ladder that went down underneath the booby hatch at number two hatch. It had also a kind of a skylight and it was down through that that this bugler aimed that bugle."

Tom MacFadyen: "The way they found the bugler, the first night we went on board, they had a big [meeting] down in the classroom which was the upper number three, made all the cadets sit in the square of the hatch. The upper class sat around. They had this background information on every cadet that came in. So they'd call you up there individually and harangue you and shout at you and everything and they knew, apparently, a couple of guys could play a bugle. So they'd just throw the bugle at'em. You better catch the damn thing. Some of them couldn't play too well, they only got a wail out of it, but one guy, Doc Savage, could play it well enough that he became the bugler and he was pretty good.

"Savage had a flair for doing things a little differently. So, one morning, right in the top of the number two hatch, it's ten feet below, all the cadets sleeping, a hundred fifty of us, he got a slide trombone to play reveille on. That was a little different. And he got away with that. Then later he played taps on two bugles at one time. And Severin came out and said, "Give each one of those men ten hours' detention. So Doc got twenty hours of detention. And that was marching out on the pier with a rifle back and forth to work the hours off."

Roger Putnam: "Jim Muhlstein was the best bugler. He'd play jazz, he'd do jazz taps and reveille. There was a lot of talent up there."

Tom MacFadyen: "The ship had a mascot, sort of a cross between a German police and a husky. His name was Soogee."

Roger Swain: "Soogee was everybody's pal. He held reveille every morning with the bugler, howling along with him."

Don Peterson: "I remember Soogee blowing reveille, too. A cadet bugler would blow reveille down the hatch in number two. A few minutes before six you started hearing him warming up a little bit, sort of tuning up, quietly you know, and you'd hear Soogee warming up, too. He'd sort of howl. You had the bugler warming up and Soogee warming up and then a little howl, then when the bugler let go, Soogee would howl at the same time. The bugler blowing the damned reveille down the hatch and Soogee howling at the same time, it'd wake <u>anybody</u> up."

Tom MacFadyen: "Soogee got so much attention that he was really indifferent to us most of the time. He would stay on the main deck. He could go down the ladder to the berth deck, but why bother. But, the thing that he would do, Saturday mornings we'd have drill out on the pier and then after that we'd have inspections so we could go ashore for liberty. That's when Soogee would walk up and down the ranks rubbing his fur on the navy blue uniforms."

Don Peterson: "He disappeared while we were still in the school. He could go ashore any time he wanted and they'd go find him up at the waterfront bars where he'd get food or something. Finally he just didn't come back one time. We never found out what happened."

Reveille was the signal to begin the day. But on board ship the day never really ends.

Reveille was at 0600 every morning. Credit California Maritime Academy, courtesy Rod Marshall.

Watches are stood around the clock, both on deck and in the engine room.

Tom MacFadyen: "At the very aft end of the house, on the main deck, on the port side, you'd step into the upper engine room, there was a refrigeration compressor there."

Don Peterson: "On the four-to-eight watch, one of the first things you had to do when reveille blew was to get that ice machine [refrigeration compressor] started. You shut it down at night time. So, twenty minutes or so before you're ready to go you went up and lined up all the valves and so on. Woe betide you if you didn't get that engine cranking over at the first note of reveille. Dwyer would be down there on your tail and want to know what the hell happened, how come you didn't get it started. I guess he didn't sleep very well anyway. He just laid there looking and he'd listen to the sounds of the guys draining steam lines and opening valves and getting it cranked up and ready to go. You threw that throttle open at the first note of reveille and if you didn't you were in trouble."

The war and the move to the Ferry Building apparently brought an improvement in both the quantity and quality of the food.

Jack Summerill: "Mayo had contacts in the Navy. During the war everything was first class. Money wasn't a problem."

Harold Huycke: "I recall butter, lots of butter, lots of everything. We just came from home where rationing cards were governing our lives and here there was plenty of everything. Garbage cans filled up with food. . . Shocking change. . . Scrambled eggs, cold cereal, hot cereal, gee there was no shortage of food. It was all good."

Tom MacFadyen: "It wasn't home cooking, but there was variety and it was reasonably good."

Don Peterson: "All the lower classmen had to stand mess watches. They brought the

Training for deck midshipmen included the traditional use of the ship's sextant. Credit California Maritime Academy, courtesy Rod Marshall.

food down from the galley. It was up on the next deck. It came down on a dumb waiter kind of thing. The cadets had to pack it out on trays to each table."

Tom MacFadyen: "The mess tables were these kind that four people could sit on one side and five the other. The oak ones that the service uses, the legs fold down and you'd stand and then they'd put an oil cloth over them, which was wide enough to come down to about the length of it."

Harold Huycke: "The first classmen sat up near the inboard end and the second classmen and the swabs were down at the other end, outboard end, next to the skin of the ship. And you worked your way up as time went by, naturally. As you gained seniority, you became a petty officer, you worked up to the head of the table. Nobody sat on the ends."

Don Peterson: "Upper classmen would get the first cuts, and what was left would be left for the swabs.

"I don't remember losing any weight at CMA. It was a different kind of food, certainly, than home cooking, but we ate pretty well."

Tom MacFadyen: "There was one fellow, George S. Carl. And Carl, I'll say this for him, in later years when I met him at a forty or fifty year reunion, he was about as smooth and polished as could be, but at that point, his table manners were lacking. I mean he'd get everything on his plate, and then catsup all over the top of it and then dive into it. One upper classman thought, well, hey, you know, he could improve on that. So the upper classman happened to have some chopsticks. So he gave them to Carl and says, 'Eat with these.'

"So Carl ate that meal with them and threw them away and the next morning, the upper classman said, 'Where are the chopsticks? Oh? Well, you're not going to eat without them.' So he went out and found an orange crate and whittled out some chopsticks and he ate with chopsticks for the rest of the time he was a lower classman."

Don Peterson: "So did I. I remember eating with chopsticks. And I can still eat with chopsticks to this day because I had to. That was part of the hazing. Eating with chopsticks was one thing, and the other one was a square meal. And woe betide you if you didn't do that. I was allowed to have a spoon for soup, but that was it. You learn or starve to death."

Dick Jenness: "The cant of the deck in the mess hall made it possible for the upper classmen to order the swabs to 'eat a square meal' while holding up the oil cloth to make a trough for the ice water or hot coffee that traversed into the lap of the swab. As swabs, we knew what was happening. The 'square meal' bit required that you looked straight ahead, raise your fork straight up to mouth level and hence horizontally to the mouth (all the while wondering what else was coming your way)."

During the war years the school's curriculum was severely curtailed. Training cruises and foreign ports were no longer possible. The three-year course was compressed into eighteen months. Classes, training and discipline became densely concentrated. There was little time for anything else.

Engineers were given hands-on training in the ship's engine room. Credit California Maritime Academy, courtesy Rod Marshall.

Harold Huycke: "Everybody lived aboard. That was the school. It was the school ship and it was the school. Everything was centered there, the offices were elsewhere, I guess, but the classrooms were all on board the ship and in adjacent offices in the Ferry Building. There was a gangway that led off the fo'c'sle head up into one of those long waiting rooms that leads down from the northern part of the Ferry Building. There were various waiting rooms that had been converted to classrooms with desks. We studied in a long room with a slope that had banked sloping seats. We studied seamanship, we studied navigation. That's where we got our signalling because it was a long room."

Roger Putnam: "I remember class in the Ferry Building. We had some signalling instruction in one of the lounges on the ship.

Captain Claude B. Mayo, foreground, at the con, with Lt. Cdr. Chester H. Tubbs to his right. Midshipman Kenneth R. Orcutt is at the helm. Credit The Oakland Tribune, *courtesy Alvin Gregory.*

Most of us got pretty good on blinker and semaphore."

Harold Huycke: "Class was at eight o'clock and, of course, everybody went to class, first class, second class, third class, then navigation was rotated between first, second and third class.

"Some were in the Ferry Building and some were in the ship. I think most of us went to the Ferry Building. I know we spent a lot of time in the Ferry Building, and then we came back to the ship, coffee time. They instituted a coffee time, that was part of our daily life.

"During our swab year, the routine was pretty thick. The classes were intense. There was no time for fooling around. You paid a price for not studying.

"We had good instructors. Jack Summerill was class of '38 and he was the signaling instructor. He also taught Rules of

the Road, Tankers and Rules and Regulations. A guy by the name of Chester Tubbs, who was class of '38, Santa Barbara, was the navigation instructor. There was another officer who was kind of the exec. His name was Hugh Severin, Naval Academy class of '23. Severin had put in some time in the Navy, got out, became a stockbroker, was in the Reserves, was called back when the second war broke out, and Captain Mayo, who liked to 'dabble in cotton,' as he said, needed a stockbroker for an exec. Out of the Reserve list, put him aboard the ship. Severin was a little bit hard, but he was a levelheaded, likeable guy. Before we graduated he was transferred out and we got a couple of other jokers in there that we had nothing but dislike for. There was nothing wrong with them as officers, they just didn't come out of the tradition of schools or training academies. I think they were Naval Reserve officers that had come out of some university that had other disciplines."

Tom MacFadyen: "Tubbs was Irish, and sort of cocky, quiet, but not that inflexible. We'd go down to the South Bay on Monday and come back on Friday. Well, Captain Mayo would do his thing about being captain and bring us in [alongside]. We come up from the South Bay, pick a slack tide, you get out as far as you could and go dead in the water and then try and come in. He had no steerage. And, somehow or other, we were in the process of coming in and here was a new C-3 flattop coming along, and I think even Mayo started watching.[5] The next thing the *California State* wound up starboard side to, the ass over here and the bow over there, and finally they tie her off to stabilize her and all the cadets were up on the foredeck laughing, and they order all cadets below. We had to get out of sight and go below. I guess he backed her off or did some god damn thing and finally got her into the slip.

"OK, now that's Scene One. Scene Two. In the berth deck they'd cut ports into the side of the ship, so you could look out and see what was going on. Also, the after berth deck was at the bulkhead where the engine was. And you could actually learn to hear the rattle of the chains in the telegraph and the bells to get a sense of what was happening. I was down on the berth deck and Mayo, to train his junior officers, which was a very important thing, had let Miller bring her in one time and then it was Tubbs' day to bring it in. So Tubbs is coming in, and you sense what's going on, and I'm standing here on the port side and I can look out and see through the port here on the starboard side, see these diagonal pieces of wood on the slip? And no bells. And these god damn things are going by, like zing, zing, zing. All of a sudden you hear the bell, you know, more emphatic than you would a series of bells, Full Astern, and all of these things just stabilized and stopped. They dropped the lines over, put the gangplank over and we were done. And Mayo never let Tubbs bring it in again."

The training and the personalities of the faculty have a lasting impact on the students. Decades later, they vividly recalled many of their instructors and incidents related to them.

Harold Huycke: "The deck officer was really kind of a First Lieutenant. His name is on every rock and every corner post over there at the [Vallejo] campus. He taught seamanship and he was the guy on the bow when we tied up, name was Ed Miller, class of '34. He was the seamanship instructor and was really probably about the most reliable, one of the best instructors. The story I heard was that Ed Miller, soon as he graduated, had gone to sea when there was a strike of Masters, Mates and Pilots, in fact he was a strike breaker. When the strike was over he got blackballed by Masters, Mates and Pilots, was never allowed to join, and he had no place to go in the merchant marine. He wound up being an instructor at CMA. He was there throughout the entire war. Ed Miller was the one that carried the load and after the war he went in active duty USN, got command of a ship, did his time there as a commander."

Roger Putnam: "Miller was a hard man to know. He was very strict."

Don Peterson: "Dwyer was the Chief engineer and Dave Warwick was a first assistant or machine shop instructor, nuts and bolts . . ."

Tom MacFadyen: "Wasn't Dave a Welshman? He had an accent."

Don Peterson: "Yeah, he had some kind of an accent. He was a machinist and he knew his stuff. He taught us a hell of a lot, especially in the machine shop in number four. There was a machine shop with lathes and drill presses and we learned machine tool operation, such as we had to have it, from him. But Dwyer had his own text, his own little pamphlets. He wrote a whole series of pamphlets on marine engineering."

Tom MacFadyen: "He was commissioned by the Maritime Commission to write

---

[5] Many of the Maritime Commission-designed C-3 cargo hulls were used as foundations for aircraft carriers, called "baby flattops."

these for the entire Maritime Commission training program."

Don Peterson: "It was a guide that we studied that would prepare you for the license exam and if you knew that stuff you could pass the exam. So we spent our days academically and then also in practical work in the engine room every day."

Tom MacFadyen: "Dwyer worked in the shipyard. He told us a number of stories. One was about a ship he was on, a four screw ship. He was chief engineer. He was up in his room and all of a sudden he noticed his pitcher of water was jumping up. Nobody in the engine room noticed anything wrong, but apparently one of the propellers had lost part of a blade or a whole blade and that vibration was transmitting through the ship.

"He told another story which was more mechanical. In the shipyard when you put the engine in place, you line up the shaft and the whole works. The final thing to see if it's all properly aligned is the shaft has been coupled all the way through, right up to the engine, but not coupled to the engine. And then you've got the engine. So, you got these two flanges. To test for alignment you take feeler gauges, and you put 'em in and if it's the same distance all the way around, you know that those flanges are parallel. Well, they found out that it wasn't [lined up] too good, so what they did, as there was lighting going down the shaft alley, they unscrewed a few bulbs, they got a big muscular guy way down there and they gave him some jacks and they went through a rehearsal and this fellow could look up the alley and he could see when the feeler gauge is going in here, and he would jack these jacks and he'd make that alignment come out all right. So the ship passed, they buttoned it up, and he said they never had any problem with that shaft."

Dick Jenness: "Fifty years later I still have the notebooks from our classes. I learned best by outlining and making descriptive drawings. It was accelerated learning but nothing was left out."

Some of the personalities were not fondly recalled. Tom MacFadyen: "They had a second and third engineer and one of them had been a graduate a few years before and he was like a spoiled kid. Some of our classmates were as old as he was and just looked on him that way. Of course, he was wearing gold and he was an officer. When we graduated, our valedictorian was a guy by the name of Donohue and he was one of the older guys then, so in his graduation speech he commented on all of the officers and just skipped this graduate totally. That was his way of getting back at him."

Don Peterson: "That graduate was kind of a funny guy. One time, in Stockton, he came back aboard. He had a woman with him. He was three-quarters drunk but he was showing this woman his way around the engine room or how big of an engineer he was. He came down into the fire room, and one of the things, if you don't do it right, is you get a flare-back when turning on the oil. If you do it right it works and if you don't you can get a flare-back and you get a puff of flame out of the port that's open. And that happened to him.

In this case, signal practice is from one of the ship's boats and definitely not "Asiatic." Credit California Maritime Academy, courtesy Rod Marshall.

He was showing off to his girlfriend and he lit off and got a big puff of flame right back. He went around with singed eyebrows and singed nose and all that kind of stuff for a few days afterwards and embarrassed himself in front of his girlfriend."

The curriculum clearly reflected the wartime conditions. Harold Huycke: "We had a warrant officer assigned to be a signaling instructor. He had just gotten off the battleship *South Dakota* and she had taken a real pounding down there in the Coral Sea, one of those big battles way down there near the Solomons. I've read since that the *South Dakota* took a few direct hits and gave as good as she got. They brought it right to San Francisco and did some repair work.

"And so this warrant was detached from that ship and brought over on temporary duty. He was a heck of a sight different instructor than Summerill was. Summerill was a precise, good signal instructor. He was a good signalman, he taught us the light, he taught us flag hoists and he taught us semaphore. Those were the standard three media that we had to learn for signalling to pass the license exam and for practical use. In the semaphore everything was precise.

"This guy came aboard with his hat cocked over his right ear. He was an old pro, he was an old China hand, because he started teaching us what he called Asiatic. He was out on the China coast, up the Yangtze River in the old prewar fleet. They were always in port, he said, with Japanese ships. Japs were always looking through binoculars watching every single move on those American ships. So these American signalmen developed a style of signalling they called 'Asiatic' where their arms never stopped. They were constantly flailing like a windmill, and they'd only stop on a letter. But they were moving, moving. And he said the Japs couldn't read that, but we could

'cause we practiced with each other. That was the first time I'd ever heard about 'Asiatic.' And that was something that the old hands out in China and the Orient used because the damned Japanese were forever looking at them."

Other courses had less obvious implications. Harold Huycke: "Severin used to drill us with the rifle out on the dock, that's when we had the Springfield. He taught us drill, plain old marching up and down, manual of arms. It was so-called Naval Science, marching

"The right flank HARCH, the left flank HARCH, to the rear HARCH and that was Naval Science."

around on Saturday with a Springfield on my shoulder — the right flank HARCH, the left flank HARCH, to the rear HARCH and that was Naval Science. All the Naval Science you can get out of a Springfield was all we got. We were taught a little bit of Navy nomenclature and Naval traditions and Navy history and if there was any Naval Science in there I don't remember. It never made an impression on me.

"But after the war when I went back to USC, I had all my credits transferred from CMA down to USC. I got twenty-one units, transferable units, fifteen of which were Naval Science. Navigation didn't amount to a thing, Rules of the Road didn't amount to a thing, and the other courses which the University of Southern California did not teach were ignored, so we got fifteen or a dozen units for marching around with a rifle. What I lost one way, I gained back and it was the equivalent of a year-

and-a-half of college, so I did gain on it but it was a badly distorted recognition of courses."

Tom MacFadyen: "Every Saturday morning we had to go out on the pier and march. There were two deck groups and two engine groups. When we were first classmen, I was in charge with one of the engine groups. I had never run a group of anything. Each group was about thirty cadets. And, of course, we went to the movies and we saw all this wonderful stuff they do in the Marines, who are superbly trained. We'd go out onto the marching area in front of the Ferry Building.

"There were advantages to wearing a uniform. A lot of these doors would open for you with a uni- form."

"The first time, we were upper classmen and I had this group. When the drill was done, they would rate them and we came in last, very nicely last. And then, no holding back on the criticism. So, after, I turned to some of the guys that had gone to military, 'What the hell do we do?' One guy had a marching book and on the third Saturday we came in first. The prize for coming first was you got extended weekend leave. Instead of having to come back at seven you could come back at ten or maybe you could leave Friday night instead of Saturday. And we took that [first place] for the rest of our term.

"But it isn't who was leading the group, part of it was the nature of people. Now, the guys that went into the schoolship 'cause they wanted to go to sea and be an engineer were homogeneous, but the ones that went to sea because they were avoiding the draft or didn't know what else to do, or were sailing ship buffs, wound up going deck. All the guys in the engine room had worked on their cars or bicycles and they were mechanically inclined, so there was a cohesion. In the deck group there wasn't that same cohesion. Not to put down the deck guys, it was just the reality. They could never win [at marching]. One of the reasons I think we did well was we would go out and do what was easy and simple. To the rear march and a few things. But we a- voided all this fancy stuff they were seeing in the movies that some of the other guys were trying."

Part of the crew of the training ship includes nonteaching personnel. On cruise this staff included a radio operator and a doctor. But while the ship was confined to the Bay during the war years, the staff was limited to laundrymen and stewards. Recruited from traditional seafarers, they were sometimes among the more colorful people on the ship.

Harold Huycke: "The petty officers, like the galley crew, steward, messboys, each one of these guys had his own stateroom. These were paid crew. And there was a guy, I think his name was Morgan, he might have been the chief steward. We had two or three Chinese cooks and they were in the galley above us, on the boat deck. Two, three or even four, Chinese cooks."

Paul Marin: "The steward was red-headed and, of course, we called him 'Red.'"

Dick Jenness: "I can still hear 'Red' Morgan saying, 'Good stuff, boys, good stuff,' all the while shaking the grease off the pork chops. I went from 140 pounds to 181 pounds with the help of Red's food."

Tom MacFadyen: "We also had a laundry man on board. They'd do our laundry for us. You had big safety pins, each one had your own number on it. Then you'd pin your socks in a bag and all that. They had a steam press for pressing uniforms and the laundry man'd get pissed off at us because the guys would forget to ask him to do it when he could do it, then they'd go down, they're using his press, he'd get real upset."

Roger Putnam: "Harry Cannon was the laundry man. He would drink anything, shaving lotion, or anything."

Liberty was all-important. It was the one chance to get away from the hazing and strict regimen of the ship. The cadets looked forward to it, lived for it. Movies on Market Street were nearby and inexpensive. Trolleys, busses, ferries and cable cars were inexpensive transportation which brought the attractions of San Francisco within reach: Chinatown for numerous small restaurants, North Beach for Italian delis, Fisherman's Wharf for fresh crab, Coit Tower to watch ship traffic, Golden Gate Park, the museums.

Left to right, Harold Huycke and Roger Putnam. Photo courtesy Roger Putnam.

Paul Marin: "Those weekend liberties, they were nice. They were really nice. About every two or three months we were told there was going to be scheduled a four day leave. And that's something that we really looked forward to."

Roger Swain: "That Ferry Building was a pretty good place for a base, handy for liberty. Cadets being unpaid, we had to be pretty resourceful to pursue any kind of liberty ashore."

Harold Huycke: "The watches changed on the weekends. Those crew that were assigned to gangway watch, galley duty, engine watch, whatever watch you were going to be assigned to for the following week, you got off on Friday afternoon. You were gone Friday night. You had to be back on the ship at eleven o'clock on Saturday morning. That's when you had to report for watches. The turnover time was noon Saturday. The rest of the midshipman corps, including those that were going off watch were then allowed the weekend off. Depending on whether they were first, second or third class, you got off at ten, eleven or twelve. Each class got one hour advantage over the others.

"You were off and you could go off and do whatever you wanted to, but always wore your uniform. There were advantages to wearing a uniform. A lot of these doors would open for you with a uniform. Very few kids reverted back to civvies. Some of the kids that lived in San Francisco just went home, but a lot of the kids lived out of the San Francisco area, and they went wherever they could. Damn few of them ever came back to sleep on the ship 'cause then you fell right back into the routine, when the bugle blew, you got up, even if it was a weekend, and you were still subject to a first classman or a second classman's call. So you avoided it, and you didn't come back until you bloody well had to.

"A lot of them went to night clubs. Some of them just wandered in groups, just killing the weekend until they came back. This may sound kind of crazy but I used to go over to Oakland Creek and crawl over the steam schooners. I went to the San Francisco Public Library and went through the Coast Seamen's Journal, copying that old, old, old, old records of ships' arrivals and departures in the 1890's.

I went to Sausalito and crawled over the wrecks over there. I went to secondhand book stores."

The lack of money was a constant concern. Enterprising cadets took their liberty as an opportunity to earn some cash.

Harold Huycke: "Once I went up to the Longshoreman Hall and hired out and loaded ships one weekend. I went down in the lower hold of a Liberty ship and wrestled airplane engines with a very friendly old black preacher from Mississippi. I did some longshoreing and stayed in a flea-bag hotel in lower Market Street. When I was going to go longshoreing I had to be at the hall at five o'clock in the morning to get picked so I stayed in the Sunset hotel. I had my dungarees and my leather jacket and working clothes with me. All the money I got longshoreing I went up to Lieberman's book store on the lower end of Market Street and bought about four hundred pounds of Lloyds Registers."

Dick Jenness: "The longshoreing jobs were our real source of money. Tipping over (breaking down) fifty-five gallon drums weighing three hundred fifty pounds plus was character building. One learned fast to get the toes out of the way."

Roger Swain: "I remember working as longshoreman for ATS [Army Transport Service] at Fort Mason. That was backbreaking work, loading box cars. That's how I earned my fee for my class ring. Otherwise I made my fortune two bits at a time being a barber. Ralph Moon and Carl Severance got

Paul Marincovich of the indomitable spirit. Photo by Roger Putnam.

paid by the California Youth Authority for being buglers."

~~~

The philosophy of most military and maritime schools is that you can't lead and give orders until you learn to take orders. This is in training for life-and-death situations when one must obey unquestioningly the orders of the leaders, depending on their knowledge and experience for survival. This is especially true in the merchant marine aboard a moving ship hundreds of feet long where the time it takes to question an order may mean the difference between avoiding a collision or not, passing safely through a narrow channel or going aground, breathing fresh air or poisonous fumes from an improperly-cleaned tank. In wartime, the danger of the profession is exacerbated by the added risk from enemy planes, ships and submarines, bombs, torpedoes and kamikazes. The training begins by reducing everyone's self-esteem to one common denominator — hazing.

Harold Huycke: "Part of the routine when we first got there was to lose our identity. We were called swabs. That was the first year. We came in as third class and within hours of going aboard ship we were swabs."

Dick Jenness: "The swab status, a key part of the CMA system, introduced us to hazing. At the time we accepted it as reducing everyone to the lowest common denominator status before teaching us to be leaders. Looking back, I think it also instilled in us the discipline needed to learn."

Harold Huycke: "There was hazing. The officers knew there was hazing. And because they had gone through it in the early pre-war years, they felt that, especially in this compact era, where we had to be whipped into shape, they allowed it to go on as long as it didn't get out of hand. The rule was you couldn't lay a hand on anybody. You couldn't touch them, but you could haze the hell out of them by extra duty which could confine you to the ship on a weekend. Extra duty was a pet punishment for the infraction of any kind of a rule, real or imagined. If an upper classman didn't like the way you crossed your eyes, or you did something that offended him or you broke a regular shipboard rule, he could assign you to an hour of extra duty. Sometimes that extra duty took the form of marching up and down the dock with a rifle on your shoulder. And you could only do two hours on a Saturday before you could go ashore and if you got three hours of extra duty, you did two hours now, you stayed aboard and you worked the last hour off the next weekend. Which means three hours confines you to the ship. Seldom did I see anybody get three hours. They had to be pretty mean to take a guy's weekend away. But it happened."

Roger Putnam: "The first few weeks was just a heck of a lot of hazing. They turned the fire hose on you when you had to do push-ups.

Harold Huycke: "Paul Marincovich was the one that took the worst hazing. Marinc took an awful lot of hazing and he smiled and he laughed about it and he aggravated the upper classmen because they couldn't subdue him. He had that unquenchable spirit. Uncomparable spirit. He was a real tough hombre when it came to taking physical abuse. He was a good boxer, he was strong, he was in good shape and he could take all this."

Roger Putnam: "They couldn't break him. He laughed, he could have whipped anybody there."

Paul Marin: "Sometimes in the middle of the night, midnight, one or two o'clock in the morning, there would be a handful of swabbies awakened. We'd be told to go walk up on deck and there was kind of an extended plank like a little gangway at the end of which

would be tied one of the ship's dinghys. We would be told to walk the plank. We'd have to walk this plank and take a dunk in the cold San Francisco Bay waters, swim back to a ladder and climb up, go back in the showers, rinse off and go back to bed."

Alan Dougall: "We had to memorize a lot of things, one I remember is 'Life aboard ship differs from the more irregular and confused life ashore.' There was PT [physical

"I did forty pushups and the last ten his foot was in my back."

training] late at night, push-ups and that sort of thing. But we survived."

Harold Huycke: "At six-twenty out on the deck, out on the dock, down the gangway and lined up. First classmen were back here, looking like they didn't care whether they were out there or not. The swabs were all in the front row, our hats all were square, white sailor hats. And they looked us over very carefully, the first classmen and the second classmen. It was a caste system in the most primitive sense. And it was for a purpose. The hazing was to see whether you could take it. These guys wore their hats and they may come out in their bathrobes, they might come out any way they wanted to, but the third classmen, swabs, came out immaculate. Nothing out of whack, nothing wrong."

Tom MacFadyen: "They had rules we had to learn, Swab Rules, and I think in the first week you had to have memorized the whole page-full and be able to recite any of them on call. The other thing that was a prime disciplinary tool was push-ups, I mean, just do twenty push-ups."

Don Peterson: "Yeah, particularly in the lower compartment. We were woke up at two o'clock in the morning and taken down there and do push-ups for an hour and a half and things like that, you know, were supposed to shape you up.

"Of course, there's nothing like a common bond of misery to bring a class together. That was part of the militarism, more like West Point or the Naval Academy at that time."

Roger Putnam: "There was a basement in the Ferry Building. Upper classmen enjoyed throwing dances for the swabs as part of the hazing process. Only the swabs danced, by request, and since there were no girls, with each other."

Harold Huycke: "When I was a swab, I was sitting on the outboard end of the table in the galley, in the mess deck, just about second or third table down. A big affable guy by the name of Johannessen was sitting up here, a big friendly guy, didn't have a mean bone in his body. He was a good Joe, everybody liked him, he wasn't mean or vicious as some were. He looked at me and he said, 'Swab, what's his name?'

"The guy that was sitting next to me was a second classman. Well, you had to know everybody's name, yeah, quickly [snaps fingers] you had to know his name. But this guy had a nickname that he did not like. And Johannessen was just setting a trap. 'Swab, what's his name?'

"Well the other guy'd been given the name of 'Peepee' when he was a third classman and he hated it. He looked at me and he said, 'Don't you say it.'

"'Swab, what's his name?'

"You know, hammer and the anvil, what are you going to do. You're damned if you do, you're damned if you don't. The seniority guy you better pay attention to. The second classman, you're a loser, but you lose less. So I said, 'Peepee.'

"This guy's name was Knutson. He said, 'After dinner,' he says, 'I want to see you at my bunk.'

"This was a Friday. So, after dinner, after we finished, I went down, he says, 'All right, on the deck.'

"I did forty pushups. I didn't think I could do 'em, I did forty pushups and the last ten his foot was in my back. And I pushed against that foot. When I hit fifty he says, 'Get out.'

"That night I was in the hospital. I was in the hospital all weekend. I was there Sunday, I was sick as I could be. I shouldn't have been but it was something else. I guess I was catching a bug. But then the pushups didn't help matters. The doctor came in, 'What's the matter with you?'

"I never said a word about Knutson. Because I could be doing the same thing by pointing the finger at him as the cause of this. That was the unhappy part of it.

"It broke your spirit down to the point that they had a common denominator they could rebuild upon, and then, when you were finishing your third class year, they began to rebuild you. But they had to find out if you could take it."

The incoming cadets weren't completely bereft of compassionate attention, however. To help overcome the confusion when third classmen came aboard they were each assigned a "shipmate."

Tom MacFadyen: "They got the list of all the new cadets and whatever city they were in, some cadet from that area, who was already on board, was assigned the responsibility to find out about this kid. So when we showed up, we were not unknown. They knew that their dad was in the police department or this or that or they knew that you'd been an athlete or some other thing . . ."

Don Peterson: "He was your 'ship-mate,' your mentor, sort of. He was to show you the ropes and, of course, take care of you even though he was an upper classman. If you needed help in anything, or questions answered he was supposed to help."

The shipmate, to some degree, reduced the bewilderment of the new swabs. At least there was someone, hopefully with a sympathetic ear, they could go to when things didn't make sense.

Harold Huycke: "We, in the second class, were assigned a name and a swab to help and guide. I was assigned a redheaded kid, not more than eighteen, a wispy sort of boy. His name was Bob Cornish.

"I was still only twenty years old. I thought to myself, these kids in this class are greener than we were. How are they going to fare in this compacted training period and come out of here as third mates?

"There was plenty to learn, almost too much to learn about this ship, even in six months. Cornish had plenty to learn. I thought in one uplifting moment, we'll both learn this ship together.

"'Swab!'

"'Yes, <u>Sir</u>!'

"'I want you to learn something new about this ship every day and come back to me at the end of the day and tell me something you have learned on your own. How many holds are there, how many bulkheads are there, where are the watertight hatches, where are all the ladders, where are the fire hydrants and hoses . . .'

"Well, Cornish went off on these little private expeditions and in the evening he came back, 'Sir!'

"'Yeah, Cornish?'

"And then he'd wave his arms a bit and describe where he had been and what he had learned. And that way he gained a lot more in the way of indoctrination of this old ship than

THE SONOFABITCH OF A SCHOOLSHIP
This song started in the '30s and was added to over the years until there were twenty-eight verses. Some of those fit to print:

The world's a sphere Magellan found
　　For no good reason we're going around
Back to Frisco we are bound
　　On the sonofabitch of a schoolship

The food we get is not much good
　　And all the cadets they wish they could
Eat the eggs that taste like wood
　　On the sonofabitch of a schoolship

The cook up in the galley square
　　Is slowly shedding hair by hair
We know, we find them everywhere
　　On the sonofabitch of a schoolship

Of schoolships we have got the worst
　　Most of the time we are in reverse
We start a race and are never first
　　Oh, the sonofabitch of a schoolship

Her engine is a standing joke
　　At nine-and-a-half along she pokes
And half her oil goes up in smoke
　　Oh, the sonofabitch of a schoolship

Oh a thing of beauty is our scow
　　With bulging sides and square cut bow
And all the graces of a cow
　　The sonofabitch of a schoolship

Oh Crossman is a dizzy guy
　　Who thinks we'll look him square in the eye
And say "I'm the guy who stole that pie"
　　Oh, the sonofabitch of a schoolship

The mate he is a jolly tar
　　He shoots the rangelight for a star
And wonders where in the hell we are
　　On the sonofabitch of a schoolship

We always seem to be on the alert
　　The cadets they claim they never shirk
We always dig in and do the work
　　For the sonofabitch of a schoolship

the rest of his classmates and he was really excited about the assignment and seemed to enjoy telling me what he had discovered."

Some weren't cut out for the seafaring life. They simply couldn't take it. Harold Huycke: "Devoto was a good-hearted guy but he was all left hands and left thumbs. One time he was on gangway watch at twelve, and they had a big bell on the main mast right over number two hatch, a great big bell about eighteen inches across, welded right on to it with a trip gong on it. You'd pull it and it would go click-bang, bang, bang. They'd ring the bell, eight bells, you know, all through the day and up till nine o'clock at night they'd ring the bells. So here Devoto was on gangway watch and he had to go up there at twelve o'clock, stood by, the second mate gave him the nod: ring the bell. And Devoto grabbed this thing like the sexton in a church, one, two, three, four, five, all the way to twelve, just like the church up town. Pretty soon you could begin to see the officers sticking their heads out the porthole. Pretty soon here comes Miller sticking his head out in the passageway wanting to know what in the world is going on. And within a week Devoto was back in civvies again.

"I can remember . . . sneaking into their wardroom and looking for pieces of pie."

"Unhappily for Cornish, he washed out for other, unknown reasons. But when he came to say good-bye, he said, 'I really learned a lot from you, doing this. Thanks.'"

Tom MacFadyen: "Our class started out with fifty-two and within two or three days four guys had gone home."

Roger Putnam: "We went up the river to Stockton and out on the Bay. Some of the guys washed out because they got seasick on the Bay."

Harold Huycke: "There was a fella, at the time I didn't like him. He was very even-handed, level-headed. He was fair, but he was strict. He was a first classman. He belonged to that ethereal level of the all-mighty. You didn't dare cross 'em. He told me to do something and I mouthed something that he read. He read my lips. Kept a straight face and he said, 'Come on down to my quarters.'

"I knew I was in for it. I could've really caught hell, but he said some of the best advice that I had received up to that time and I never forgot it. He put a good levelling element on this whole compact idea of eighteen months making an officer out of you, taking the rough clay and making something out of you.

"He said, 'Now, listen. We're not here very long. You guys have got a lot to learn in six months and you got a lot more to learn in the next six months and you've got a whale of a lot to learn in the next six months. By the time you get out of here you better know enough to get by. You better do what you're told and learn to take orders. This is not done to you out of spite. It's done for a purpose, to make you conform to a more restrictive shipboard life and to learn to take orders and bite your lip and keep quiet about it.' He says, 'If I give you an order it's not for you to decide how sensible it is or if you want to do it. Did you get that straight?'

"'Yes, Sir.' And he let me off. And it did more good from that point on than to have the extra duty, or some other more vindictive punishment he could have inflicted on me."

But there were ways to get back at the upper class. Harold Huycke: "One of these upper classmen at breakfast said, 'I want some honeydew melon.' Well, there's no honeydew melon within five miles of the ship, let alone in the galley. So there actually was a precedent for it. You take grapefruit and you put honey on it and you give it to him. Somebody had gone through this and class after class, year after year, this had become a tradition. But if you don't know the secret you're groping. When they said it to me I thought of honeydew melon. Now where am I going to get it. So some guy said, 'Grapefruit with honey on it. But before you give it to that son-of-a-bitch,' he said, 'rub it on the deck.' So I did that. I got a half a grapefruit, I rubbed it all over the deck, I give it a squirt of honey, and gave it to him and he ate it."

As always, food was rarely far from the cadets' minds and, fear and hazing notwithstanding, good food was worth risking a few demerits. Don Peterson: "I can remember standing messenger watch, too. As a swab, you had to do that. If you were on deck you had to stand messenger watches. In the middle of the night there'd probably be just a second classman as an officer and an OD [cadet Officer of the Deck] when they called him, and the swabs as messengers. One of the messenger's duties was to scrounge up some night lunch."

Tom MacFadyen: "It was pretty standard. Kraft cheese came in those five pound boxes and there was plenty of bread. There was a big toaster so you'd put a piece of cheese between two slices of bread and throw it in the toaster. Probably very tough to digest, but being as young as we were it didn't matter."

Don Peterson: "Or, one of the things you'd do was sneak up in the wardroom which was in the deck up above the boat deck. I can remember tippy-toeing, scared to death, you know, some officer's going to find me, I'll be in big trouble. Up into the officers' country on the bridge deck and sneaking into their wardroom and looking for pieces of pie. They'd leave pies out there for night lunch. I remember tiptoeing carefully in the dark in the wardroom, not daring to turn on the lights, and scrounging around to see what I could find in the way of food. Pie was great, if you could find that."

Tom MacFadyen: "The cooks baked pies, that was a specialty. There was one occasion they tossed the pie down to the guy on the berth deck, upside down."

The *Golden State* was home to the cadets while they were in school. They got to know every rivet intimately. Interviewed half a century later they pictured the ship vividly. Harold Huycke: "Each guy had a footlocker and a steel hanging locker where you could hang your uniform up and your clothes. It was about eighteen inches by maybe eighteen inches by probably eighteen inches, with a steel door to hang things up in so they wouldn't get wrinkled. The footlockers opened up back to back. They were wooden capped. Above them were bunks that folded up in the day time."

> *" . . .warm bare feet on the cold wet deck, right now . . ."*

Paul Marin: "These bunks were on metal stanchions and they folded up, they folded down. There were two sets, a set below and a set above, one on top of the other with a passageway on each side."

Harold Huycke: "Heaven help you if you ever let those bunks down during the day except on Sunday. It was a stuffed mattress, sheets, one or two blankets, depending on the season, chain bunks, pipe frames, hinged in the middle right down the back."

Tom MacFadyen: "There were two lockers under the bunk, one for the upper and the lower bunk, and the bunk hinged together so your mattress met the other guy's mattress. I think the mattresses were, hell, only two feet wide."

Harold Huycke: "When you got out in the morning you better not linger when the bugle went off. Get out, warm bare feet on the cold wet deck, right now, and quickly the bunks were triced up. You made up your bunk, you triced them up and you hooked the chains over a hook up on top. There were footlockers and two tiers of bunks, and they all triced up. Always third classmen in the upper bunk, second or first classmen in the lower bunk. Swabs were always up above."

Paul Marin: "Every Saturday, after breakfast we would all line up at our lockers in the passageways next to our bunks. We would then stand at attention as the duty officer, one of the Naval Officers, Lt. Summerill or Lt. Miller or Mr. Tubbs, whoever it was, led the cadet officer down the row inspecting all the open lockers of the midshipmen. In the lockers we had all our clothes, our whites, our dungarees, our hats and everything all in tight-rolled fashion."

The head consisted of a stainless steel trough with wooden seats that folded down on it. A chain ran overhead which, when pulled, flushed the whole trough. Although there were no doors, there were partitions between the seats.

Harold Huycke: "Up forward there was a row of heads. As you graduated from third to second to first you were able to move up farther along. But when you were a swab you sat on these two [nearest the entrance] and don't get caught on these [farther inside], unless you had diarrhea or you got special dispensation from somebody. You weren't in everybody's view, like those in front of the door.

And as you got farther forward, why you just got away from the public view. It was all progression, you know, you just didn't start out with all these luxuries, you worked your way up. The showers, I think, were on the port side, tile deck, all these little white octagonal tiles. Everything was painted white."

Cargo holds 1 and 2 were located under the forward 'tween deck. At first No. 1 was used for rope and canvas storage and practical training, physical exercise and recreation. No. 2 held supplemental water and fuel tanks. Later on they were seldom used for training. Harold Huycke: "They just used it for a dumping ground for mooring lines and whatnot. It wasn't disorderly, it wasn't a junk heap, but we seldom, if ever, got down in there."

On the port side aft in the way of no. 3 and 4 and along the starboard side were the petty officers' quarters. No. 4 contained a machine shop. Aft of it was the steering quadrant. The steam engine that moved the quadrant was just inside the midships house and turned a drum on the outside on which the steering chains were wound. From the drum, the chains ran through troughs along the deck to the quadrant.

Harold Huycke: "They had rod and chains that went back to the quadrant along the deck in a kind of a U-shaped open trough, just like a channel iron. Lying along the deck underneath the hatch on the starboard side and the port side, was a big black chain that was coated in grease. The more grease you put in it the easier it pulled back and forth as the ship was steered. It was part of the basic steering. Quite often we'd have to get in there and scrape out the dirt and surplus grease and then we'd put a new slather of grease in there so this chain could work up and down. And that came out on the midship house and came down who-

Cruises on the Bay and to Stockton gave the midshipmen ample time to polish their small boat handling skills. Here they go over the side to the waiting boats. Photo by Harold Huycke.

knows-where through a bunch of conduit and then it emerged out on the number three deck, and back to the poop."

Berthed in San Francisco Bay, the students had a unique element to adjust to. Don Peterson: "One of the climatization things was the foghorn out at the end of the dock. A lot of the nights were foggy and they had two different levels of foghorns. They had a little tooter out at the end of the dock, kind of tooted away and the bigger heavier one was blasting away, and your fog bank out there it's echoing off of. So you had this kind of a chirping noise and a blasting noise. And the first night or two it kept you awake. After that it was just like a lullaby. You just sleep and hear this thing all night long, you know, and just rocked you to sleep like a lullaby. You got so used to it that you missed it if you didn't have it."

~~~

During the war years cruises were confined to San Francisco Bay, Stockton and the Carquinez Straits.

Roger Putnam: "We went to Stockton and I remember a lot of fun. We met the people from the University [College of the Pacific]. Met some real nice girls."

In this photo the midshipmen board the Golden State *over the boat boom. Credit California Maritime Academy, courtesy Rod Marshall.*

Harold Huycke: "Twice a year, at least once during each of these six month semesters, we went to Stockton. It was just a means of going up the river, everybody having a chance to learn how to steer, to put the boats out. We were damn good at rowing boats. We had four whaleboats and we learned how to row those boats, drop them in the water, pick 'em up. We became very good at that. We became so good and so confident that we could take the boats out with little or no supervision other than a good coxswain either at the oars or at the engine and we would be allowed to go run these boats up and down the river."

Tom MacFadyen: "We'd go up the river and the engineers had all kinds of throttle time. It'd be hotter than hell down there, of course, in the middle of summer. Having watches, securing and getting underway and

Trips around the Bay and to Stockton gave engine midshipmen a chance to handle the Golden State's *power plant. Under the watchful eye of the instructor, center, a midshipman answers the telegraph, right, while another handles the throttle, left. Credit California Maritime Academy, courtesy Rod Marshall.*

Cruises in the South Bay and up the San Joaquin River to Stockton gave midshipmen a chance at wheel watches. Credit California Maritime Academy, courtesy Rod Marshall.

The Golden State *in wartime grey. Note the guntub on the boat deck, midships house aft. Photo by Harold Huycke.*

anchoring and doing that stuff all the time, we had experience, lots of throttle experience on that big old reciprocating engine."

Harold Huycke: "My recollection is we always went up in the Spring, sometime in April. We'd stay in Stockton maybe a week. Whether it was a PR program that Captain Mayo cooked up or whether it was just something to provide us with a change of scene, I don't really know. The routine went on and we still had classes. We invariably got acquainted with all the local girls. They liked the ship and all these good-looking kids in uniform. Pretty soon we were invited out to parties, to homes and generally made a good impression. Nobody got hauled back in disgrace. We were told 'mind your manners' and we did."

Unfortunately, this happy situation was short-lived. The outbreak of war brought another major change in the way the school was run. Tom MacFadyen: "As soon as the war was declared, we went on inactive midshipman status."

Don Peterson: "They started paying us, instead of us having to pay them. You had to pay tuition, but after the war started we were midshipmen and getting paid, like on a real ship."

Harold Huycke: "As I remember, we got $50 a month from the government. Because we were in the Naval Reserve as midshipmen while we were in school. Capt. Mayo was partial to 'midshipmen.' They emphasized 'midshipman' whereas before the war I think they used to say 'cadets.'"

Maintenance was a never-ending job, even in San Francisco Bay. Credit California Maritime Academy, Courtesy Rod Marshall.

Tom MacFadyen: "My folks had to lay out 235 bucks to get me in the school. That was for the uniform costs, book costs and etc., etc. So, as soon as the war started we were then entitled to midshipman pay of $65 a month. Well, the captain was Captain Mayo, he was an Annapolis man. Couldn't drive a car, couldn't hardly drive a ship. But he was the figurehead. Around January or February or something, it was our first pay period and it so happens we had arrived in Stockton and Mayo wanted to impound all our pay and put it in a bank account for us. He found out he couldn't do that so we got our first pay check which was $87.50 'cause it was for a month and a part of a month. Here we are going on liberty in Stockton and they pay us in cash! I went home to Palo Alto, but I heard some of the stories about what transpired that weekend in Stockton. I was a young, naive high

school kid. We had some other high school kids that weren't too naive. They knew the ways of the world. They went ashore, some of them took a hotel room and invited the girls in and the City of Stockton had it in for the entire cadet corps. After that we were never welcome again."

Don Peterson: "There was a bar called Matty's or Mattioni's in Stockton where we kind of hung out. I don't know if it was the first weekend or not, but I know we were getting paid and going ashore there. Remember winding up in the College of Pacific campus and we meet some girls. It was the first time I got really drunk, I think, was that weekend, some place on the COP campus and somebody had a few bottles of something or other and we picked up some girls someplace and we just had a big old party out under the trees. That was, ah, an educational experience."

Tom MacFadyen: "We were quarantined the moment we stepped back on the ship. We couldn't leave."

Harold Huycke: "The other cruises were in the South [San Francisco] Bay, underneath the bridge. They could practice dropping the pick. We didn't all get to stand wheel watches, because we just weren't out enough and evidently the guy that was seen to be a good quartermaster was kept on the wheel for safety's sake. That was a major shortcoming. There was no night steaming at all. At the end of the day, drop the pick, put the gangway down. The next morning, pick up the pick, go somewhere else in the Bay, up to San Pablo. There would be a steaming period of several weeks up and down San Francisco Bay giving us practical sea time and the feeling of at least being away from the pier. It was minimal but it was all we could do because they wouldn't let that ship outside the Golden Gate."

Dick Jenness: "The true test for the deck jockey was docking the ship. With

Pre-drill assembly at Morrow Cove. Note the puttees (leggings) on some of the midshipmen. Photo by Roger Putnam.

suitable regard for the war effort and the docks, we practiced docking the *Golden State* alongside a moored camel in the South Bay."

Paul Marin: "We had ribbons made up. We got little pieces of cloth and fashioned them into the size of a wartime medal ribbon and took some coloring and colored it. So then we were veterans of 'The Battle of South Bay.'"

The remains of the four-masted schooner Bangor *with the "new" administration building in the background. Photo by Harold Huycke.*

Roger Putnam: "We did a lot of rust chipping. I can truthfully say I spent many hours in the bottom of the bilge with a light, scraping rust. That was a good experience. We had the cleanest bilge afloat."

Roger Swain: "We maintained and operated the ship ourselves. The cadets were the crew. The time taken off for classrooms was more the exception than the rule. The emphasis today is more on the academic side, whereas ours was predominantly ship maintenance. We did a lot of chipping and scraping of paint."

As cadets progressed to upper classes they found themselves on the other end of hazing. Some, like Harold Huycke, dished out hazing with a bit too much enthusiasm. "I was known as a SOB at times. I found a whole jar of honey in my bunk one night. Some of the

The Golden State *at Morrow Cove with steam up departing for a cruise on San Francisco Bay. Courtesy California Maritime Academy.*

guys, the lower class had dumped honey in my sack because of some hard-nosed attitude that I had on. I learned from a first classman how to treat the third classman, and when I got to be a first classman somebody stole my pea coat and dumped honey in my bunk. So I got it from both ends and eventually began to learn, some lessons are harder than others."

Ownership of the *Golden State* was again transferred in 1943, this time to the War Shipping Board.[6] Funding was found to develop new academy facilities, and a permanent location, at Morrow Cove in the Carquinez Straits at the south end of the City of Vallejo. The facilities were completed and the new campus (the present site of the school) was opened and occupied in August of 1943.

The campus was located just below the Carquinez Bridge in a canyon which shelved out (with the help of landfill) from the local hills to the entrance to Carquinez Straits. The shoreside approach to the campus, lined with eucalyptus trees, led to a series of temporary buildings: classrooms, offices, three barracks,

---

[6] In 1947 the War Shipping Board was dissolved and ownership of the *Golden State* reverted to the Maritime Commission. This entity was renamed the Maritime Administration in 1950 during a widespread reorganization of the federal government.

an engineering building, recreation hall, store room and mess hall. Of course, the facilities included a pier at which to berth the training ship. The view of the Straits was, and is, stunning; the ship traffic to and from Stockton, Sacramento and the oil refineries on the river a constant reminder of the students' chosen profession.

Harold Huycke: "We were the second class to graduate from this base. The class of December '43 was the very first. We graduated in June of '44.

"We moved to Vallejo in August. You could see the old ferryboat, that old *Contra Costa,* was shoved up there in the mud and another old four-masted schooner called the *Bangor* had been used as a pontoon for the building of the Carquinez bridge back in the '20s. When they finished with her they just shoved her up in the mud. She was still intact.

"There was an administration building, then a dirt road that led down to the pier and the ship. They had only begun to build the officers' quarters up on the hill. There were very few trees, only what naturally grew up in the gully, and this old pier left over from who knows how far back, way back in early history. There were several classrooms, all in this one story building, wooden siding, simple desks. I think they used the ship for the machine shop because we were herded back down to the ship. Regular watches were also stood on the ship to a minimum degree. The engineers were back on the ship quite often, every day undergoing formal instruction in the engine room and then the machine shop. We did our turn down there, some maintenance on the ship, too.

"Towards the end of the year, before the end of our second class year, we took our usual cruise again out in the Bay and up to Stockton. And in our first class year, it was the same thing, but by this time we were a good part of the time ashore in the barracks and a good part of the time on the ship, dividing it roughly evenly."

Roger Putnam: "It was quite a thing when we moved over to Vallejo because we had more room. The barracks life was different, we had a chance to study more."

Harold Huycke: "We had just turned first class, it was in early January '44. The hierarchy as a first classman was that those that were either scholarly or those that had just emerged as natural leaders in the group were picked by the regular licensed officers with the old man's approval. I wasn't in the top of the class, but when it came to the practical side of seamanship I was a little bit better than some. I could row and splice and tie knots and I was just a little bit more at home 'cause I'd been in small boats in Southern California. So they sort of weighed that against my mediocre scholastic achievement and they made me cadet adjutant."

Roger Putnam: "Harold's talents showed up early. They used to call him 'Pretty Boy.' He was a handsome guy. We also called him 'Horace' or 'Sails.' They passed these names down from class to class."

The "caste system" was not limited to lowly swabs and lordly upper classmen. Harold Huycke: "Now, the cadet pecking order: There was a cadet commander, and that was Walt Bernhardt. Walt was about twenty-four, smoked a pipe and looked 'senior.' Equal to him but a little bit lower in the traditional order of things on ships was the cadet engineer and that was Tommy Lewis. Below that was the cadet adjutant, that was me. Then down here were petty officers which were almost like division officers. For Saturday drill, you had puttees on and gunbelts or ammunition belts, and our blue uniform or white, depending on summer or winter. They all line up and the second classmen would take the count. 'All present and accounted for, Sir,' turn around to the division leader, the first class petty officer, 'All present and accounted for, <u>Sir</u>.' We're on a wooden platform, right in front of the barracks. They built a little wooden platform up there for the officers to stand on, while the rest of them were in the street. So we're standing on this wooden platform, first classmen all turn around, 'All present and accounted for, <u>Sir</u>. All present and accounted for, <u>Sir</u>.' I did a right about-face, got my foot caught in the planking and went right on my butt.

"There was another time, it was about our first week as first classmen. Everybody was out on the dock getting these assignments. The third classmen were, of course, routinely out in front. The first classmen were there and nobody ever counted the first classmen. You didn't dare count your classmates absent. The second classmen bloody well better be there, the third classmen, there was no question but that they were going to be there. They were going to do the work. But the first class may or may not be there. Well, I wasn't there. Four of us decided the hell with it. We're first classmen and we can do what we want to do, so we all went down and we hid out underneath the berth deck in the water tanks. And Summerill counted a lot of vacant spaces up there. Well, Summerill had gone through the ship and he knew where the water tanks were, too. Pretty soon here's a flashlight beam, Summerill reached over the tanks, there's Huycke, and there's Don Tedsen and the other two I don't remember. Summerill, with a sigh of despair, said, 'All right everybody out.'

"Wrote us up on report. We knew this was serious business because we hadn't had our stripes sewed on but a week and already we're caught. We tried what others did the two previous semesters, had never gotten caught. I thought sure as hell we're going to lose our stripes. I thought we would be disciplined and rightfully so. In due course we were ordered to go up and see Capt. Mayo,

where the air was thin. It was the captain's mast and that's a damn sight worse than just being chewed out by one of the watch officers, Summerill, or Miller or Tubbs. That was bad enough. But now we're going up to the four stripe level, the ultimate judge in this hierarchy and nobody wanted to face him. The day came. I didn't mind going up but I sure wanted some company and these other three guys were all ready to go with me. At the appointed hour we put on our dress uniform, and got ourselves all cleaned up and shined our shoes, and where's Tedsen? Well, Tedsen got a special liberty to go ashore to a dentist he had in San Francisco. Fortuitously it happened to be the day he was to meet the old man. And the other guy, he got a special liberty and he disappeared. That left two of us to face the music. So we climbed the stairs and knocked on the door and here's old Mayo sitting there at his desk. He'd probably given this speech a hundred times, but to us it was the first time. The impact was devastating. I'd never been chewed out by the captain before. Not this way, anyway. 'Mah bloojackets would never have let me down like this.' He had a Virginia accent. "Gentlemen, Ah'm ashamed. You have been appointed, as you know, as leaders of this cadet corps and one week from getting your stripes you have shirked your duties, you have hidden out down below when you should have been an example to the second and the third classmen.'

"He shook his head in a very impressive way, he looked right at us. 'Mah bloojackets would never have let me down like this.'

"'Yes, Sir. We won't do it again.' Our knees were knocking to a certain pitch.

"'All right. You're on probation. You've got only a short period of time to become officers.' And he let us off, and nothing ever happened after that. But the effect was tremendous. We did shape up. We didn't do that any more. It was a bad example and we lost the game."

Roger Swain: "Claude Banks Mayo. He was a small man in stature, big in commanding respect. He had talks with us on occasion. We'd be assembled in ranks and it would start out, 'In all my thirty-eight years in the Navy...' He had been commanding officer of the *Ramapo* before the war and started a volley ball game with a medicine ball called 'Ramapo.' He was very instrumental in getting the present base at Morrow Cove, did a lot of the leg work, and was involved in the legislation."

Jack Summerill: "I came back during the war as XO. Mayo was retired out of the Navy. He was a nice guy but he didn't know one end of a merchant ship from another. He told me, 'You run it the way it should be run, John.' That was my sole order from him as XO."

Harold Huycke: "After the end of eighteen months we went out to shorten the war or lengthen the war, however you look at it. We had a third mate's license and an ensign's commission in the Navy."

Roger Putnam: "It was a fantastic experience. We got very close. It was stressful but not impossible. We made many good, close friends. It was a good growing experience. I wouldn't trade it for anything. I wouldn't be the same person today if I hadn't gone there."

Dick Jenness: "The bottom line was that CMA was charged with educating and bringing the cadets' maturity to an acceptable level in only eighteen months. Many of us were seventeen year old kids when we entered CMA and nineteen when we took full responsibility eight hours a day for command of a ship, cargo and lives of a lot of men, most of whom were considerably older. I tip my hat to the officers and CMA system that accomplished this almost impossible assignment."

The *Golden State* made its final cruise as a training ship in 1946. The war having ended, she once more traveled outside San Francisco Bay touching ports on the West Coast of South America. The ports of call were San Francisco/Vallejo, San Pedro; Acapulco, Mexico; Balboa, Canal Zone; Callao, Peru; Valparaiso, Chile; Balboa, Canal Zone; Magdelena Bay, Mexico; Long Beach, Santa Barbara and San Francisco.

Meanwhile, a search was underway for a replacement and the year-old attack cargo ship *USS Mellena* was selected. Stripping of the *Golden State* began as soon as the 1946 cruise returned to port.

The last entry in the log for the Training Ship *Golden State* was dated August 12, 1946 at 0800. The student watch officer of the day wrote, "Farewell dear T.S.G.S. May God be with our 'Iron Mother' and her gallant crews of C.M.A." That same day the ship was towed away to the Reserve Fleet at Suisun Bay.

With a tug at each quarter, the Golden State *leaves the Academy for the Suisun Bay Reserve Fleet. Credit California Maritime Academy, courtesy Alvin Gregory.*

CHAPTER 5

THE *GOLDEN BEAR* I

The first *Golden Bear* was laid down as the attack transport *Mellena* (AKA-32) on September 25, 1944. Built under contract to the Maritime Commission by the Walsh-Kaiser Co., of Providence, Rhode Island, she was launched seventy-seven days later on December 11. Mrs. Paul P. Neal broke the champagne on her stem, christening her *Mellena* after an astronomical body. Acquired by the Navy on January 20, 1945 the ship was commissioned the same day.

Following a quick shakedown cruise out of Norfolk, Virginia, the *Mellena* carried cargo by way of Guantanamo Bay and Panama to Pearl Harbor, arriving in the middle of March. This was followed with three weeks of training in Hawaiian waters and a quick run to San Francisco and back for cargo. Amphibious support training exercises occupied the new ship's days until June 13 when she sailed for the Philippines. The *Mellena* spent the closing weeks of World War II in the Western Pacific running cargo to the Palau Islands, the Marianas and the Admiralty

Islands. In August she sailed in convoy for Iwo Jima and was anchored there when the war ended. After transporting Seabees to Saipan she returned to Leyte Gulf, Philippine Islands on August 28.

Newly-assigned to Transport Squadron 24, the *Mellena* embarked 242 MPs and Army Engineers of the XIV Corps at Manila, sailing in convoy for Japan on September 7. Arriving at Tokyo Bay on the 13th, she steamed up the Honshu coast and unloaded her troops at Shiogama (Isinomaki Wan) two days later. Receiving a typhoon warning she shifted to a safer anchorage at Mutsu Kaiwan, then proceeded to sea to ride the storm out.

Assigned to the 7th Amphibious Group, loaded with units of the 1st Marine Division, she sailed for Mainland China (the Tientsin area) on September 29 where she aided the U.S. program of helping the Chinese Nationalists regain control of the mainland.

The *Mellena* anchored in the Gulf of Pohai (with lookouts warned to be especially alert for mines) on October 3 and spent a week unloading the 1st Marines who were ordered

From the deck log of the USS *Mellena*:

September 18, 1945.
0350 Underway from Isinomaki Wan, Honshu, Japan to Matsu Kaiwan, Honshu, Japan in company with
    U.S.S. SAN SABA (APA-232), U.S.S. ALHENA (AKA-9) and U.S.S. GANDY (DE-764) comprising
    Task Unit 32.6.5 and in compliance with ComThirdPhibsForce Dispatch #170512. Movement orders
    due to threatening typhoon. Maneuvering on various courses and speeds to form convoy.
0544 Changed speed to 11 knots.
0600 Wind and sea increasing.
0800 Steaming as before. Wind force 6 from 145°T, sea rough and ship rolling easily.
0945 Commenced maneuvering at various reduced speeds when U.S.S. SAN SABA (APA-232) stopped
    because of engine trouble; made preparations to take U.S.S. SAN SABA in tow.
1008 Increased speed to 8 knots, U.S.S. SAN SABA underway under own power.
1100 Wind increasing in intensity - force 9 - direction 170°T. Sea very rough and ship rolling moderately.
1135 Wind veering slowly to right.
1200 Wind force 10, direction 185°T; sea very high and ship pitching heavily; visibility one mile.
1530 Wind moderating somewhat; visibility improving. Barometer rising.
1600 Steaming as before. Wind veering to the westward and moderating - force 8 to 9. Barometer rising.
1843 Speed 4 knots.
1900 Wind force 5 and veering to northwest. Ship pitching more easily in lengthening swells.
2000 Steaming as before.

to take control of the Tientsin area until Nationalist troops could be brought in to replace them. Her next port was Haiphong, French Indo-China where she discharged 906 troops of the 52nd Chinese Army and support equipment, by boat. Sailing on October 30 for Darien, Northern China, the *Mellena* was part of an eight-ship troop convoy. Dodging mines enroute, the ship's destination was changed to Chinwangtao where she discharged her troops. Returning to Taku Bar (Gulf of Pohai) two days later she waited at anchor until assigned to "Magic Carpet" duty.[1] She sailed for the West Coast on November 25 with a capacity load of returning troops.

From December 14 to January 9, 1946 the *Mellena* was drydocked for repairs at Willamette Iron and Steel Co.

Designated for conversion as a survey ship, she made San Pedro her home base while awaiting conversion orders and was part of

Service Force, Pacific Fleet. On March 6 orders were received to dispose of the ship rather than convert it.

The Maritime Commission learned they would be receiving the *AKA-32 (USS Mellena)* from the Navy and offered it as a replacement for the *Golden State*. Captain Claude B. Mayo, Superintendent of the Academy, and Dr. Richard C. Dwyer, former Dean of Education, traveled to Seattle, where the *Mellena* had shifted, to inspect the ship and see if it would serve their purpose as a training ship. They agreed it would do nicely.

Steaming south, the *Mellena* made her last voyage in the open ocean as a Navy ship. Arriving in San Francisco, she went to anchorage and on April 17 shifted to Mare Island.

Cadets from CMA immediately began the process of stripping and refitting the ship. Ralph Swany '33: "We had fifteen or twenty stools in the *Golden Bear* [*Mellena*]. What

---

[1] "Magic Carpet" was a major logistic effort that brought the fighting troops home to the United States after the war.

we did before we got rid of it [*Golden State*], we went in and stripped all the toilet facilities off that. We took all the ports that we had in the hull. Took them all off. So when we got the *Mellena* we installed them all back in there, like great big portholes. I don't know how many, but they went down both sides of the berth deck. They just made cutouts in the bulkhead and welded them in.

"We had a lot of superfluous Navy bridge gear that we had to get rid of. We got it all fixed up so we had bridge classrooms there for navigating classrooms."

On May 10 the *Mellena* went into drydock No. 3 at Mare Island. Sea trials were conducted May 24 on San Francisco Bay with the entire Midshipman Corps on board. On May 30 the ship was shifted to a commercial pier, the Sperry Flour Dock in Vallejo. She was decommissioned on June 11, 1946 and simultaneously transferred to the War Shipping Administration (WSA) for delivery to the California Maritime Academy.

The final Navy deck log entry reads:

1200 - Received Commander H. Clifford, 55210, USN, Twelfth Naval District decommissioning officer, aboard. The U.S.S. MELLENA(AKA-32) was decommissioned, Commander H. Clifford officiating, and delivered to War Shipping Administration.

The first log entry of the new ship recorded the same ceremony. Dated June 11, 1946 it records the official transfer of the ship from the Navy to the Academy, indicating Cdr. H. Clifford, USN, as decommissioning the vessel while alongside the Sperry dock after which it was accepted by Capt. Claude B. Mayo, USN (Ret.), for the Academy.

The weeks that followed were busy, with cadets swarming over the ship as she moved from one location to another in the process of outfitting for training. Bulkheads were burned out, washrooms and heads removed, all Navy berthing, lockers, etc. were taken out. In July we find the vessel at United Engineering in Alameda. There, new berthing, heads, passageways and portholes were added.

The *Mellena* was struck from the Navy list on July 3, 1946.

From the date of transfer of the ship to the Academy it was referred to in the log as the *Golden State*, but from July 30, 1946 and ever after she is the *Golden Bear*.

~~~

The ship returned to the Academy at Morrow Cove on August 24, her new coat of gleaming white paint punctuated by stylish buff trimmings. She was completely reconditioned and on September 6, 1946 was rechristened the *Training Ship Golden Bear* by Virginia Warren, daughter of Governor Earl Warren.

On December 5, 1946 the ship shifted from Morrow Cove to Pier 62A in San Francisco to prepare for the upcoming cruise. Her master would be Ralph Swany, who graduated from the California Nautical School in 1933. Ralph Swany: "I was on the original training ship [*California State/Golden State*] when I first went to the Academy. In '46, that's when we got this, the *Mellena*. And I put her to bed, up in the Reserve Fleet. So I was a student in the old one, and then we got this one and I was skipper on her for eleven years."

On January 10 the *Golden Bear* shifted to the Union Oil dock in Oleum to fuel and sailed on its first training cruise three days later. Ports of call were: Long Beach, San Diego; Balboa, Canal Zone; Cristobal, Canal Zone; Vera Cruz, Mexico; New Orleans; Kingston, Jamaica; Cristobal, Canal Zone; Balboa, Canal Zone; San Diego, Long Beach, Santa Barbara, Monterey, San Francisco, Oakland, Stockton and Vallejo.

Reconditioned, freshly painted and ready for service, the Golden Bear *alongside the pier at Morrow Cove. Courtesy California Maritime Academy.*

Virginia Warren, daughter of Governor Earl Warren, rechristened the ship for her new service. Credit The Binnacle, *courtesy Alvin Gregory.*

The first *Golden Bear* was a twin-screw, turboelectric-propelled vessel of all-welded steel construction. She had a straight, well-raked stem, a cruiser stern, a midship house and two streamlined stacks. She was considered a medium-sized shallow draft vessel with one continuous steel deck, the main deck extending aft for about 85 per cent of the vessel's length. The machinery was housed in two engine rooms separated by an auxiliary machinery space. There were three cargo holds, one forward of the machinery spaces and two aft. She had a balanced rudder and two four-bladed screws. There were two steel masts.

How a ship rides is of great interest to her passengers and crew. The comfort and enjoyment of living aboard depends a lot on a vessel's sea keeping abilities. An integral part of how a ship rides is the way she handles. A ship's handling and riding characteristics are among the first things a new captain tries to determine.

Ralph Swany: "She was high-speed, shallow draft. That's what she was designed for originally. Twin-screw turboelectric. But she only drew about twelve feet of water. She was so shallow, she didn't have any weight. So you get any seaway or anything and you're at the mercy of the weather conditions. She was rough riding. She'd take and roll all the dishes off the tables."

Chester Ferguson '52 had a different reaction: "I think she rode O.K. She was pretty fair in that respect, a good sea keeper. There was quite a bit of permanent ballast in the forward and after holds."

Ralph Swany: "She would make fourteen knots, but you couldn't afford to run it. So we'd cruise about ten, on one engine. Then we'd hook up both engines when coming into and out of port so we'd have full advantage of twin screws. We'd get out and get her stabilized and steady away, then we'd switch over to one engine and one screw."

John Keever '70 (later master of the *Golden Bear* II): "She was relatively slow. Twelve knots on a good day was probably pretty good. Most of the cruises were down in the ten knot range. She handled pretty well because she was twin-screw. Most of the dockings were done without tugs. In fact, during a tugboat strike, while I was here, Capt. Bowman actually took the ship to a shipyard and put it in a drydock in Richmond without tugboats. So it must have handled pretty well. Even though it was only a little over four hundred feet it was still a fairly good job to get that into a drydock. A lot of people have trouble getting into drydock *with* tugs."

There were two main engine rooms and an auxiliary engine room with more than enough equipment to train future ships' engineers.

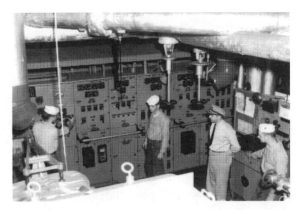

One of the Golden Bear*'s two engine rooms. Courtesy California Maritime Academy.*

Rod Marshall '51: "It had turboelectric drives. Two fire rooms and two engine rooms and an auxiliary engine room. The auxiliary engine room was between the two main engine rooms. That was where the salt water evaporators and all auxiliary electrical machinery were."

Don Lipman '51: "To me, one of the main highlights or attributes of the ship was that it did have two engine rooms and the auxiliary engine room. That gave lots of training. We could be trained on many locations at the same time. You had two watch engineers and two oilers and firemen. There was enough to do that you didn't have to make work. It was an ideal training ship in that respect, much more opportunity for training than on a single-engined ship. One of the big advantages was that we had one engine set up to use Hagan equipment, [combustion control equipment] and the other set up to use Bailey controls. This gave the midshipmen experience in two types of plants instead of one. These were common types of plants used in the industry at the time."

Chester Ferguson: "It was good training for engineers 'cause the two engine rooms were similar."

Don Lipman: "Another big advantage with that ship was that it was AC [Alternating

Current] powered and the U.S. merchant marine at that time was shifting over to AC [from direct current]. That gave the students on that ship a huge step up compared to others. I thought that was a big, big advantage."

Larry Teague '63: "We [deck dept.] got down in those as lower classmen to help wipe up oil and things like that. We got down there just to see the big things going around. There wasn't too much as far as sharing duties with deck and engine."

The berthing arrangements were similar to those on the *Golden State*. Midshipmen slept in tiered bunks in the forward compartments. Chester Ferguson: "We slept forward, two and three high. In the morning if you didn't get up they'd unchain the racks. So everybody was up. We had big showers forward. We were sleeping in troop quarters and had little wooden lockers. It was a lot like enlisted men lived in World War II."

Larry Teague: "Number one hatch was the berthing area, a converted cargo hatch.[2] It was set up with just rows and rows of bunks and I think they were just three bunks high. That was mostly third class and second class. The first class had a berthing area forward of that, they lived up there, and they were a much smaller class than the rest of us. Heads and showers were in the after end of that forward area."

Because of the large crews carried on Navy ships, the new vessel had ample room for classes, recreation and navigation.

Ralph Swany: "The whole bridge area was all classroom areas, for navigators. I never had to worry about where we were because I had enough navigators. I had two real crackerjack navigators — Roger Swain and Fred Neid."

Chester Ferguson: "The cadet chart room was twenty by ten. It was set up well for navigation. Those were good days, morning stars, noon stars and evening stars, every night. The credit goes to Fred Neid. He was a tough instructor. We learned a lot."

Roger Swain '42: "The *Golden Bear* was very well laid out as a training ship with adequate quarters for all hands. It even had a boxing ring in the square of the 'tween deck hatch. I remember our ship's doctor was William Nugent Scott who had been in the Navy, just came out of the Navy in time to make this cruise. He was a former Golden Gloves champion and was pretty handy as a boxer. I used to box with him but he had the edge even though I was bigger."

Bridge watch on the Golden Bear. *Note the dress khaki uniforms which were not worn in earlier years. Courtesy California Maritime Academy.*

John Mena '51: "I got knocked around that ring because I had no experience. We had a lot of fun there, young girls came aboard and we gathered there. The juke box was there.

"Classrooms were below the sleeping quarters. I don't think we spent a heck of a lot of time in the classrooms. We had a first lieutenant who believed the ship should be in tip-

---

[2] Thirty and forty years after the fact, many of those interviewed were understandably hazy on some aspects such as the number of hatches or holds. I have edited their interviews to reflect the correct configuration. Author.

top shape. As swabs we spent a lot of time on labor, not much in class."

Chester Ferguson: "Underway, it basically was bridge watch and navigation with handling small boats. We had a couple of whale boats, a couple of monomoys on board.[3] All we had to learn about small craft we had to learn on the cruise, which we did. Of course, there was a never-ending maintenance job. They couldn't figure out what to do about the soot. We soogeed day and night to get the soot off."

Rod Marshall: "The 'tween decks were outfitted to classrooms and general storage. We had ample storage spaces for anything they were going to take for a foreign country. In the after hold, in the lower deck, was installed a donkey boiler used for steam heat in port. It was quite large and was installed and operated by midshipmen."

Larry Teague: "There was also a barber shop and a snack bar and a laundry room; they were set up aft somewhere."

Phil Laudenschlager '51: "We had that laundry on the ship and it was luxury living. We'd toss our clothes into a bag and four or five days later we'd get them back."

Larry Teague: "The laundry was run by the midshipmen. But a lot of us would tie our laundry on a rope and toss it over the side for a mile or two. Ten minutes was about right. If you left it out too long you would bring back threads. You had to trail it out a long ways. But what bothered me is there were always seasick guys vomiting over the stern."

The CMA staff was complemented by some civilian crew. Rod Marshall: "The mess decks were amidships on the main deck. There was a huge galley to support the troops the

The galley was "the kind where you walked through and they flopped it on your tray." Courtesy California Maritime Academy.

ship carried when it was a transport. We also had a civilian crew who did the cooks' work, and some seamanship was taught by ex-boatswain's mates types."

Larry Teague: "We had five or six civilian employees in the galley force. Of course, our officers were the actual instructors at the school. Probably a dozen, I guess, because every division had an officer-instructor in charge and there were eight divisions. And, of course, a captain and an XO.

"And we had a bosun, a permanent year-around guy, typical old bosun, had been there for years, everybody liked him. I think we had to carry a civilian radio operator and a doctor."

---

[3] Monomoys are double-ended boats used in training at most maritime academies. They can be rowed with up to ten oarsmen or sailed with a single, removable mast and sails. Their use is due to their configuration which closely resemble ships' lifeboats.

Phil Laudenschlager: "We originally had the full crew aboard — the sail maker and the carpenter, the old original carpenter, but they got cut back as the budget got cut. The bosun stayed but when the other two left that was the end of those two positions."

Larry Teague: "All the officers' quarters were forward on the upper decks, and the galley and messroom were accessible from the berthing area. There might have been a couple of little offices in that area, too. The galley was strictly the kind where you walked through and they flopped it on your tray."

Phil Laudenschlager: "There was a special small hatch, maybe five or six foot square, against the face of the deck house and it had a couple of one ton or ton-and-a-half booms and we'd bring the pallets of food down directly into the chill box or reefer box or for dry stores."

The cruise of 1948 was to be a goodwill trip. Just before Christmas 1947 the California Maritime Academy suggested to Governor Warren that the *Golden Bear* carry a relief cargo of food and clothing to some of the countries it would visit in the Mediterranean on the annual training cruise. Governor Warren approved the plan and appointed Maurice C. Sparling, State Superintendent of Banks, as Chairman to organize the trip and collect relief cargo. The State Junior Chamber of Commerce was pressed into service. It was decided that canned milk would be the major portion of the cargo and the *Golden Bear* became known as the "California Milk Ship."

Roger Swain: "In '48 Dr. Dwyer called me and offered me a job as a teacher. We made a training cruise, Russell Ihrig was commodore, and he originated the idea of this Marshall-like plan to Europe. We took milk to war-torn Greece, Italy and France."

Ralph Swany: "We took a thousand tons of milk, donated by the people of California."

Governor Warren presents several cans of milk to Capt. Swany for the cruise of the "California Milk Ship." Courtesy Ralph Swany.

The humanitarian voyage appealed to everyone in the maritime industry. Arrangements were made for free loading services at Stockton, Oakland, San Francisco and San Diego. The U. S. State Department arranged for free port services on the receiving end at Marseilles, Genoa, Naples and Piraeus. The Navy Department fueled the *Golden Bear* at Gibraltar and Algiers.

The *Golden Bear* sailed from CMA on January 14 and arrived, loaded and sailed on schedule from five California ports (Vallejo, Stockton, Oakland, San Francisco and San Diego). Governor Warren and other officials gave the voyage a colorful send-off with numerous civic ceremonies.

Ralph Swany: "Governor Warren's son was an honorary student on board. The governor rode with me from San Francisco down to Long Beach, so we got a chance to talk with

Among the many civic ceremonies attending the sailing of the "California Milk Ship" were departures from Vallejo, above , and the Naval Supply Center, Oakland, right. Credit for both photos goes to San Francisco Maritime National Historical Park.

Although the sign in the right foreground identifies the berth as "3rd Street" it's unclear what port this is, possibly San Diego. Courtesy California Maritime Academy.

him. Then, while enroute down the coast, they had the son working with the rest of the kids. His dad, when he went down there and found him, where was he? He was up there in the head scrubbing toilets. That was Earl Warren, junior.

 "Before we left, his mother came up and talked to me, says, 'Take good care of my boy.' And his dad gave me an extra hundred dollars in case he got caught short and needed money."

 On January 25, 1948, the *Bear* cleared her last California port, San Diego, loaded to capacity with a cargo consisting mainly of

The school children of Marseilles greet the Golden Bear. *Courtesy Ralph Swany.*

A guided visit to Notre Dame de la Garde was part of the stay in Marseilles.   Courtesy Ralph Swany.

canned milk, canned goods and clothing, and 300 tons of whole dried milk belonging to the United Nations International Emergency Childrens Fund for delivery to Italy and Greece.

Enroute to Gibraltar the *Golden Bear* received an SOS calling for medical assistance from the *SS Joseah Snelling*. Backtracking 270 miles, the ship picked up a sick seaman and the *Bear*'s doctor performed an appendectomy.

Roger Swain: "We rendezvoused with an American merchant ship in mid-Atlantic. We got a member of the black gang off the ship and our doctor operated on him for peritonitis. All-in-all, it was very successful." Six days

later the seaman, John Murray, was able to go ashore under his own power in Gibraltar.

The relief cargo was delivered at the ports of Gibraltar, Marseilles, Genoa, Naples, Piraeus, Algiers and Funchal, Madeira.

Roger Swain: "That was a very successful cruise. We had a lot of notoriety from the State Department and other sources that we worked with."

Ralph Swany: "We were under the auspices of the State Department. They acted as my agent and would get me through if I had a situation where I had to go though customs or something like that. We'd go into these ports and they would get pilotage and berths.

While in Rome, CMA midshipmen received the blessing of Pope Pius XII. Courtesy Ralph Swany.

Sometimes I'd have to pay for pilotage, sometimes I'd have to pay for wharfage, sometimes it was *gratis* to me."

The Communist Party was strong and powerful in postwar Italy. As national elections were to coincide with the *Golden Bear*'s visit to Genoa, it was thought best to get the cadets away from any potential confrontation.

Ralph Swany: "In Genoa, they had Togliati, he was a Communist organizer, and they were getting ready for elections. We came in, the Rotary Club took all the students on a tour down to Apollo, down out of Genoa, while they had a big Communist rally there. Got them out of town."

Most of the midshipmen were from small towns in California and had never been outside the state. For them the trip was one colorful, exciting adventure after another. In Rome they spent their time viewing the ruins, the fountains, the Coliseum, galleries and museums as well as enjoying the food and the exuberant friendliness of the Italian people. Italian girls were attracted to their uniforms; the midshipmen were attracted to the girls. Traditional ambassadors of good will, they performed their duties with enthusiasm.

Ralph Swany: "The time we went to Rome, all the fellas that were ashore got an audience with the Pope. I didn't make the audience at that time because I had to stay down in Naples to go with the prefect to the opera house to see 'Salome' as his guest. But the next morning they sent me to Rome, they had an audience set up with the Pope. And going up, the train ran into a cow so we were twenty minutes late getting to Rome. The people that were taking care of me in Rome, one took my bags to the hotel and one got me up to the Vatican, and we got in for my audience with the Pope. And it was a twenty minute chin-chin there. He talked about our

The Golden Bear *and its goodwill mission are welcomed to Piraeus. Courtesy Ralph Swany.*

project, what it was for and where it was going, my family, and wife and all. It was just a really nice, general conversation. And you figure, it's the head of the whole Catholic Church."

Rome was but one example of the welcome received by the California Milk Ship. In Naples, Piraeus and Marseilles, the receptions were just as warm, the gratitude heartfelt. In every port there were welcoming ceremonies, parties and dinners with dignitaries; grateful children, appreciative elders and caring citizens. The midshipmen were on their best behavior, smiling, trying to answer questions, breaching language barriers with cross-cultural nods and gestures.

Back at sea, the glory that was Rome gave way to the more mundane problems of dealing with the weather.

Ralph Swany: "It was a rough trip. We was burning fuel all the way and I didn't get fueled up until I got into Gibraltar on the way into the Med. I got fuel there and then in Algiers on the way out for my trip across the South Atlantic, then I fueled up again at Curaçao to get me home. She had a tendency to be wild, in other words."

The ship returned to her home port on May 19, ending a unique mission of good will

in which not only the midshipmen of the California Maritime Academy participated, but also the people of the entire State.

~~~

Funding problems at the California Maritime Academy were almost a tradition, dating back to the *Jamestown* and the original California Nautical School. The era of the late 1940s and early 1950s was no exception. As a state agency, CMA, like other state agencies, was financed through state legislation. Unlike agencies such as the Department of Fish and Game or CalTrans, however, its reason for existence was difficult to justify to a Legislature that felt little impact from the merchant marine, if they even knew what it was. The general population had little or no understanding of just how they received goods and raw materials from around the world. They enjoyed the cachet of "imported" fashions, wines, automobiles and the thousands of other commercial products without any appreciation of how these goods had arrived at their local stores and dealerships. There was a constant battle to prevent the school from being closed by overzealous politicians who saw an opportunity to enhance their own reputations by closing a little-known school and reducing the state budget.

Chester Ferguson: "I went in in '48. I no more get into school than the legislature wants to shut it down."

Nonetheless, each time, those who knew the importance of the school battled diligently and succeeded in preventing its closure and ensuring its continued existence — until the next threat.

John Mena: "In '49 we took out a DDE [destroyer escort] known as the *USS Colahan,* prior to our cruise, to break in some of the midshipmen. It was a destroyer escort [actually not a DDE but the DD-658] out of a reserve group out of Treasure Island. We went

Valparaiso has always been a favorite port for CMA midshipmen. Here a cadet and friend look down on the Golden Bear *at her mooring. Photo by Phil Laudenschlager.*

to Monterey and everyone was sick, including me. We were all so sick … And then there were the cadet predators that would try to make you sicker by telling you stories about bodily mutilations and so on. The toilets on the DDE were set on a trough and, of course, the upper classmen would ball up the toilet paper and set it on fire and float it down under the guys throwing up."

Rod Marshall: "That was our first sea cruise. They had a skeleton navy crew and the preponderance of the crew was midshipmen and midshipmen instructors. We went on a full power trial and that was exciting. You seldom have an opportunity to see that, the engines running full out to see that they maintain the proper pressures and be sure that everything is functioning properly. It was a good training exercise."

~~~

The cruise of 1949 included the ports of: Callao, Peru; Valparaiso, Chile; Balboa, Panama; Acapulco, Mexico; San Diego, Long Beach, Santa Barbara, Oakland and Vallejo.

Phil Laudenschlager: "On my first cruise we went to South America and that was another real exciting thing for me, my first time away from home. That was a very enjoyable cruise even if, as swabs, we worked our tails off. It was a very enjoyable trip. I made all the side trips: in Valparaiso, to Viña del Mar where we spent the day, in Acapulco we took the train to Mexico City and enjoyed that. And, of course, Acapulco was always highly anticipated."

John Mena: "Capt. Swany taught me boat etiquette in Callao. The liberty boat was already gone and Swany took us ashore in his boat. The captain is supposed to be the last one in and the first one out. When we got to shore I jumped off first and got sent back to the ship for not observing the etiquette."

Ralph Swany: "Then in Peru, we had a nice gathering there with the embassy people. We were invited out to dinner at one of the consular places. He had a big round dining room, big round table and sideboards all around. They had all this beautiful silver. All the fittings were silver, the door pulls and the hinges, everything, all silver. I asked him, 'Hey, what gives, you got everything silver.'

"He says, 'Hell, that's cheaper than brass. All brass is imported and the silver is mined here.'"

Phil Laudenschlager: "We had several diplomatic parties. As a matter of fact, that was part of the trip to Valparaiso. We had been invited over to a big luncheon and the same thing in Mexico City. I don't know if that was because we were all Naval Reservists or not. All in my class had to be Naval Reserve.

"We brought back a bunch of miniature penguins, about a dozen of them, and dropped them off at San Diego [for the zoo].

That was interesting because they were only a foot-and-a-half tall and they had a corral behind the radio operator's room for them. They came from the Galapagos and we picked them up in Peru. They were some special breed of penguin that was a warm weather type."

~~~

Before World War II, students were attracted to the school by a combination of necessity brought on by the Depression and a sense of romance of the sea which they got from the writings of Howard Pease and Guy Gilpatric. During the war years, the students' draft status entered the equation. Now, we find some of them simply wanting to get away from home or looking primarily at a Navy career.

Phil Laudenschlager: "I was interested in going in the Navy. Mainly I just wanted to get away from the family or out of the house and I wanted to go in the Navy or the Naval Reserve, but I wanted to go in as an officer, not an enlisted man. And I wanted to get into the submarine corps, which is where I spent my Reserve time. So I happened to see an advertisement in the paper for the Maritime Academy and it offered Naval Reserve commissions if you went. I guess it was fairly common because a lot of my classmates wanted to go on in the Navy."

John Mena: "I was sort of a family boy. I had never left home, under the thumb of my folks all the time. It was my first time away from home. I was awed. It was sort of regimented and everybody was trying to sell you paraphernalia to sew canvas. The upper classmen, everybody, pounced on the first year guys selling them everything, telling them they would need it."

Rod Marshall: "My interest in going to sea came mostly from talking to CMA upper classmen when I was in high school. I was working in a produce store in Vallejo, and we'd hear about the ship. Also, there was a family tradition. My father and his father and his father were in Navy and merchant marine. I talked to upper classmen, found out how to get in. I took the entrance exam and passed and went in."

Phil Laudenschlager: "I went in right out of high school in '48. It was a new adventure into the world. I was happy because I could live there and I didn't have to depend on going home and all that kind of stuff.

"I was excited to get busy, going on to school and get educated. I didn't know a lot about the reputation of the school except the catalog."

But others still came to be merchant mariners. Don Lipman: "I was a young boy of sixteen. In 1945, '46, I got interested in going into the merchant marine. I got in touch with the maritime service and went into a training program and went into Sheepshead Bay, New York. They placed me with Army Transport Service where I sailed for a year-and-a-half. I decided if I was going to be sailing I should go as an officer. So I applied to CMA and was accepted."

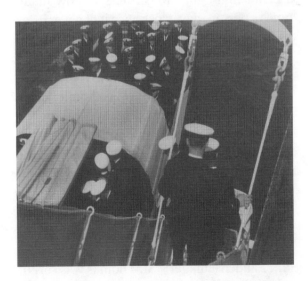

When at anchor in port the liberty launch was the only way ashore and back. Here, midshipmen board for a day ashore. Courtesy California Maritime Academy.

The training cruise of 1950 went to: Long Beach; Balboa and Cristobal, Canal Zone; Houston, New Orleans; St. Thomas, Virgin Islands; Curaçao, Dutch West Indies; Cristobal, Canal Zone; Balboa, Canal Zone; Acapulco, Mexico; San Diego, Long Beach, Santa Barbara, San Francisco and Vallejo.

Once again, young midshipmen from the farms and towns of California were seeing tropical beaches and foreign cultures for the first time and they eagerly welcomed the opportunity. They enjoyed the food, culture and, of course, meeting the girls in the many ports they visited.

The cruises have always been the highlight of the CMA education. In 120 years, that has not changed.

The Panama Canal transit was always a major highlight. Regardless of how many times a person may experience it, it never loses its fascination – the massive locks, the rapid raising and lowering of large, ocean-going ships, the electric mules, the lush tropical vegetation and the fact that it was all built before 1920 and still functions perfectly.

Rod Marshall: "The cruise through the Panama Canal into Houston and New Orleans and to Curaçao was the most interesting. It was so different going through the Canal. We had time to stop in the cities and do our shopping in a trade-free or tax-free zone."

There were some disappointments. Phil Laudenschlager: "St. Thomas was sort of a dud. It was when St. Thomas was beginning to become a tourist attraction. They were just building the first hotel. Now it's quite a major vacation spot. But we went up to the Bluebeard Castle and, of course, the bay in there is beautiful, just as clear as it can be.

"That was one place where there was a Russian fishing trawler in for repairs. One of my classmates spoke Russian, so we went over and talked to them a little bit. When we left, his comment was, 'They're more than just fishermen.' They were too intelligent to be just fishermen."

Meanwhile, the campus at Morrow Cove continued developing. Some of the temporary buildings were replaced with permanent ones: a new mess deck (cafeteria), indoor swimming pool in Mayo Hall, a classroom building, a student library, a residence building and a main gate.

But the cruises have always been the highlight of the CMA education. In 120 years, that has not changed. Although most of the school year was spent on the land campus — attending classes, holding formations, studies, hazing, "bull-sessions," hi-jinks, school and extra-curricular activities — the ship has always been the focus of the education and the cruise the highlight, the foundation of the CMA experience. It is the ship, and the annual cruise, that changes boys from the cities, farms and suburbs of California into seasoned mariners.

Chester Ferguson: "The cruises were some of the happiest times of my life. We were a jolly bunch."

John Mena: "The cruises were as much for letting the students know that the instructors were human as anything else. Several of them championed our cause, several were really well-liked. We had a group of instructors everyone was really stuck on. Noel Martin was very popular. The navigators were Fred Neid and Roger Swain. They were very well-liked. We had a great bosun by the name of J. Renick. He was a sort of father confessor to those who got into trouble. Our seamanship

The California Maritime Academy campus, probably sometime in the 1950s. Golden Bear I is at the pier, lower right. Off its port quarter is the campus, relatively devoid of buildings (see page 159 for comparison to 1993), barracks partway up the hill and, above them, the houses of senior administration. The highway leads from the Carquinez Bridge, off camera, right, through Vallejo, upper background. Courtesy California Maritime Academy.

instructor was Don Pederson, he was a great guy. These same guys that you learned to appreciate at sea were the ones that went with us to the foreign gatherings and taught us how to act. That helped us get along better in later years with our instructors."

Larry Teague: "One of the highlights, as far as our instructors, was Bill Aguilar, I think you could say that the midshipmen really loved him. He was the navigation instructor. Everybody thought the world of him. He was kind of like Mr. Roberts, just the good guy that everybody loved, you know. And I think he was one of the first graduates ['34]. Everyone called him 'Ags.'"

The fifth cruise of the *Golden Bear* (1951): Portland, Seattle; Vancouver, Canada; Honolulu, Territory of Hawaii; Hilo, T.H.; Acapulco, Mexico; San Diego, Long Beach, Santa Barbara, San Francisco and Vallejo.

Phil Laudenschlager: "We went to Vancouver and Hawaii and to Acapulco and up the coast. We were short on fuel, didn't have that much money for it. And that was part of what made it not as good as the prior cruise, we spent a lot of time at sea and dilly-dallied to use up the time. We were in Hilo, Hawaii. I always liked Hilo better than Oahu. We went down and saw the black sands beach."

John Mena: "There were several of the cadets that knew how to cut hair. Not too good. Myself and two classmates needed haircuts, and the barbershops were not open. We decided to cut each other's hair. After the first one was done, it looked horrible. We had to go ahead, but we weren't any better off than the first guy. We had a horrible time passing inspection to go ashore.

"While in Honolulu I had dinner with a family and they had a mango tree in the back yard. They said go ahead and pick some. I went up this tree and picked mangoes. Three or four days later I broke out with blisters. I went to the infirmary and the doctor put a salve on me that just spread it. The electrician was an old timer and he recognized it. He said, 'You got Mango Rot, try calamine lotion.'

"After a week of calamine lotion I got better."

The adventures were not confined to foreign ports. Later in the year the ship went to Todd Shipyards in Alameda for routine repairs. John Mena: "While in the shipyard we'd stay ashore in a personnel barge. Those were hard-working days. It was the first time I ever went AWOL. An upper classman talked me into going to a strip joint and we only had a small amount of money between us and I fell in love with a stripper. Later I found out she was a female impersonator."

~~~

The quality of the food on board apparently improved. At least, no longer was there mention of the infamous "Below Standard" sticker. Chester Ferguson: "The food varied. Sometimes it was pretty rough, although it probably was healthy. They didn't really care how it looked but it wasn't all that bad. We survived on it."

Don Lipman: "It was good, for institutional-style food. We ate Navy-style off of steel trays. It was pretty good. I gained weight, I think everyone else did too."

Larry Teague: "The food wasn't good, but I don't remember it as being terribly bad. The thing that most of us looked forward to was the night lunch. They had a night cook and baker and he would make hot sandwiches. We looked forward to that. Sometimes we'd get up, even if we weren't on watch, just to get the night lunch. Of course, we had to work it so they didn't catch on. Too many people eating the night lunch and he'd realize there weren't that many midshipmen on watch. It sure seemed good at the time.

"The rest of the meals were mediocre, the breakfasts with the artificial scrambled eggs and so on. If it was the same food we got the rest of the year at the school [mess deck], then it was prepared better because <u>that</u> was terrible."

John Mena: "I think whether you liked the food or not was a result of how hardy or how particular you were. And whether or not you were really tired or had worked up an appetite. We had SOS [creamed chipped beef on toast] a lot. We had greasy eggs. Everything was greasy. But I thought it was good.

"There was sometimes a lot of bitching about the food. The steward was named Morgan. Everybody called him 'Mother' Morgan. They wanted to get rid of him."

Phil Laudenschlager: "I thought the food was good. A lot of the other guys complained at the time. I thought they never had it so good. 'Mother' Morgan tried to put out good food, but he couldn't satisfy them all."

But there were other compensations. John Mena: "Phil Laudenschlager ran the ship's store. Every night after dinner he would open up and make root beer floats. We'd go down and get these root beer floats and sit on deck and watch the lights go by. He never cheated on them and they were always full."

Phil Laudenschlager: "The ship's store was run by a second classman and I would sort of help him out now and then. On the cruise we had the soda fountain just forward of the galley in the mess hall on the *Golden Bear*. So we'd open up for a couple of hours after dinner. We were just inside the hatch where they loaded the stores. Mostly it was ice cream cones, a few milk shakes. We'd do it in the evening just before the movie.

"The engineers would get all the movies going. They ran all the projectors and they put on the movies about twice a week. And

Part of the daily routine at anchor was colors on the fantail. Courtesy California Maritime Academy.

even at that they had to run some of them twice."

Don Lipman remembers it differently: "We had movies every night either from the Navy or from a rental agency, films every day. That was a big event because it gave everyone a chance to let off steam and express their personality."

The shipboard routine was the same as in earlier years, except the reveille bugle of the *Golden State* was gone, replaced with a more prosaic public address system.

Larry Teague: "One of the most difficult things I remember was every morning at six: reveille. Someone on watch over the bridge would say 'reveille, reveille' over the PA system. Then we'd sweep down and swab the decks. The third classmen did the work and the second classmen were in charge of them."

John Mena: "We'd get up around six or earlier in the morning and as swabs we'd be delegated to polishing urinals and cleaning the captain's area. We'd work for about forty-five minutes then have breakfast, then classes."

Phil Laudenschlager: "Reveille at six, of course. If you had a watch you got to sleep in an extra hour. There were so many of us we didn't have watches every night. At six we did cleaning stations, hose and wash down the ship. Then go to breakfast."

Larry Teague: "Breakfast must have been at seven-fifteen or seven-thirty or something like that. Then you'd muster outside, wash, clean up and turn to at eight o'clock. Of course, as a third classman you were basically an ordinary seaman. As a second classman you were more like a bosun or an upper level AB. You'd have to do some work but some more supervision."

Phil Laudenschlager: "All the deck people had to do a morning sun line and a noon latitude."

Larry Teague: "Classes on the ship, as I recall, were in the afternoon. We always had general maintenance in the morning for the second or third class. Most of the first class were doing navigation or whatever and then in the afternoon we had classes, seamanship, knot-tying and that sort of thing.

"All three classes stood watch. On the deck side a first classman was always in charge of the watch. He was the officer of the watch and there would be two second classmen, who had mid-level duties and we had a third classman steering, and a couple of lookouts.

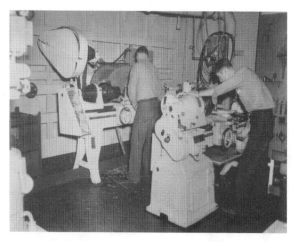

The daily routine for engine midshipmen included work in the ship's machine shop. Courtesy California Maritime Academy.

When entering and leaving port a second classman would become helmsman. It was a quasi-military group on the bridge as far as numbers go.

Pictured in engine room working uniform, midshipmen Todd Hale, left, and Rod Marshall each went on to become captains in the U.S. Navy. Courtesy Rod Marshall.

"On arrivals and departures we always had a fresh group, which was one of the more interesting things, otherwise watches at sea were boring. We didn't get enough watchstanding experience. On the other hand, that ship was great for engineers because they had two engine rooms for twice as much experience."

Rod Marshall: "Engine rooms were on the 'hot watch' all the time. They were never shut down when operating because of the short amount of time in port. We also had a steering engine room and many emergency fire pump rooms. Each fire pump was driven by a diesel engine. Part of the training was keeping those engines up and repaired. We also maintained the emergency generator and the boat motors

Lowering the lifeboats was not a job to be taken lightly. Courtesy California Maritime Academy.

in all the small craft the ship carried. Your practical instruction went from the smallest to the largest engine. It was a full-time job."

Larry Teague: "As we got into our first class year we did some shiphandling. They'd throw drums overboard and we'd come alongside, do a Williamson turn, and so on, with a first classman in charge. It gave us a feel of how difficult it would be to maneuver.

"Once, during the lifeboat drill we put the lifeboats out and we were going to lower them. Everybody had a job. One of the guys was in charge of the Fleming gear and he gave the order to release it, and someone misunderstood and released the releasing gear. The boat just fell to the water. Man, it hit and the bottom just caved in and there were midshipmen sprawled all over the place. It impressed me with how hard it hit and the fact that it happened so fast. There was no, oops, or rethinking it. It made an impression on me how dangerous it could be."

Don Lipman: "We also had cruise books to prepare and all that type of thing. Any time anyone had any extra time they'd fall down in a hunk and try to get some sleep. Sleeping was a high priority."

Phil Laudenschlager: "Actually, the work schedule was much lighter at sea than at the academy. Chipping out the fan rooms was the worst we did. During the second year Rustoleum came on the market and that was a big improvement. Just scrape it clean and spread that over it and it soaked up the rust. Just paint with this clear Rustoleum.

"At school [on campus] we had classes in the morning and worked on the ship from one to four-thirty. Worked more then than at sea."

John Mena: "Then noon lunch, then form up and march to the ship for the afternoon and exercises. We did lots of small boat exercise. We used to get in a lot of ship work as well as practical seamanship, rowing and boat races."

Rod Marshall: "The emphasis was on practical training. We were called the 'school ship sailors.' That meant what it said."

Hazing was far less physical than in the early years. Larry Teague: "Being a third classman you had to answer to everybody. If they called your name you had to answer their questions. The Selby refinery across the Straits from the school had a tall brick smokestack. [See the photo on page 121] and you had to know how many bricks were in it. Well, I'm sure someone came up with a number and that was passed down from one class to another.

"Of course, on the cruise the hazing eased up, but it went on a lot and you always had to be aware of an upperclassman calling your name and having to respond. The system was to find out how to not fight it and get by. From my point of view it never seemed brutal or bitter, but it went on a lot. And, of course, the uniform bit, the shined belt buckle and shined shoes."

Phil Laudenschlager: "When we were swabs we got a good dose of what the school was all about during that first year. I didn't have any particular problem, I don't know if there was any real hazing. Some of the freshmen were a little older and had been through boot camp and all that and didn't want to go through it. I didn't really recognize any of it as hazing. Oh, we had to get the haircuts and had the encroachment on our rights and privileges and so on . . ."

Don Lipman: "That was an interesting point, when I came there as a third classman, the State of California had banned hazing as illegal. They couldn't do anything physical but they could do mental stuff. Well, they'd try to torture you mentally, threaten you with working in the bilges for the rest of your life. That technically wasn't hazing, but if you had to face it every day it might seem like it. The upperclassmen were pretty clever at that. But they stopped all physical hazing."

But some of the old traditions went on. Larry Teague: "At every meal you'd go to when you were at the Academy, you'd go through the line at the mess deck and you had to report to a second classman at a table and ask permission to eat. They'd ask you a question and if you didn't know the answer you'd have to eat a square meal. Eating a square meal was not only a difficult thing to do but sometimes you didn't eat what you wanted to eat. You might have a piece of meat with a lot of fat on it or something like that.

"On board ship, we were segregated, I think second and third classmen ate in the same area but we had separate tables. As a third classman you were always under the view of a second classman. First classmen always had their privacy."

Don Lipman: "When I came back as an instructor, I noticed the attitudes were cycling. Sometimes they were fighting the system and sometimes they went along with it. And it seemed to rise and fall about every three years.

"I was an instructor in 1955. I spent seven years all together as an instructor. Some of the things that happened to me as a midshipman I came to understand as an instructor. One good example was working on the ship you didn't have any time to yourself at all. What do you do with 250 guys that are over average intelligence locked up on a ship for weeks at a time? You don't want them to have time to themselves, they just get into trouble."

The sixth training cruise (1952) included the following ports: Manzanillo, Mexico; Callao, Peru; San José, Guatemala; Acapulco, Mexico; San Diego, Long Beach, Santa Barbara, Oakland and Vallejo.[4]

Don Lipman: "We went to South America. That was a highlight because we went to places I hadn't been before. I'd already been out to the Far East before I went into the academy."

Of course, the South American Cruise included crossing the equator which meant a visit by King Neptune and a renewal of the ceremonies for another generation of pollywogs. From the deck log: "On 2/13/52 "Held Neptune party on deck. Crossed at 88-00.0 W."

Chester Ferguson: "Our Shellback ceremony was the roughest ever. It started with a gauntlet, you're on your hands and knees and they'd wash you down with fire hoses, forcing

---

[4] The training ship cruises generally follow set patterns. There is a West Coast of South America Cruise, a Caribbean Cruise, a South Pacific Cruise, an Australian Cruise and a Far East Cruise. So as not to be repetitive the remainder of the cruises are listed in Appendix B. Otherwise, only ports in which unusual incidents occurred will be mentioned.

or Navy time. People that were on watch when the ceremony was scheduled thought they would be excused, but the royal court had them relieved so they participated anyway."

Larry Teague: "We had quite an extensive equator crossing. They hadn't done it for two or three years so there were a few first classmen that had crossed but most of the school had not. It was a large ceremony. It was sort of typical. A large wooden pool erected on the foredeck in number one hatch with wooden seats built up by it for the royal

Above, King Neptune and the Royal Court in their finery. Courtesy California Maritime Academy. Right, foreground, a lowly pollywog awaits sentencing while in the background punishment is meted out. Photo by Phil Laudenschlager.

Below, a pollywog receives the business end of a fire hose in the process of becoming a shellback. Photo by Rod Marshall.

you back to where you had to start over. Then we visited the royal physician, he had you hold a foxtail wired to a magneto. They put throw-up medicine in dough and made you eat it. Before the ceremony we were standing in garbage cans of salt water keeping watch with coke bottles.

"There were signs all over the place, 'Them's that dies is the lucky ones.'"

Don Lipman: "The Neptune ceremony was pretty nervous. I can still remember getting that paddle on my butt. And the meggar hooked up to the foxtail. Later on I participated in it as an instructor. As a viewer."

Rod Marshall: "We had the equator experience on our first cruise to South America. In the third class we had several shellbacks, people who had merchant marine

court. We had to kiss their bellies, kiss their toes, ask their forgiveness for being pollywogs, then wade through a pool of garbage that had been accumulating for several days. Those that talked back had their mouths washed out with soap. Each one of us had a specific charge, when we went up to the royal court we had a charge against us thought up by the upper classmen.

"There were no hard feelings whatsoever. It was kind of rough but it was all in so much fun and the weather was so good, there were no hard feelings at all."

John Mena: "Crossing the line, I remember I was a pollywog. I took my share of nasty-tasting drinks and some of the first classmen hadn't been across, but some of the second class had been in the Navy and they got even for demerits."

Phil Laudenschlager: "We went across the equator and that was a big anticipation because no one knew who had been across. No one would tell anybody, so we didn't know who to trust. It was a lot of fun. You had to crawl through the tunnel and get swatted on the behind. They were all growing beards at the time and we had a big beard growing contest. Then after we got toward Callao everybody had to shave."

Acapulco was a favorite port with its warm ocean waters, tropical beaches, lovely señoritas and inexpensive and tasty food and drinks. Ralph Swany: "Acapulco was usually a good spot, but then in Acapulco, though, I had to pay the pilot. I always did the work. I'd bring her in and take her right up in the little basin right there off the city dock right in the center. They could have only a little short haul ashore. But the pilot, Mexican pilot, when they were doing it, they'd always anchor way out farther. I didn't like that."

Chester Ferguson: "On my first class year one guy that didn't make it was Marvin Dewey Burroughs. He was a real handsome guy, red-haired, six foot tall. There was a rule nobody was allowed aboard after six p.m. So, Elizabeth Taylor and Nicky Hilton [her first husband] and their entourage came alongside in a boat, wanted to come aboard. Marvin

chased them away. When we found out we beat him to the deck with our hats."

If the cadets didn't paint the ship in Acapulco, there would be a layover on the coast of Baja. Capt. Swany fondly recalled: "We used to go into Magdalena Bay with the training ship. That's above Acapulco. Go in there and paint the ship for the cruise, and come back into San Diego, everything all bright and clean. And when we were painting the ship, you'd get the PA system going with music. Slow music going like that and the damn paint brushes, they'd go like that, too. Take and speed up the music, take and speed up the painting, save a half a day."

Phil Laudenschlager: "We painted the ship at Magdalena Bay. Even that was kind of nice. It was all ship work, but there were fishing parties. It was a beautiful place."

As with military schools everywhere, attrition was high at the California Maritime Academy. The discipline, hours, swab work, hazing and, sometimes, the academic requirements, served to winnow the entering classes. Chester Ferguson: "There were fourteen or fifteen people in our deck class and twice as many engineers. By graduation there were nine of us. Only three followed the maritime. Most guys in the barracks wanted to go in the Navy. The Union hall in San Francisco had two thousand mates registered in the MM & P."

John Mena: "We started with eighty and before the first year was up we were down to thirty. Thirty of us graduated, ten deck, twenty engine. Guys just didn't like the regimentation."

The cruise of 1954 was down the West Coast of South America. Capt. Swany recalled: "We'd been in Valparaiso and getting ready to sail and the agent came up and told

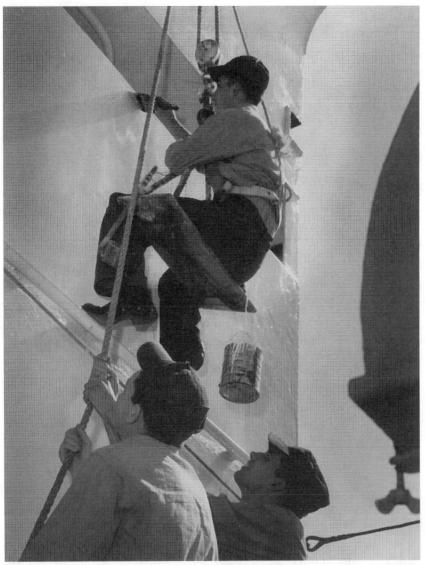

Painting any ship before her return home is a maritime tradition. Acapulco and Magdalena Bay were the favored paint stops before the first California port. Courtesy California Maritime Academy.

God damn Chileños, when I was down there this time they took and nailed me.'

"He says, 'I'll get'em.' So, when they came up the next time he took and socked them for all San Francisco port fees."

~~~

In 1958 Capt. J. Anderson relieved Capt. Swany as master of the ship. He was relieved the following year by Capt. E. Turpin who, in turn was relieved by Capt. C.G. Bowman in 1961.

Larry Teague '63: "Captain Bowman had been a Coast Guard guy and I believe he had commanded the [Coast Guard] sailing ship *Eagle*. This was a retirement job for him."

~~~

me they want port dues, dockage. I said, 'They've never done it before.'

"He said, 'I know, they want it.'

"So I says, 'OK.' So the two of us went to the safe and got some money out. We went ashore, we went up to the black market and exchanged it to the currency of Chile, went up to the custom house, paid off the bill and they sent us out.

"So, when I got back up to San Francisco and I checked in with the custom house there, I told the Deputy Collector, I says 'Hey,

By the 1960s and 1970s another change was coming about. Once again, as in earlier years, the cadets were entering the school for the traditional reason of wanting a career in the merchant marine.

John Keever '70: "What first got me interested in the sea was a geometry instructor in the eighth grade who was a retired naval officer, Naval Academy type. That matriculated into getting interested in big ships and then finding out I had a next door neighbor who was a merchant ship captain. I saw his ship one day, a States Lines ship, and asked him how he got to do that and he said you go to the Maritime Academy. I had no idea what it was. In fact, I really didn't have an idea what the merchant marine was. I kind of had the Navy and merchant marine lumped into one category. Lo and behold, I ended up at California Maritime Academy a few months later instead of becoming an electrical engineer at UC Santa Barbara, which is what I intended to do before that."

Larry Teague: "I was born in Oakland and raised in Sunnyvale. I was a typical senior in high school with no direction. My mother grew up in Vallejo and was familiar with the Academy. Mother saw an ad in the paper about the entrance exams and suggested I take the test. I didn't know the difference between deck and engine, but I thought engine had to do with engineering and that would be harder."

The wartime practice of having cadets choose their field at once continued.

John Mena: "You had to decide immediately whether you wanted to be deck or engine. Since I didn't like heat I stayed away from engineering. Of course, once you got out there were more jobs for engineers . . ."

Larry Teague: "You declared what you wanted right away, deck or engine. You could change after a semester or so but you actually did start out as deck or engine.

"My first impression of the ship, I was sort of in awe. I had never been on a ship before and within my first few days I found myself on a bosun's chair hanging over the bow working on an anchor. It put me in a world I wasn't familiar with at all or aware of.

"It had cargo gear which was just great. I think we all got a lot of good exposure to cargo gear. This was another mysterious thing, how did all these booms and all this gear work. Having this cargo gear on the ship was really beneficial to us all."

Rod Marshall: "It was a ship that was probably in service at the Maritime Academy a couple of years when I first saw it. From the point of view of a novice, which I was at the time, it was in excellent shape. The turboelectric power plant was probably the state of the art at that time, in the late '40s and early '50s.

"There were several holds forward and two holds aft all fitted with conventional cargo rigging and winches which required a lot of repair and maintenance."

The cruise of 1961 included calls at Papeete, Tahiti and Honolulu, Hawaii. For some it would be a lifelong remembrance. Larry Teague: "Tahiti. That was my first foreign port. I was seventeen years old and I said, 'This is it. I have found heaven.'

"We were scheduled to stay there, I think, two days and later the trip was altered so we were there four or five

Tahiti, a favorite stop for the Golden Bear, *was considered "heaven on earth" by many. Courtesy Ralph Swany.*

days. This was before they had an international airport, so things were still primitive. Everyone rented scooters. There were Vespas all over the place. We hit the main two bars, Quinn's and Lafayette, every night.

"One of the things I had never seen or been close to before, Quinn's had a coed head or bathroom. That was an eye-opener at that age and at that time.

"While we were there the sailing ship *Bounty* with her crew was there. They were in the midst of filming the movie, 'Mutiny on the *Bounty* [starring Marlon Brando].' One of our guys, Rick McCloud, got to know the crew. Later, he was offered a job so he took a year's leave of absence, worked on the *Bounty* and came back to school a year later."

Larry Teague: "Honolulu was a big highlight because when we arrived they had the girls on the dock in grass skirts and leis doing the hula."

In 1962 the *Golden Bear* made its first trip to the Galapagos Islands.

Larry Teague: "One port I remember more than any was going to the Galapagos Islands. We spent several days there, anchored. We went ashore, saw iguanas and turtles and all kinds of sea birds. Looking back, that has grown in my memory as a major highlight."

On February 22, 1962 CMA cadets escaped disaster when eighty-six midshipmen were aboard a train to Cali, Colombia which was wrecked. Larry Teague: "We went to Buenaventura and it was arranged for us to go to Cali. I went the first day and had a wonderful time and came back. The next day, the second group went and that was when the train wreck occurred. That was just a major event, luckily no one was killed, the one hurt the worst was riding the engine. The people that got hurt were the natives. They were in the less well-constructed cars in the center and the steel cars accordioned on through. Of course, the first

word we got down at Buenaventura was that everybody was killed. But as time went on we got better information filtering through."

Steaming homeward, there was the usual stop in Acapulco to paint the ship.

Larry Teague: "We came back up the coast and I remember we did stop in Acapulco on our way homeward bound, and painted the ship. Anybody who had any demerits was held aboard to paint."

John Mena: "You could get demerits for unmade bunks, dirty uniform, etc. Demerits had to be worked off."

The cruise of 1963 included transiting the Panama Canal and sailing down the East Coast of South America.

Larry Teague: "One of the highlights was going through the Panama Canal and on into the Caribbean. I remember being so excited in seeing the ship going up and down [in the locks]. It was inspiring to see that amount of water moving. Also, I was impressed with how busy it was. We were just one ship in line with other ships. There was a long line of ships in our direction and a line coming from the other direction.

"The thing I remember at Rio was guys trying to get ashore, and at night sneaking out the portholes and going down the mooring lines. I don't recall just how they did it but they did and they came back the same way."

One of the many items that must be attended to in preparing the *Golden Bear* for its training cruise is getting permission from the countries and ports on the ship's planned itinerary for the ship to enter those ports. The process for the 1964 cruise began on October 8, 1963 with a letter from J.T. Everett, Supervisor for State Maritime Academies (of the Maritime Administration) to the Chief of Protocol for the Department of State.

It is requested that arrangements be made for clearance of the training ship, GOLDEN BEAR, to visit the foreign ports listed in Captain Richter's letter of September 18, 1963 (copy enclosed) and the courtesies of the ports listed be extended to the training ship, GOLDEN BEAR.

The 1964 cruise had a unique mission. The California Maritime Academy was called upon to transport sixty-seven scientists and their equipment to the Galapagos Islands. The

---

Midshipmen were required to keep a daily cruise journal. The following pages contain extracts from John Athanson's ('63) journal which give a representative sampling of the cruise of 1962:

18 January 1962

LOCATION: Port Costa, Calif. to Galapagos Islands, Ecuador.
WEATHER: Moderately cool due to cold winds.
BAROMETER READING (NOON): 30.19
STEAMING TIME: 24 hours.
VISIBILITY: Restricted due to low haze on the horizon.

I was roused for my 0400-0800 Q.M. watch on the bridge, at 0325. I reported ten minutes before the hour and instructed the third class on their job responsibilities. Since this was to be my first watch this cruise, I soon found that I had quite a lot to learn. Among the new responsibilities I was to receive were such items as getting the sea water temperature, taffrail log reading, seas and swells, compass corrections, and R.P.M.'s. At first I was a little confused as to what was expected of me, but soon I felt that I was learning my job. We sighted nothing new during our watch, which I suppose could be classified as normal and routine. I was relieved at 0750, but did not leave the bridge until 0815 since M/S Young, the OOD, wanted me to help him fill out the log.

I spent the rest of the morning cleaning the berth deck and at 1053, I took my morning sun sight. We held a Quarters Formation and inspection in the early afternoon. At 1320 the chemical alarm bell rang signifying a man over-board drill. I reported to life boat #5 and proceeded to take the cover and strong back off. Boat #4 was instructed to lower away at 1330. Within a matter of minutes the boat had picked up the "dummy" and lay off waiting for the T.S. Golden Bear to make its turn and come alongside. As the ship bore down on the lifeboat, the wind forced the ship onto the boat forcing the crew to pull away and make another attempt at landing the small craft. At 1355 the boat was raised and preparations were made to secure. The ship was back on its course and underway at 1410. I noted the time of detention to be approximately 50 minutes; using this for navigational purposes. I went topside for another sun line. After getting my navigation notebooks and materials out to make my noon fix, I was surprised to hear the chemical alarm go off again. This time the lee side of the ship was to be stbd. meaning that our boat #5 would be launched into the seaway to make the rescue. All procedures went normal until the after falls had become fouled. We had to bring them on deck and try to unfoul them so that we could raise the boat when it came along side. However, when we dropped the falls over the rail, she became entangled again. On the second try we managed to get the falls straight enough to raise the boat. Once secured, the falls were led out on deck again and re-run through the block. We secured at 1554, just in time for cleaning stations. Since I was the acting MA [master-at-arms] today, I handed out the cleaning assignments. I secured the crew at 1645 and lay below to work on my neglected navigation. After dinner I finally plotted a satisfactory noon fix and decided to work on my cruise note book and journal. Retired at 2100.

LESSON FOR THE DAY: A "water-light" is a metal canister, usually secured by one end to a life ring, used because of its chemical reaction with sea water to give off a smoke signal.

29 January 1962

LOCATION: Port Costa, Calif. to Bahia Wreck, Galapagos Islands, Ecuador.
WEATHER: Very humid, with early and late afternoon rain. Calm sea.
BAROMETER READING (NOON):
SAILING TIME: 24 hours. (Noon, 28 Jan. to Noon, 29 Jan.)
VISIBILITY: Good in morning; poor in afternoon.

Reveille. At 0545, brought us all out of our racks. A good look at the first islands belonging to the Galapagos. I have never seen such barren, god-forsaken land in all my life! As we passed these islands during our morning run, I could only make out sparse patches of greenery and plant life. We saw plenty of "rocks" jutting out of the water which contributed to the mysterious and desolate appearance of the Galapagos.

I spent the morning taking land bearings and plotting them in the second class study room. At 1300 we approached Bahia Wreck. Rain slowly closed in and visibility was limited to a few hundred yards. As a result, our first landing proved to be too far from the actual bay itself, so we had to back off and try again. We finally succeeded in landing, and by 1300 we had dropped our "hook". At this time it was still raining, so Division One turned-to, cleaning our area. At 1600 I was secured from work. At this time liberty was granted, but I had some letters to catch up on so I decided not to take advantage of the two and one half hours of liberty given us.

We had put the Captain's gig and liberty launch over to use while we spent our short stay here. We also rigged an accommodation boat boom to service these boats.

LESSON FOR THE DAY: The boat boom is rigged to accommodate small craft while a ship is at anchor. The boom serves as a "mooring post" for such boats and is usually not used for loading purposes. The boom itself is attached to the side of the ship by the use of a goose neck. Stays lead fore and aft and there is also a topping stay. A handrail rope follows the boom out and a small light is situated at the very end to give indication of the boom's presence. A jacob's ladder is located about three-fourths of the way out on the boom. Lines, attached to the boom, trail in the water so they may be easily picked up by boats wishing to tie along side. At night, this boom may be seen servicing numerous crafts, ready to be put under way in the morning at a moment's notice.

scientists were taking part in the Darwinian Galapagos International Scientific Project. The ship left Vallejo on January 10 and arrived a few weeks later at Academy Bay, Santa Cruz, in the Galapagos Archipelago. The midshipmen unloaded the scientists' cargo and two days later the Darwin Research Station was completed by the scientists and dedicated. The next day the ship, *sans* scientists, left for Callao, Peru and later for Papeete, Tahiti. They returned for the scientists on February 27.

David Perlman, Science Correspondent for the *San Francisco Chronicle* and part of a team of scientists, made the following observations regarding their "cruise ship" and the sea-borne curriculum and activities of young officers-in-training:

The passenger quarters and the dining room are like no cruise that ever was: four tiers of canvas bunks with sleeping bags; a clattering mess hall where everyone lines up for chow served on GI steel trays.

Food ranges far: breakfast, for example, may include anything from the time-honored and ill-reputed GI creamed chipped beef on toast to a wildly improbable, but expertly prepared, eggs benedict, served in individual casseroles.

23 February 1962

LOCATION: Buenaventura, Colombia to Acapulco, Mexico.
WEATHER: Rain and overcast.
STEAMING TIME: None (1200 22 Feb., to 1200 23 Feb.)
VISIBILITY: Fair.

This morning everyone has seemed to calm down from the Colombian train wreck of yesterday and things returned to the normal Friday "in-port" routine. Word was passed that we would cast off for Acapulco as soon as the Captain and remaining M/s returned from Cali. There was no liberty for the corps today. At 0800, we had a turn-to formation on the fwd. weather dock. I spent the morning cleaning the bulkheads on the superstructure deck and secured at 1150.

After lunch, we were told that we would have a quick cleaning of our Division area and at 1400 we would have a meeting in the rec. room with the American consul and Colombian representatives wishing to thank us for our aid during the wreck. However, the meeting never came about, so we were secured until 1600. At this time we were told to remove the rat guards and gear from the lines and get ready for sailing. It was not until after dinner that we actually pulled away from the pier. Captain Bowman was still not on board so we were going to pull out into the stream and anchor until his return. Division One took its line handling station aft and had little trouble bringing in the lines. By 2000 we were secured from station, and I laid below to get some sleep. Soon, however, the captain arrived and the anchor was brought up. As we headed out of the harbor, another ship was coming in. Since we were on a collision course, the pilot ordered hard right rudder, and then to meet her after we had started to swing. The helmsman was unable to meet her in time and we ran over a lighted buoy. The buoy scraped along our stbd. hull and took a few trips around our stbd. screw. We were afraid that we had entangled the buoy's anchor chain in our screw and the order was given immediately to stop both engines. After a careful examination in the engine room, we started out of the harbor again, hoping that no damage was done to our ship. Unfortunately, the buoy was wiped out. After seeing what all of the action on deck was about, I retired at 2300.

LESSON FOR THE DAY: In leaving the wharf this evening, it was noted that the tide was slowly coming in. Our stern faced the on-coming tide. Therefore, the stern lines were all brought in, as well as our spring lines, and we swung around easily on our fwd. head lines. As we were perpendicular with the wharf, the lines fwd were let go and with the aid of a harbor tug pushing out our stern, we were able to make a complete 180° turn, facing out of the harbor.

...how incredibly well trained these young men will be when they graduate and start serving aboard America's fleet of freighters and passenger vessels.

On the Golden Bear, for example, fire and boat drills are earnest, full-scale affairs. Everyone stands muster, midshipmen go through their assigned duties under the watchful eyes of the ship's 24 officers, all of whom are veterans of sea duty in the Navy, the Coast Guard or the merchant marine.

A man overboard drill was as near to the real thing as possible. "Oscar," a battered, stuffed dummy with a woebegone face, was tossed from the stern. Someone shouted an alarm.

Instantly one group of midshipmen raced to the fantail while an emergency life raft, packed into a white, sealed canister, was shot automatically over the stern rail. In the water it popped open, revealing a roomy, canopied home for "Oscar."

Other midshipmen scrambled into small life boats to port and starboard. The half dozen who manned the port boat were lowered to the water. The boat was released and the midshipmen hauled at the oars, heading for the raft.

The Golden Bear, meanwhile, cut her speed and circled through the long tropical Pacific swells. Eventually, the lifeboat returned, after a sweaty row of a couple of miles, with the raft and "Oscar" in tow.

When they're not on watch, life for the midshipmen and their occasional fellow voyagers is easygoing; it smacks a little of the old days.

Out on the foredeck, with shirts off, all hands may gather around a couple of guitars harmonizing; harmonicas play. Scientists birdwatching, and midshipmen girl-watching via tattered magazines look over each other's shoulders, exploring mutually alien worlds.

At night the ship's ham radio operators gather in the radio shack forward, chattering over their station WB6IWB through the vast skies with friends in Antarctica, across America, and out over the Pacific from Tahiti to Australia. Other midshipmen watch ancient movies in her recreation lounge.

At meal times the lowly third classmen are subject to indignities in traditional form. Each must present his tray in front of an upperclassman before sitting down. The tray must be held at eye height, smartly at attention. Then a ritual is intoned

"Sir, prim and prissy polliwog XXX, who is lower than whale's feces, which is the lowest thing in the briny deep, dutifully requests permission to sit and eat at the royal table."

Crossing the equator, near the end of the voyage to the Galapagos, was a truly ancient mariner affair. Midshipmen horseplayed the roles of King Neptune, his Queen, and Davy Jones. Lowly polliwogs were hosed, force-fed revolting concoctions of dough and pepper, smacked on their backsides with lustily applied straps and paddles,

A [THIRD CLASS] SAILOR'S PRAYER

Now I lay me down to sleep
 I pray the Lord my soul to keep
Grant no other sailor take
 My shoes and socks before I wake
Lord, guard me in my slumber
 And keep my hammock on its number
May no clews nor lashings break
 And let me down before I wake
Keep me safely in thy sight
 And grant no fire drills to-nite
And in the morn let me awake
 Breathing scents of sirloin steak
God protect me in my dreams
 And make this better than it seems
Grant the time will swiftly fly
 When myself shall rest on high
In a snowy feather bed
 Where I long to rest my head
Far away from all these scenes
 From the smell of half-baked beans
Take me back into the land
 Where they don't scrub down with sand
Where no demon typhoon blows
 Where the women wash the clothes
God, thou knowest all my woes
 Feed me in my dying throes
Take me back, I'll promise then
 NEVER TO LEAVE HOME AGAIN!

But, three years later —

Our Father who art in Washington
 Please, dear Father, let me stay
Do not drive me now away
 Wipe away my scalding tears
And let me stay my thirty years
 Please forgive me all my past
And things that happened at the Mast
 Do not my request refuse
Let me stay ANOTHER CRUISE.

Courtesy John Athanson '62.

and confined to foredeck watches standing in water-filled garbage cans.

The scientists, too, were initiated — without bruises, but without much dignity either.

Capt. Bowman reported it this way: "Neptune in all his glory, including a sea-green Davy Jones, came aboard as we crossed the line and properly initiated the pollywogs (including, by request, most of the scientific party). The color film should be marvelous."

David Perlman continues:

But work is foremost aboard the Golden Bear, from reveille at 5:45 a.m. to taps at 10 p.m. Cargo handling, navigation, marlinspike seamanship, rules of the road, meteorology and emergency radio operation are only part of the curriculum for would-be deck officers. Aspiring engineers learn engine maintenance, electrical operations, pump handling, pipe fitting and lots more. Everyone stands watches — on the bridge or in the engine room.

The midshipmen will have learned a full measure of seamanship by then — and for the first classmen making their final cruise, the day when they go to sea as licensed, highly-trained ship's officers is not far off. They will have earned the job.

Midshipmen weren't the only ones required to keep cruise journals. The master's responsibilities extended to a detailed account of everything transpiring on the voyage to keep the administration fully apprised of every aspect. Unloading at the Galapagos caused some problems. From Capt. Bowman's letter to the Superintendent, Harry E. Richter.

The unloading, as we expected, was a real wingding but was finally accomplished with the loss of only one crate of mayonnaise. Everybody turned to muley-hauling the many tons of gear up the beach and stowing it in the station where it can be sorted. I doubt that half this amount of plain work has been

done by all the other PhDs in the world since the degree was invented.

The only fly in our friend's ointment was the presence of over a hundred distinguished persons who had been flown out to witness and participate in the grand opening and dedication of the Darwin Foundation's permanent station and laboratory. There were endless speeches, most in three languages, which became rather rough as the sun climbed higher. However, I improved the opportunity to become acquainted with our Ambassador to Ecuador, Consul-General at Guayaquil, and, most important, the Chief of Staff of the Ecuadorian Navy, so all the suffering may not have been in vain.

Some of the frustration in running the ship was expressed in another letter from Capt. Bowman to Superintendent Richter, dated 28, January, 1964.

It would probably be better if I could write this letter a couple days hence when I have had time to regain my perspective and perhaps my sense of humor. Right now I'm frustrated and mad.

In the first place, our communications completely broke down. Your letter never arrived and my radio [telegram] which I sent three days out, was never received by the Naval Attache. The radio was duly delivered to the ship yesterday in a sealed envelope. The only things which did arrive were a letter from the Vallejo Rotary Club saying that they were forwarding large amounts of clothing for distribution by the Lima Rotary Club to the poor and a press release from Washington with a picture of the ship (presumably the one you sent in haste). I had a nice visit with Ambassador Jones this morning who freely admitted that he had forgotten about our coming until he read about it the Sunday paper. Had the Naval Attache taken an earnest interest in our welfare, much could have been saved, but he didn't, at least not until this morning.

The real and most serious difficulty is getting fueled. We kept people aboard all day yesterday to handle fuel promised from hour to hour. It finally arrived at 0900 this morning, 2400 of 4000 Bbls we need. The barge has just finished and the skipper has told Otto, 'no mas until mañana.' There will be a slight interruption in this epistle while I salle' a la muelle [walk out to the pier] and have a few words with Mr. Esso — Another exercise in frustration. Señor Layseca has gone to Callao, presumably to come out to the ship and confirm the bad news, perhaps to change the barge skipper's mind. The time, and date, of our departure will tell you. The boat trip plus writing my woes seems to have me feeling better already.

The first of Otto's real troubles came today, we have ruptured two fuel lines while fuelling. Not from excessive pressure either since the fuel in them was being moved by gravity from the settlers to the tanks for fear of such trouble. Devcon (epoxy putty with iron filings in it) is a wonderful development of the plastic age and will probably suffice to make repairs that will bring us home but the outlook for the future is not good, there is no reason not to expect similar trouble in other lines since the proximate cause is plain old corrosion.

So long as our one available boat continues to run, being out at anchor has definite advantages. The crews get a lot of training, we have much better

control of the midshipmen with no possibility of jumping ship, and the climate is much better out here away from the fish docks and the fertilizer loading facilities.

On the return voyage to the Galapagos from Tahiti, Captain Bowman was feeling more cheerful:

The trip from Tahiti to Galapagos was uneventful, completely so. The ship's routine proceeded without interruption, ship's work and instruction went as per schedule. We averaged .739 barrels per mile vs. .823 on the way out for a mean of .781 on the trip which is a little better than we had anticipated and helps make up the deficit occasioned by the rise in price at Callao.

We arrived at Galapagos on schedule and embarked the remaining Scientific party including two Lady Scientists. I really had no choice in the matter. Nate Cohen assured me that they had chartered a boat to take them the eighty miles to the island where the airport is. They spent all day on this little fishboat only to find that the plane had departed several hours ahead of schedule and before their arrival. They then spent the night aboard the boat and returned to Academy Bay the next day. No one knew when there would be another plane and the next "ship" was due in several weeks. Since we had no one sick at the moment the only decent thing to do seemed to be to bring them along, letting them sleep in the ward with a mental reservation to turn over my place to them if someone turned up sick. Looks as if all will be well, no one is sick yet and we should be in by noon tomorrow. I am also giving passage to the Ecuadorian Naval Lieutenant who has just been relieved as Captain of the Port at Academy Bay and was very anxious to get to his new job. In addition to the local goodwill he may engender, he is also familiar with the new port and its approaches.

The Scientific party seems to be in good spirits and well pleased with their accomplishments. We have fifty-eight aboard (including the gals). Some flew home early while some came down by plane for a net gain of four, among whom is Dr. Ussinger. It now appears that thirty odd will come to San Diego with us. I have to go to the bridge now so will sign off until after our arrival.

John Keever: "Captain Bowman was the captain at the time. He was about ten years master. He was interesting. He was quite an excellent seaman and shiphandler, I would say of the old school, a seat-of-the-pants type operator, but with a very talented seaman's eye. Very matter-of-fact about his orders and directions. And no news was good news. He wasn't one to run around complimenting you although he might think you were doing well. But if he didn't think you were doing well you probably might hear from him."

Not least among the training opportunities on board ship are the unusual or unanticipated events which, by their nature or circumstance could never occur on campus, but which also serve to train young midshipmen to handle the unforeseen. A bizarre occurrence from one of his cadet cruises was recalled by John Keever. "We hire temporary people to man the galley staff during the cruise and we had a temporary cook on board. We were a day or so out of Mazatlan and this cook decided to go back to the stern and pick up a life ring. A student told him he shouldn't be playing with a life ring so he handed it to the student and

proceeded to jump over the side. It was a flat calm sea. The student threw the life ring over the side. The alarm went out relatively quickly and we turned the ship around. It was very interesting how hard it was to find that small little head floating around in the ocean in a flat calm sea. It really makes you appreciate how difficult it would be to find that same head in a rough sea.

"We sent a boat out with an officer in the boat. We do man overboard drills often and this was toward the end of the cruise and all went very well and they got the person in the boat. The officer in the boat called up on the radio and says, 'I have a little problem here, seems as though Fernando decided to take all his clothes off.' He tried to jump out of the boat so the officer had the students put him under the thwarts of the boat. The officer sat on him while the students pulled the boat back to the ship.

"We got into Mexico and were going to try to repatriate Fernando and it turned out that when God had told Fernando to take his clothes off when he was in the water, he forgot to tell him to take his wallet out of his pants. So he didn't have any documents. So we confined him to a room and had a guard on him. He tried to climb out the window a couple of times so we actually had to put him under medical restraint to keep him on board. In those days the Public Health Service Hospital was still functioning so we sent him back for psychiatric evaluation. He was back on a ship in about a month and a half."

The final cruise of the first *Golden Bear* was in 1970 to Tahiti, Australia, New Zealand, the Fiji Islands and Hawaii. One of the highlights was the arrival of Queen Elizabeth, Prince Philip and Princess Anne in Suva, Fiji Islands while the ship was there. Another well-remembered highlight was the weather. John Keever: "My last student cruise on the first

Golden Bear was my senior cruise. We hit quite a storm coming from Hawaii back to San Francisco, which was the ship's final cruise, as it turned out to be. It was a relatively shallow-draft, flat-bottomed ship, designed for the invasion of China. It was never used for that, obviously. But putting it in a pretty good size storm with a beam sea, on that particular cruise we were rolling up to fifty-two degrees, which is pretty good. We had special watches through the two nights that this all took place because things were breaking loose. I was in charge of one of those watches as a senior and I remember making my rounds through officers' country and hearing a noise coming from the captain's cabin. I stuck my head in and he was trapped behind his desk which had broken loose from the deck. He was trying to hold on to the desk and the bulkhead to keep the desk from moving. We went in and rescued him from his desk. Then we went by the wardroom and there was an officer who had slipped on some water on the deck there and he was sliding back and forth across the wardroom hitting his head on each side as he went. He ended up with about eight stitches in his head. The jumbo boom broke loose, the boat boom fell over the side. It was quite an interesting last trip for the old boat there."

~~~

Vallejo Times-Herald, sometime in 1970:

After 23 training cruises in which midshipmen were instructed firsthand in the arts of seamanship, the Golden Bear has come to the end of her career.

The Golden Bear, a 6,000-ton vessel, has carried countless California Maritime Academy middies on training cruises which are scheduled each year

The skyline of Sydney, Australia, presents a handsome backdrop to the Golden Bear *on her last cruise. Courtesy California Maritime Academy.*

as part of the students' practical training as future deck and engineering officers in either the Navy or the Merchant Marine.

The Golden Bear made her final training cruise early this year, and now is tied up at the Maritime Academy dock, where midshipmen are busy stripping the vessel of her usable parts.

Once that is done, the gleaming white ship will be towed away and eventually is destined to be sold for scrap by the Maritime Administration.

The Golden Bear *was placed alongside her replacement and the process of removing usable equipment began. Courtesy California Maritime Academy.*

In August the *Crescent City,* the new *Golden Bear,* was towed to the Academy and docked alongside the [former] *Golden Bear.* Transfer of usable equipment from the old to the new was the priority.

On May 14, 1971 the first *Golden Bear* was pushed by two tugs away from her berth in the Carquinez Straits on her last voyage to National Metals Co. at Terminal Island, California where she was scrapped. The sale price of the ship was $65,000. During her twenty-three years of service to the students of CMA and the state, the ship steamed over 250,000 miles. She served as a training laboratory to more than 4,000 midshipmen, almost 2,000 of whom received their first professional experience on her decks and in her engine room.

Larry Teague: "When I first went there I really had no idea what I was getting into. As the years progressed, I knew what it was but didn't know if I would like it. But now I look back on it fondly. I loved going to sea and loved the maritime industry. I really am glad I went there. My son went there, I still have a soft spot for it in my heart."

John Mena: "It was a good education, worthwhile, especially for a guy that was reared so close to the family. It was certainly an eye-opener on becoming independent. You run into all kinds of people. It was a good learning experience, a good life experience."

Larry Teague: "I respect the school for the training it gives. And now we are the leaders of the maritime industry on the West Coast. Look at any part of the industry, it has some of us in it."

The leaders of the West Coast maritime industry, before they were leaders. Credit San Francisco Maritime National Historical Park.

CHAPTER 6

THE *GOLDEN BEAR* II

The *Crescent City* had a distinguished war history. Built as the *Del Orleans* for Delta Steamship Co. of New Orleans by Bethlehem-Sparrows Point Shipyard in Maryland, the ship was assigned two hull numbers: 4338 by the Yard and 49 by the Maritime Commission. Her keel was laid on May 8, 1939, she was launched on February 17, 1940 and delivered on August 23, 1940.

Loading a full cargo and filling her 26 passenger cabins, the *Del Orleans* sailed from New Orleans on her maiden voyage September 5, 1940 for the South American ports of Pernambuco, Rio de Janeiro, Montevideo, Buenos Aires, Santos and Bahia. She returned to New Orleans on October 24.

With a turnaround of one week the ship then duplicated her first run and was home just before Christmas of 1940. She made two more voyages to South America before returning to New Orleans for the last time as a commercial ship on June 5, 1941.

The initial contract from the Maritime Commission for the *Del Orleans* was part of President Roosevelt's plan to revitalize the merchant marine which culminated in the Merchant Marine Act of 1936. But the requirements of the Navy superseded all others in the pending war and she was taken over on June 9, 1941. Placed in Alabama Dry Dock and Shipbuilding Co. for conversion to a troop carrier, she was commissioned on October 10, 1941 as the *Crescent City* (a popular nickname for New Orleans) with Cdr. W. C. Calhoun in command. Originally designated AP-40 she was later reclassified as APA-21. Late in October she sailed to Charleston, South Carolina, for completion of her conversion to a troop carrier.

Accommodations were modified to carry more than 1,100 troops with the equipment and supplies needed for their support. To serve the needs of her crew of 500, a ship's store was installed as were a soda fountain, cobbler shop, tailor shop and barber shop. Armament consisted of twenty-three antiaircraft guns (four 50 cal., seventeen 20 mm, two 40 mm) and a 5"-51 as defense against submarines.[1]

---

[1] Five inches is the diameter of the shell fired, 51 means the length of the gun's barrel is 51 times the shell diameter.

The Crescent City *as AP-40 while serving as a troopship in the far Pacific. Credit National Archives.*

By the time of the attack on Pearl Harbor, she was completely outfitted and sailed for Norfolk, Virginia the next day. Fueled and provisioned to capacity, the *Crescent City* steamed in convoy from Norfolk on December 15 for the Canal Zone with troops and equipment of the 301st Barrage Balloon Battalion and Patrol Wing Three.

Her first contact with the enemy occurred Christmas Day when a German submarine was discovered close aboard. The threat was thwarted by the quick response of her escort and the convoy continued to Panama without further incident. There, passengers were discharged and the ship proceeded to San Diego to load Navy and Marine personnel for Pearl Harbor. From Hawaii she returned to San Diego with civilian evacuees and immediately turned around, returning workers and equipment to the damaged Naval base at Pearl Harbor. During the next few months the *Crescent City* was involved in setting up an advance base at Efate, New Hebrides. She then returned to San Diego on April 22, 1942 for a brief overhaul.

Sailing July 1, 1942, the *Crescent City* took part in the first landings at Guadalcanal. While off-loading her troops on August 7 she was subjected to heavy Japanese air attacks.

On August 8 a major torpedo plane attack developed with forty enemy planes approaching the anchorage from the direction of Florida Island. The concentrated fire from the screen and transports was so intense only one plane escaped. The *Crescent City* was credited with destroying four of the enemy bombers. She remained at anchor for two days unloading supplies essential in holding the beachhead, then sailed for Espiritu Santo to unload material needed for a forward base to supply Guadalcanal. The following months were occupied dodging enemy forces as the ship delivered men and equipment from Brisbane, Australia and Wellington, New Zealand to advance bases at Noumea and Espiritu Santo. As the Allied offensive swung north through the Solomons in early 1943, the *Crescent City* continued her transport duty to the newly-established, hard-won base at Guadalcanal. On August 13 she assisted in repelling an air attack in which the *John Penn* (AP-51) was sunk.

October 28, 1943 found the ship sortieing for the invasion of Bougainville. There, she landed troops at Empress Augusta Bay under air attack on November 1. On the 13th she helped repel a torpedo bomber attack and landed support troops brought from Tulagi and

In 1943, as APA-21, the Crescent City *shows a trimmer-looking silhouette. A two-tone gray paint scheme gives her a more streamlined appearance. Credit National Archives.*

Port Purvis. She then took part in the assault landings on Emirau Island on April 11, 1944 and returned to Guadalcanal on April 30 to prepare for the Marianas operation.

As the war progressed the *Crescent City* spent so much of her time in the company of the *President Hayes*, *President Adams* and *President Jackson* that the quartet was dubbed "The Unholy Four."[2] Fleet members and ground forces could be sure that whenever The Four gathered, a new offensive was in the works.

Held in reserve during the attacks on Kwajalein and Eniwetok, the *Crescent City* then landed her troops and took aboard casualties at Guam from July 21 to 25, 1944. She returned to Guadalcanal on August 16 for

the staging of the Palau operation and took part in the landings on Peleliu on September 15, then sailed for Humboldt Bay, New Guinea, where she arrived on October 16, sailing immediately for the invasion of Leyte in the Philippines. After landing troops of the 6th Army at San Pedro Bay on October 22, she brought reinforcements from Leyte to Hollandia and arrived at Manus on November 20 to take on passengers for the United States.

Returning to San Francisco, the ship underwent an overhaul, then departed February 25, 1945, arriving at Pearl Harbor March 4. Following conversion to a temporary hospital evacuation ship she sailed for Kerama Retto, Ryukyu Islands, where she arrived on April 6. Taking the wounded from the beaches

---

[2] The four ships were sisters in design as well as in war history. In 1938 the basic Maritime Commission C-3 hull was modified to produce a cargo-passenger liner designed to carry 52 passengers as well as five holds of cargo. For wartime use the passenger-carrying C-3s were further modified to become attack transports. Each of "The Unholy Four" was this same design.

of Okinawa and other ships, she transferred them to the hospital ship *Hope* (AH-7) for evacuation. The *Crescent City* remained at Okinawa receiving the wounded and transients until the end of the war.

The ship then took part in the same support effort as her *Golden Bear* predecessor, *USS Mellena*, carrying troops for the occupation of China. She ferried the 1st Marines to Taky between September 30 and October 6, 1945, and Chinese troops from Hong Kong to Chinwangtao and Tsingtao in November. Returning to Okinawa on December 1, she embarked soldiers eligible for discharge and sailed for Seattle, arriving on December 20.

Sailing December 23 from Seattle, the *Crescent City* arrived in Norfolk, Virginia on February 14. She operated from New York and Norfolk on training duty in the Caribbean until October 10, 1947, when she sailed for San Francisco. Arriving there on November 1, the ship was taken out of commission in reserve on April 30, 1948 and transferred to the Maritime Commission on September 3, 1948. She was then placed in the Reserve Fleet at Suisun Bay, California.

For her war service she was awarded the Navy Unit Commendation and received 10 battle stars. She downed eight Japanese planes during her career.

~~~

Searching for a replacement for the *Golden Bear*, the nearby Reserve Fleet at Suisun Bay was the first place the school administration checked, and the last. According to Capt. Bowman: "When one of our people discovered this ship [the *Crescent City*] in the Suisun anchorage, he said it was like finding grandpa's Rolls-Royce after it had been jacked up in a garage for 20 years."

Originally, the estimate for conversion to a training ship was $1.2 million. This was

Looking like a ghost from the past, the Crescent City *is towed from the Reserve Fleet at Suisun Bay under the Carquinez Bridge to its new home at Morrow Cove. Courtesy California Maritime Academy.*

whittled to a bare-bones figure of $460,000. The actual cost was $287,000 (which, not coincidentally, was the total amount of federal funds allocated to do the job) due to the diligent efforts of the midshipmen and staff at the Academy. Of that amount, $280,000 was spent on engine repairs and to paint the ship.

From the *Vallejo Sunday Times-Herald*, March 28, 1971:

> *They said it couldn't be done, but the faculty, engineering students and even a pair of graduates of California Maritime Academy have done it — the new Golden Bear's boilers are fired up and she has been pronounced as well as if her engines had been shut down only yesterday rather than 24 years ago.*
>
> *The ship — labelled by CMA critics the worst sort of waste, because, they alleged, it would cost too much money to get her to run — was fired up for the first time on Wednesday, when she ran for two half hour periods without difficulty.*
>
> *According to those who were there, it was a sight to behold, the steam from the funnel after those more than two*

decades and the propeller clearly visible as it slowly began to churn up the water.

At first the big prop turned about one revolution per minute. As the throttles were opened slowly, the propeller began to turn faster and faster until it was making 30 rpm — and the engineers were satisfied that the new Golden Bear would run and perform.

"There are still adjustments to be made, but her machinery compartment is basically ready to go," said Capt. Carl G. Bowman, the Golden Bear's skipper, receiving a nod of agreement from chief engineer, Commander Otto H. Bruhn.

In fact, according to Bruhn and Bowman, the ship actually is likely to have a longer serviceable lifespan than any the academy might have obtained — at considerably more cost — brand-new.

Those currently criticizing CMA have contended that her acquisition by the school was a waste of money — some had even said she would never run again because of costs. But CMA has, with the starting of the engines, taken the wind out of the sails of Crescent City critics.

"You don't see a lot of cast iron on her," Capt. Bowman pointed out. "It's all bronze and metal, and materials assembled prior to the war shortage years. If you tried to build a ship like her today it would cost you $20 million."

The work by the cadets was not only a means of economy, it added an invaluable amount of practical training to their future careers. Capt. Bowman: "Restoring her to running condition has provided a lot of valuable experience for the boys, although the kids doing the scraping and chipping might not be too sure what value it has. But, on the other hand, part of their duties as officers will be to supervise this kind of work, so without this experience they would either have to just stand by and do nothing or else interfere at the wrong time.

"Practical knowledge has always been one of the big sales points of this school. In laboratories we give them the theory of automation, whereas if they don't know what to do with the actual machinery, it's all just a couple of red lights flashed here when such and such happens and so on. This way they know the actual components."

The new Golden Bear ex Crescent City made her first trial run after the boneyard in the week of June 15, 1971, achieving speeds of up to 15. Academy Superintendent Rear Admiral Francis T. Williamson USN (Ret.) said on the trial run, "Feel the ride. There's hardly any vibration and the ride is as smooth as silk. And there were those who said this ship wouldn't run. I know I can take this ship anywhere in the world and bring her back without trouble."

Capt. Bowman, repeating the phrase that had caught on: "It's like finding a Rolls Royce that grandpa blocked up 20 years ago and all it needs now is a new battery and some lubrication."

The living conditions on the second *Golden Bear* were a great improvement over the previous ship. There were more berthing areas, showers and heads. John Keever '70, later master of the *Golden Bear* II: "The first *Golden Bear* was rustic, at best, compared to the current *Golden Bear* [*Crescent City*]. It had been built as an AKA. It had quarters for

TUITION
In 1971 tuition was $3,680 for California residents and $4,580 for those from out of state.

At first the hull was painted black, the superstructure white and the stack buff. Courtesy California Maritime Academy.

about three hundred marines and the rest, navy crew. For the two hundred fifty cadets or so who went on the ship there was one head facility, which we all shared, which usually meant waiting in line in the morning. And there were two basic berthing compartments with a few small cubicles elsewhere. So most people lived in large compartments of about a hundred people each, three high, small lockers, very close quarters. The current *Golden Bear* [II], although it's certainly showing its age and was older than that ship, with eight separate living compartments and eight separate head facilities was quite an improvement from when I went to sea on the training ship."

Robert Stewart, professor: "For the officers the quarters aren't too bad. But, except on a cruise to Alaska, you're living in the tropics in an un-air-conditioned space. You are dependent upon the student engineer literally for light and heat and hot water. There are many occasions when you get up at three o'clock in the morning and you turn the water on in the shower and there isn't hot water. Well, because in the engine room they're teaching something that has impacted the hot water system so they have it turned off. So, who's it going to bother at three o'clock in the morning?

"The rooms aren't bad-size, but with the lack of air-conditioning and the variability of the hotel services, sometimes the living conditions aren't the best. You compare it to a merchant ship, there are no room stewards. You make your own bunk, you do your own laundry, you clean your own room, and so it's not a Hilton."

Holly Fuerstenberg '87: "The women used to be back in the old crew's quarters. It was the main deck right below the stack, over the steering gear. That's where we were. We had a common area about twenty by twenty. And that was lined by lockers. The racks were two high and two deep and then the first class had their own separate area. You were lucky if you had an inside locker. My first cruise I had an outside locker so I was in the hallway. Everyone knows what's in your locker."

Cadet-midshipman, instructor or master, most who sailed on the second *Golden Bear* enjoyed the experience and developed an affection for the ship. She really was like a well-preserved Rolls-Royce or Duesenberg, well-proportioned, with beautiful lines. And she took to the seas in a kindly manner. Robert Stewart: "She's really a good ship. It's not a big ship. If you come off a tanker which rides real solidly, the first response I had to the training ship was, boy, she rocks, she rolls, she responds. As you think about it, well, we got five hundred feet of ship in comparison to eight hundred feet and seventy thousand tons of tanker. I mean, there's not a lot of horsepower here. This is not a navy frigate; five hundred feet long with thirty thousand horsepower or anything. She's only got seven, eight thousand horsepower. But because of the size of the ship she is fairly maneuverable. She is fairly responsive. But it is a steam ship, that dead slow bell, especially astern, is effectively useless. But she is fairly responsive most of the time on a backing bell or something like that and I think that's a real asset in our program. Most years in our program there are four or

The Golden Bear *outbound under the Golden Gate Bridge on her annual cruise. This photo, taken in 1974, shows the hull now painted white although the stack remains buff with black stripes. Courtesy California Maritime Academy.*

five days set aside for maneuvering of that ship by the students.

"And one of the joys of the ship is she's so consistent. I can say, when the wheel wash gets to a certain point we're dead in the water. And if you go in and look at the GPS[3] or you go in and you look at the Doppler speed logs, that is, in fact, the case. After being on a big ship it's kind of like driving a sports car. She's pretty responsive, she handles fairly well for the most part, for as little cargo as is in it, and for as little weight as is in it, in most sea conditions, unless it's right on the beam, she doesn't ride badly, either."

John Keever: "She's a relatively nice-handling ship because of her size. She's sluggish, she's a single screw, single rudder ship; not too big a rudder. Steam turbine, not a lot of backing power, not a lot of horsepower ahead when maneuvering. So she's sluggish,

---

[3] Global Positioning System. This satellite navigation system has replaced the sextant and other navigation systems. It is inexpensive and allows the navigator to read latitude and longitude directly with an accuracy of six feet anywhere on the surface of the earth.

Later in the 1970s the Academy emblem, a shield over two seahorses and a trident, was added to the stack as shown in this photo taken in San Diego. The shield was later replaced with a gold bear and the stack painted blue with gold stripes above and below the bear (see cover). Courtesy California Maritime Academy.

but I certainly have found her to be a reasonable ship to handle."

Bob Black, former student: "She's a very forgiving vessel. She rides easily in ballast. She's responsive, a nice-riding ship. She was a proud vessel with a lot of history. I liked sailing on her."

Seamen have always ascribed human personalities to their ships. Partly this is because anything as complex as a ship, with all its wiring, plumbing, machinery, shapes, spaces and noises, develops individual characteristics. No two are alike. Even if built to exactly the same plans, ships will operate with differences in temperament and personality that are immediately discernible to the seafarer.

Bob Black: "All ships have a personality, even the supposed mass-produced ships have a personality. She was designed as one of those passenger-cargo carrying ships and she's a beauty. She's a lady. And being a training ship didn't change that. She's a tough lady, but a lady."

Brandon Moser '95: "Like all ships, she's characterized as a female, but I only know this for certain because she always behaves herself like a lady. Being the oldest active American-Flag merchant vessel she was like the *grande dame* of the merchant marine. She was a little scary in rough weather, but once you realized she wouldn't roll over on you, you enjoyed it. She rode well, for a ship that you expected to behave like a senior citizen. She had a lot of get up and go. She was a classy broad."

Interestingly, at least one woman thought the *Golden Bear*'s personality, usually considered female, was <u>male</u>.

Lynn Korwatch '76: "Does the ship have a personality? That's kind of an interesting question. I would say it did. I think any ship does. I think that the personality is derived through the captain. I'd characterize the *Golden Bear* as being not a lady, but more of a man because there were so many men there, so few women. I think that it probably has more of a male personality."

Holly Fuerstenberg: "She's kind of alive. I've always thought of the *Bear* as a person. She definitely has a personality. Even when I was walking down from the Res. Hall to stand watch on her, I used to think she was such a lady. Just very elegant. She has gorgeous lines. I love to see her on the horizon. We'd be in port and we'd be anchored out and she's just so beautiful to look at. I was always over the side painting in the boatswain's chair, swinging in and grabbing on and trying to paint this thing. I thought she really has quite a figure.

"She's just so forgiving. She gets beat up every cruise. You don't know what you're doing to her and she just puts up with it. She kind of reminds me, too, of the dog in Peter Pan, Nana."

Once again times were changing. The '70s, '80s and '90s saw the coming of the computer age, the break-up of the Soviet Union, the end of the Cold War, containerization, less time in port, responsibility for cargo shifting from aboard ship to shoreside and women's emergence into the main fabric of professional seafaring.

The campus environment, too, changed. With the construction of an engineering building (Dwyer Hall), new faculty offices, a larger library with an annex, an auditorium, student commons, a new residence hall and a wardroom, the last of the temporary buildings vanished. Furthermore, the grounds were improved with the addition of trees, shrubbery, landscaping, the Golden Bear Park

Taken in 1993, this photo shows the Golden Bear II *at the Academy pier. The grounds have filled in dramatically with trees, landscaping and new buildings compared to the earlier photo on page 129. Credit California Maritime Academy, courtesy Brandon Moser.*

in the center of the campus and an upper parking lot.

And the students, as they always have, reflect the times in which they live. We find the school maturing from an all-male training school with strong Navy overlays to a mature college offering a formal, more civilian, education to both genders. The reasons for attending CMA, too, changed, with a greater emphasis on opportunity — for both men and women. Yet, underlying it all is a common thread that dates back to the *Jamestown*, a sense of the romance of the sea in all its facets . . .

Holly Fuerstenberg: "The very first time I ever saw the ship I was a Brownie. It was a little field trip and I was just totally captivated. Here was this big guy in a brown uniform and he knew all about this ship. He let me touch the wheel and the whole bit. That really made an impression.

"She was the new *Golden Bear* at that time, so it would have been '73, somewhere in there."

Lynn Korwatch: "My father was an unlicensed engineer and had been sailing since World War II and had shared some sea stories with me. The *Oakland Tribune* in 1972 announced that the school was opening its doors to women. That sounded more interesting than a normal job."

Holly Fuerstenberg: "I grew up in Vallejo. My parents bought a power boat and decided that I was going to learn how to sail. I really enjoyed it and when I was in high school I started racing a lot. My dad, at that point, had gotten into sailing, so we had a sailboat. We both couldn't be on the sailboat at the same time because we both wanted to be in charge, so he would pawn me off on other unsuspecting crews. I used to sail quite a bit with Seth Hargrave who is an alumnus. He was the port captain at Exxon at the time and he'd have classmates on board or people from work and they'd have these really interesting jobs. So

the idea of not having to be an English major or that there was just something else that I could do really started to appeal to me.

"I had sworn that I would never go to another Catholic School, never wear another uniform. CMA is the only school I ever applied to and I got in and there I was, in uniform again."

Brandon Moser: "I never had planned to go deep sea. I was aiming for the Washington State Ferries all the time. I love the boats. I've been interested in their history for most of my life and it's kind of my way of having that. I decided I wanted to get the education and training at CMA.

"They say that most sailors have a never-ending love affair with their first ship. I arrived in the Fall of '91 when they were talking about the threat of replacing the *Golden Bear* with the *Hess*. I was told I may never have the chance to sail on the *Golden Bear*. I'm sure glad I did, though. That ship was without a doubt the last of her kind and the end of an era. I instantly fell in love with it. My first impression was, Wow!"

Lynn Korwatch: "Even though I had grown up around the Bay Area I had little exposure to ships. I was awed. They had just gotten it the year before or two years before. There was still a lot of work to be done."

Robert Stewart, professor: "I left commercial shipping for a couple of reasons. One, I had by that point, two young kids. And shipping was just not real conducive to me spending time with them. Additionally, I had established a goal for myself on leaving Kings Point that by such-and-such a year I want to have a master's degree. When I saw the teaching job available here at CMA it was like, boy, this is the best of both worlds."

Although it's seldom expressed, one of the great attractions of the schoolship is the enduring fascination of the sea. Pitting oneself against the unknown, braving typhoons and hurricanes; the kaleidoscopic rapture of tropical sunsets; and the eerie glow of phosphorescent waters; sitting in cafes, bars, pubs, coffeehouses and restaurants in cities on every continent, savoring foreign cultures and customs; the wonder of watching flying fish, dolphins playfully escorting the ship, and whales spouting and breaching, are all part of the lure.

The routine of the ship — reveille, standing watches, chipping, painting — continues, especially in the first year. Holly Fuerstenberg: "You were just a grunt. You were doing the chipping and painting. You were just the helmsman. So you didn't have a lot of responsibility. I really got to know my classmates at that point. The best thing about cruise was always the friendships and that you're all in this together. Even though it was monotonous, I enjoyed third class just because of the routine. Every afternoon at four, regardless of rain or shine; clean sweep-down fore and aft; the deckies, man your brooms, the engineers, man your lawn chairs. Basically they'd sit out and sun themselves and watch us."

Brandon Moser: "Monday through Saturday the daily routine was: six-thirty reveille, the under class would get up and do the cleaning of the berthing area and the heads and whatnot. Breakfast was started about seven. And turn-to for the deck side and day work for the engineers was at eight."

Holly Fuerstenberg: "Reveille was at six-thirty. You can choose to get up and get in the head and get squared away then or you can wait until the last minute and be like me, five minutes and . . ."

Lynn Korwatch: "For us, reveille was at six. Then there was usually some type of cleaning up activity, formation at eight, and then, generally working in the morning, and then, depending on what watch you were in, you may have had watch some time during the

First year duties included acting as helmsman. Courtesy California Maritime Academy.

day or evening. We were all watchstanders in the deck department. In addition we had to do ship board maintenance, and classroom activities. When I got to be a second classman there got to be stars [star sights] and so on.

Some things never change — including applying a fresh coat of primer. Courtesy California Maritime Academy.

Engine midshipmen might spend their days checking the propeller shaft bearings, above, receiving instruction on boiler operation, top right, turning valves, bottom right, or watching the gauges at the main operating platform, below. All photos courtesy California Maritime Academy.

"It didn't seem like there was time for any recreation. We had no videos. They used to show a movie out on deck which was kind of fun. You were always so busy standing watch or studying there wasn't a lot of just hanging out time."

~~~

The reminiscences that follow may seem very different from the routine and recollections of cadets in the '30s and '40s. Half a century lies between the serious young people who came out of the Great Depression and headed straight into a World War and the "laid back" '90s. Alumni from recent years speak in the casual language of the present; those from earlier generations with the gravity and experience of age. Surprisingly, overall, the stories are the same. Only the language and the present age of the storytellers are different. And the cruises are still the highlight of the school year.

Holly Fuerstenberg: "Breakfast was served until seven your first cruise. Seniors can eat up until eight. You have to be in there by seven your first year. This is in the galley. Each division has an area. It's kind of unspoken, but it's engineers on the port side and deckies on the starboard side. Each division is broken off. And they're like, 1-D [First Division, deck] always takes the most forward of the tables, and that was my division so I'd always eat there. And then the watch has kind of their own table. The mess deck [on the campus] is kind of broken down the same way.

"So you grab a bite and then deck. It's first call the deck turn-to and that's at oh-seven-fifty, second call is oh-seven-fifty-five and then deck turn-to is at oh-eight-hundred. And that's only for deckies. The engineers are broken off into classes and watch and day work, on a three-day rotation. So they do all watchstanding or all class or all day work for three days. They just go to their stations or

Every afternoon at four the stack soot was washed off the ship in a "clean sweep-down." Courtesy California Maritime Academy.

whatever. With the deckies all the division commanders meet with the corps chief mate and Mr. Sears the [faculty] chief mate and they get their work cards for the day. We're all huddled up there and taking roll and that's when we find out what we were doing. They

One of the many classrooms on the Golden Bear. *Courtesy California Maritime Academy.*

Afternoon or evening study in the lounge. Courtesy California Maritime Academy.

send us off to do work until eleven and then we go to lunch."

Brandon Moser: "Lunch commenced at eleven-thirty for first classmen, maybe it was eleven-fifty, noon was lunch for all hands. At thirteen hundred was quarters, all hands on deck for roll call, whereas only the deck side would be out for turn-to, more day work."

Holly Fuerstenberg: "That was when we would take roll and everyone on the ship had to turn to or they'd go through and check your rack and find you. Right after quarters we'd always have a fire drill. That's when they would inspect the berthing areas. We used to have quite a bit of cleaning competition. That was kind of a divisional thing so you could get off early or stay out later if your division did real well. Kind of too bad that our only sense of divisional pride was how clean your berthing area was. That was the only sense of competition we had. Not grades or anything, but how clean is your potty . . ."

Brandon Moser: "Engineers would blow tubes between fifteen hundred and fifteen-thirty. Clean sweep-down was at sixteen hundred."

Holly Fuerstenberg: "And then at four you go back and finish your day work or you'd have classes in the afternoon, some sort of class like flashing light, or Rules [of the Road] or shipboard familiarization, or tackle, figuring out the ratios, that kind of thing. The boatswain's class you had to make a bag, a canvas bag, to learn your stitches . . . So there are classes usually in the afternoon or you finished up your day work and then the class would go off and do clean sweep-down and everyone else just kind of hangs out and waits for dinner, watches the third class work."

Brandon Moser: "Dinner was at seventeen hundred or seventeen-thirty and then you were free to do your studies, watch your nightly movie. Sunday was a day of rest."

Another difference from the early years was the increased amount of, and time for, light entertainment.

Holly Fuerstenberg: "Dinner would be at five and then it was movies after dinner, maybe three movies a night. Actually, there would be six movies a night because they would divide the ship up port and starboard and so you could watch two movies at a time depending on where you were sitting. If you were in the middle of the middies' lounge, there would be one movie going on the port side and the other TV on the starboard side would have a different movie and there would be six

Afternoon fire drill would sometimes include lifeboat drill. Photo by W. Hayler, courtesy California Maritime Academy.

actually showing throughout the night. A mix of current and old movies, a lot of blood and guts. 'The French Lieutenant's Woman' didn't draw much of a crowd but you got 'Mad Max' and 'The Terminator' and . . ."

Of course, the officers and instructors had a different routine. Without the pressure of cadet work and study, it might seem cruise time would be more relaxing for them, but the days were long.

Robert Stewart: "We [the instructors] grade papers. I take the computer out of my office and I take it on the ship with me. So I have things that I'm doing either for next semester or maybe I'm writing an article for publication or something like that. I do that in my room part of the time, or just sit and read. We play a lot of cribbage. Two-thirds of the officers at one time or another will jump in. We had great cribbage tournaments on the ship. We have a pretty good video library. We'll watch maybe a movie in the afternoon and then two or three in the evening and then maybe the folks who come off the eight-to-twelve will sit down and watch a movie after midnight. The folks who are going on the mid-watch will watch theirs just before. So from four o'clock in the afternoon until two o'clock in the morning there's a kind of rolling set of people who are keeping different hours and movies. The movie system is piped throughout the ship but the wardroom has its own VCR. So if they're watching something and we want to watch something else, we can click over and watch our own movie or we can watch whatever the rest of the ship is watching. We'll sit around and chat and tell stories and play cribbage and watch television."

Holly Fuerstenberg: "If you weren't watching movies there's always a pinochle game going on. There's always backgammon and cribbage and different card games going on and there's other stuff going down on the

Taking a bearing with an azimuth circle, another part of ship's navigation. Courtesy California Maritime Academy.

division berthing area, working on reports and whatnot."

Brandon Moser: "For some reason cribbage was the game of choice on the *Bear* the two years I was on."

Holly Fuerstenberg: "You're never bored with anything. You can always find something to do. But even with three hundred people it's amazing that it actually can be pretty lonely sometimes. And the only place you have that's yours is your rack. And sleep is so precious on cruise. It's the most precious commodity in the world. It's the only time you can check out."

Getting the ship's position with a sextant dates back more than a hundred years and is one of the most satisfying of the seaman's arts. For about a half hour before sunrise and after sunset the sky is dark enough to locate stars yet bright enough to see the horizon. A star is selected, located in the sextant and brought down to the horizon. The arc of the sextant then indicates the star's altitude. The time of the sight is taken with a stopwatch. This information is then used to enter a series of tables that translates it into a line which can be drawn on the chart (hopefully) crossing the ship's course. Three or four such lines crossing

Taking a sun line with a sextant is part of the traditional art and science of navigation. Courtesy California Maritime Academy.

at the same point give the ship's position. When wrong it's embarrassing, when right, very satisfying.

Holly Fuerstenberg: "Junior year you get a little more supervisory, you're kind of running the day work crews. We'd do ten days of nav study, morning stars, evening stars, LAN [Local Apparent Noon], sun lines, everything. That's all you did, was celestial nav for ten days. I loved shooting stars. That was one of my most favorite things. I felt like you were really part of the sea, doing that kind of thing. It's such a timeless tradition."

Brandon Moser: "If you were a first classman on your celestial leg, then you were responsible for morning stars, two sunlines and LAN, evening stars, and each of these deadlines you were to also turn in a position slip, a daily position report. You turned one in for eight hundred, noon or twenty-one hundred. Seniors did not do day work during celestial

leg because you had to get sleep whenever you can."

Holly Fuerstenberg: "If the gods were smiling upon you, you could have morning stars. Then you'd have day work, then you'd have class, and then you could pull the eight to twelve. I mean you could have almost virtually a twenty-four hour day for deckies, without sleep, and that was not unusual at all. The potential was there for a very, very long day. If you really scored you had the eight-to-twelve or twelve-to-four and that got you out of day work or class and then you had morning or evening stars so you had a nice, short, compact little day . . .

"The fun watch was the security patrol. That was the great one. That was a two- or a four-hour watch, from twenty hundred to oh-eight hundred. It's only deckies and there's a second and a third class and you just wander around the ship making sure no one's sleeping on deck, make sure that nothing's flooding, there's no fires. . .

"Sometimes the engineers would stand a more regular cycle. If you had the four-to-eight, that's all you did. Or they would be in class for eight hours or they would have day work for eight hours. So they had a much different routine than the deckies did. And it's not unusual to not see someone for two or three days, depending on what cycle they were on."

The curriculum allowed for a variety of seagoing experience. In addition to the training cruises on the *Golden Bear*, students could take a commercial cruise on one of the many ships operating out of the West Coast. Some preferred the variety of experience and instructor attention on the training ship.

Holly Fuerstenberg: "My senior year we had the option of going on a commercial cruise instead. But I wanted the extra polish, I wanted the extra kind of attention to make sure that I knew what I was doing. I wasn't ready to let go of the faculty and the student thing to be out on a commercial ship yet."

The master of the ship, responsible for everything that occurred on board, was constantly on call. His never-ending day was just that — never-ending. Capt. John Keever '70 describes a typical day at sea: "Underway, up at about five-thirty, quarter-to-six, out on the chartroom and the bridge to review the night's progress. Generally, whenever the master went on the bridge he'd ask a couple of questions of the senior cadet just to see how their ability to communicate what they knew was. Then breakfast and probably a meeting or two in the morning or maybe the galley staff planning the social events for the next port call.

"Maybe a little communication with the next port. The master acts as his own agent also. You're constantly working on making the arrangements for the next port or some other port. So you're communicating with embassies or port captains. You try to get the embassy to handle your affairs. And, of course, they need a lot of guidance and pushing.

"And then, maybe, a round of the berth decks and the ship in general to see how things are going, maybe a meeting with the chief mate and chief engineer. And, if scheduled, captain's mast and dealing with any disciplinary matters that were convening. After that, preparation for whatever courses I was going to teach in the afternoon. Usually the master would teach a course or two during the afternoon period. Maybe a meeting with a person in charge of the drill scenarios to get those planned, then lunch and, in the afternoon, teach for an hour or two. I usually stood a couple of hours of watch in the afternoon to ease the strain on the other faculty, one of the dog watches. Oh, and review tracks with the second mate for the next track or two.

"Accounting. The master did the payroll and the purchasing in each port. You had

The master's job is never done, but here Capt. Keever, left, relaxes a bit as Panama Canal Pilot Bob Gray, a graduate of the class of '63, takes the con. Courtesy California Maritime Academy.

to keep the books up to date and transmit back to the academy after each port what you'd spent. And then the evenings, usually a meeting with the corps leadership in the evenings about disciplinary issues or activities in the upcoming port, those kind of things. Generally, I also got together with the chief and the first assistant in the evening for half an hour to just talk about engineering problems and the personnel or machinery since the old ship needed a lot of tender loving care.

"About eight or nine o'clock we'd wrap up the day and, usually, due to the type of standing orders or night orders left on the training ship, you could expect two or three or four phone calls during the night. Yes, there was an officer out there but what we wanted the students to do was be able to articulate what they saw and what they wanted to do and have them do that over the telephone and be able to respond to a couple of questions. That's a learning experience.

"They were busy days. You had to be quickly able to go back to sleep. You were glad to be done with the cruises after three months."

Not all the faculty made each voyage. But those that did stood watches and taught classes. Compared to the master's, the instructors' day was more organized, less chaotic. Robert Stewart, professor: "During the course of the day you are assigned a watch, a four-hour watch, and then a series of classes to teach. I would be up at three to stand the four-to-eight. Shoot stars on the four-to-eight, whatever needs to be done and then, immediately after the watch, breakfast and then classes. Usually what you have is two hours or maybe three hours of class in the course of the morning and then, in order to make up this full eight-hour day, you have your hour of prep to do that. So the day actually starts at four and ends at noon. Well, maybe there's Paul Leyda [watch officer] whose day starts at eight and ends at four and Sam Shaw [watch officer] whose day starts at noon and ends at eight pm.

"We try to use the resources of the training ship. There was usually one slack period when nobody taught, from four in the morning to eight in the morning. Basically it was because the midshipmen were involved in other things at that point; there's cleaning, there's breakfast, there's formation and there's that kind of thing. But from eight in the morning to four the following morning there are always classes in session. Even at night. There are folks who stood the eight-to-twelve watch in the evening, the twenty hundred-to-twenty-four hundred, and then they went right on to teaching and they taught from zero zero to zero four hundred and there were students who were assigned class from zero zero to zero four hundred because the concept of a daytime ship really badly overburdens both the faculty and the students. We said, 'Well, we have twenty-four hours in the day, let's use that. So we spread that out and virtually everybody's [instructors] day looks about that way — four hours of watch, two or three hours of teaching and then some prep work.

"Usually, on the watch, you have five students. You have one first class who is nominally the midshipman in charge of the watch. You have one second class who acts as kind of quartermaster, maintaining logs, recording weather and then they do personnel management. And you have three third class. One acts as a helmsman, one acts as a lookout, and one acts as a standby or messenger. Those positions, helmsman, lookout, messenger, rotate every hour and twenty minutes or so. That's what the second class does, make sure those positions get rotated and that the people are briefed on what they need to do and all that stuff.

"You rotate within the watch so that there are three people assigned to the four-to-eight watch and during the course of the four-to-eight watch you would spend an hour and twenty minutes as a helmsman, and then you would rotate up to the bow and then you would spend an hour and twenty minutes as a lookout and then you would rotate back up to the bridge and you would spend an hour and twenty minutes making coffee, learning bridge equipment, hanging out.

"The students rotate every watch. There's six watches a day, the twelve-to-four, four-to-eight, and the eight-to-twelve in the morning and then the same in the afternoon. Over the course of the six watches each day, you have six groups of six students. At four o'clock the watch completely changes from top to bottom. Watch officer and all the midshipmen change. As a first class student, you may have a watch as a student on Monday and then you may not have another watch for three or four days. As a third class student, because there are three to a watch, you usually have watch five days out of seven."

Another thing that never changes is the interest in the food — how much there is and how good it is. Teenagers are always hungry. Put them on a ship, work them hard, limit them to three meals a day and they become healthy, hard-working and ravenous. Throw in salt air and sea breezes and appetites almost get out of hand. Holly Fuerstenberg: "I didn't mind the food. I was always amazed that they could cook anything at all on there, cooking with that kind of plant. I thought the food was pretty good. When in doubt, there was always rice to eat. People live on tuna, cans of tuna. They bring a lot of their own, those noodle things, Top-ramen and cans of tuna are very, very prized possessions. And then they steal Tabasco sauce and Kikkoman [soy sauce] from the mess deck and they'll have a little stash."

Brandon Moser: "If you went hungry it was your own fault. The food on board, my first cruise was, well, there was nothing wrong with it.

"I wasn't on the cruises where this happened but there was something about the corn dogs. They kept cropping up at every meal and the middies finally refused to eat them. They had a rebellion. So Dr. Lyons [Academy superintendent] promised 'No more corn dogs' in 1992. But what they got was bagel dogs in '92. That brought on another rebellion. The result is that to this day neither has been served again on cruise."

Meals generally were geared toward the desires of the students. That is, the ship served more hamburgers, hot dogs, pizzas, sandwiches, spaghetti, potato chips and the like than you would find at a restaurant or cafeteria ashore.

Bob Black: "Actually, aside from all the jokes about corn dogs, I can't complain about the food. The people that ran the mess deck tried to make the food creative and did the best they could. Everybody made comments about the bad food but in the end they ate it."

Lynn Korwatch: "It wasn't too bad. It wasn't gourmet by any means, but it was certainly adequate. It was the same food that we were getting in the cafeteria every day on the regular [land] campus."

The mess deck of the Golden Bear *was always the focus of one of the midshipmen's main concerns — food. Courtesy California Maritime Academy.*

Holly Fuerstenberg: "Sunday afternoons when the weather was nice, we'd have a barbecue on deck. The faculty would be up there cooking or the first class would be cooking for you and it was just kind of fun. You let your hair down and then the cruise band would usually play. That band was just kids from the campus and they usually get together for cruise. We used to have a stereo system on the fantail. You hang out on the fantail and they'd pop in. A lot of Jimmy Buffet was played in my era. And the sun setting and it's Jimmy Buffet on the fantail and you're just kicking back and life doesn't get any better than that."

Brandon Moser: "The best part, though, was midnight rations or 'mid rats,' for sure. They were prepared by a little lady called Candy Lillard. She has since retired. She would scrape up whatever she could from the leftovers of the day. One night it might be fried potatoes with peppers and onions, the next might be waffles and sausage or whatever.

"One night when I was master-at-arms we got tacos and cheese out of one of the store rooms and pounded the tacos down to make nachos. We had twenty-four square feet of nachos that disappeared in about eight minutes."

On December 16, 1971, Capt. William H. Aguilar was appointed master of the *Golden Bear*, following the retirement of Capt. C. G. Bowman. Capt. Aguilar was a native of Vallejo and a graduate of the California Nautical School in 1934.

Lynn Korwatch: "Aguilar was very well-liked. He was a very quiet, reserved man and everybody really highly respected him. Aguilar was a very calm person. We never had a sense of things being chaotic. Everything was well-managed, well-run. Everybody knew what they were supposed to be doing."

~~~

By 1972 the California Maritime Academy had evolved from a highly-regarded vocational training school to a fully-accredited academic institution and the program was expanded to four years. In addition to licenses and a Naval Reserve commission it now offered college degrees in marine engineering and maritime transportation.

Immediately setting the precedent, a year later CMA became the first merchant marine academy in the country to open its doors to women and in 1976 it was the first to graduate women.

Lynn Korwatch: "I went in in '73 and graduated in '76. I was in the last of the three year programs. Those who graduated in '77 got a four-year degree. They audited one year and had enough other college credits to graduate.

"There was one instructor, Fred Newton, the navigator or the XO of the ship. He was one of those people who always expected the best out of everybody. There was no room for error with him. You were either exactly right or you were wrong. And we rose to his expectations. I think that's why, when we sat for Coast Guard licenses, no one ever failed it. I consider him my mentor. He had a daughter who was in the Navy or who had just gotten out of the Navy, so he was very supportive of women in nontraditional roles.

"I had difficulty adapting to the discipline at first. I was twenty-one when I went in. I had already lived on my own and held a job. So, listening to some seventeen year-old tell me to put on black socks or that I had to be in at ten at night was hard to take. Fred Newton would tell me, 'You can get through this. Just go along with it.' I was very grateful for his advice."

Holly Fuerstenberg: "The hard thing about the ship for women is that we're isolated. You know we're all in that one area and so you're part of the division when there's a lot of work to do and there's watchstanding but when it's something fun like linehandling, they usually forget to come and get you.

"I was always welcome in the guys' berthing area, but you just can't hang out in there because there's thirty people or forty people trying to live in there and get dressed and get changed and you're making all of them uncomfortable. So, to study with me, we'd have to go somewhere else. You just tended to feel more isolated. And then, no one wants to go in the women's berthing area. Definitely a no-man's-land."

Lynn Korwatch: "I was in the first division. The berthing area was all the way up forward. What they did with the women, because there were only five of us, they gave us two crew rooms with an adjoining head. By the time we got to our second class year, there were more women and they designated a berthing area that the women used.

"There were three women in my class that graduated, another deck and one engine."

One of the effects of the training ship experience is that the students develop a sense of "family." Sharing the same experiences on board over a long period of time creates strong camaraderie.

The distinctive lines of the Sydney Opera House make it easy to identify this port of call. Courtesy California Maritime Academy.

Holly Fuerstenberg: "The guys are very protective. There's very much a sense of you're their classmate, you're their friend. It's very much a brother-sister thing, which I think would surprise a lot of people. In Australia, there was a very strange port. They had a dial-a-sailor kind of thing where they could call and order a middie [as a guest]. If you wanted two that were between twenty and twenty-five you could put in your order and if they wanted to go, they'd go with you. Some kids ended up on some family schooner for the weekend. It was just a welcome to Sydney. I had an order put in for me. This man had seen me somewhere on the street and he called the ship repeatedly. But even if I had wanted to go, I wouldn't have been able to go by myself. There would have been three of them with me. To be sure that I was OK."

~~~

One of the joys of going to sea is the lack of intrusion from the outside world. There are no telephones ringing with unexpected calls, no doorbells, no sirens (other than Loreleis and mermaids), no garbage trucks, delivery vans, trailer trucks, leaf blowers, lawn mowers, jammed freeways, honking horns, motor cars, motorcycles, motor scooters, salesmen, saleswomen, Jehovah's witnesses, Mormon missionaries, Hari Krishnas, rock music (unless you want it), television, taxes, faxes or saxes (except in the cruise band). One can watch the glowing green phosphorescence boiling off the bow or churning in the ship's wake and be able to absorb the grandeur of it all without interruption. You can follow the path of an albatross as it effortlessly circumscribes the ship, gliding majestically on outstretched wings. There is only you, the ship and the great dome of the sky.

And then, there are the ports.

Each cruise had its unique highlights, its unusual incidents, depending on the ports of call. Some were memorable for the excitement and anticipation of foreign lands, others for the unexpected events. Reminiscences hopscotch ports and cruises over a score of years.

— Lynn Korwatch: "The first year, in Mexico, we had some major problems with kids buying drugs. It was serious enough that several kids were kicked out of the school because they found marijuana aboard.

"My second cruise we had some problems because of engine difficulties. There was concern about warping of turbine blades, and we stayed on the hook for about a week in Panama. Westinghouse sent out some experts to look at everything. It turned out there were no problems, but as a result we missed Carnival in Trinidad and were late in all our other ports."

— Bob Black: "We went from the Tonga Islands to Sydney, which was absolutely a marvelous liberty port. We were royally treated by the Royal Australian Navy. Then we transited inside the Great Barrier reef all the way up to Cairns. It was noteworthy because it was like riding on a mill pond. And, of course, the water was exceptionally clear and just huge schools of flying fish and dolphins escorting us every step of the way. Then to the Marshall Islands, and even though it's a U.S. territory or protectorate, it's a very poverty-stricken stretch of islands. Of course,

we were going through just a year after a typhoon which leveled the place. That stop was particularly noteworthy because we went in without a pilot or a tug and came out without a pilot or a tug. It was a really outstanding demonstration of Capt. Keever's ship handling skills.

"Weatherwise, we encountered a triple low pressure area north of Hawaii and were taking white water on the bridge. We took a forty-five degree roll. It trashed the engineering office, because it wasn't ready for sea.

"Then Seattle to Astoria. Coming in over the bar there were three ex-CMA grads who were pilots fighting over who was going to bring the *Bear* in. The one with the loudest voice won.

"Out of all of them, Astoria was the best liberty port. The town welcomed the middies and the ship. The American Legion and other fraternal orders provided us transportation all around. It was a nice community."

— Brandon Moser: "My first cruise was Long Beach, Lahaina, Cabo San Lucas, Long Beach, Sitka, Valdez, Glacier Bay, Juneau, Ketchikan and Eureka. We were also supposed to go to Victoria but that got canceled. It wasn't really a stellar introduction to cruises on the *Bear* because we'd all been led to believe there was a South American cruise, an Australian cruise, a Far East Cruise.

"We went to Kodiak, Alaska. I guess going to Russia earlier in the cruise had the same effect on a lot of other people as it did on me. The first thing I did was make a beeline to MacDonald's. There were about twenty middies ahead of me.

"It was there I stumbled across one of the old Washington State Ferries, the *Kalakala*, an old, silver, streamlined ferry. The *Kalakala* had been converted to a fish processor but had been abandoned about fifteen years before.

In Alaska the Golden Bear *is dwarfed by a glacier. Courtesy California Maritime Academy.*

Seeing that was kind of disappointing to me because in pictures it was so big, but in reality it was small and decrepit.

"There is a fish processor called the *Star of Kodiak*. It was a Liberty hull. There's no doubt about that. They identified it as an EC-2 Liberty hull in one of the tourist pamphlets.

"The thing about Alaska is you look up at night and see a phenomenal number of stars."

One of the great challenges of going to sea is that of the unexpected. One must always be ready for a crisis. Situations develop quickly and when they involve two several-thousand-ton ships moving through strong currents, the absolute importance of watchstanding and constant vigilance become clear.

Capt. Keever's shiphandling skills were severely tested on an early cruise as master of the *Golden Bear*.

— John Keever: "During my second cruise as master [1984] we had gone to Portland. Coming down the river I was standing in the back of the bridge watching the mate and the pilot and the students do their thing. The helmsman started sputtering. We were in a kind of a right hand turn and going around a corner and it turned out that the helm was stuck five degrees to the right. In fact, we were steering by telemotor and the helm was physically locked. You couldn't turn the wheel. So we shifted to electric steering and nothing happened. The training ship carries an after steering watch. Normally, we have a warrant officer and a first class engineer and a first class deck; deck to do the steering, the engineer to

In dress blues, CMA midshipmen await the word to go ashore on liberty. Courtesy California Maritime Academy.

shift over. It was in the evening about dinner time and the warrant officer had gone to dinner, leaving the first class engineer in charge. So I had the chief mate get on the telephone while I checked the chart and the position and worked with the steering on the bridge to take the control aft and put the rudder hard left. He did that about three times, he said, 'Take the control aft, put the rudder hard left.'

"The response was always, 'No, the rudder's not hard left, the rudder's five degrees right.' There was a communications gap. So, seeing that wasn't going to solve the problem, I put the engine full astern. We were doing turns for about fourteen knots with a speed over the ground of about seventeen knots, with

about three knots of current down the river. There was another little river or slough that came into the river at that point and we were turning off kind of towards a mud flat river entrance. The pilot was a trainee pilot. Did not have his state pilotage and was still working for that. Because we were a public vessel and we were free they could use him on us. He knew where the channel was but he didn't know where the banks were. It was dark. He kept saying, 'You're going to hit any time. You're going to hit any time.' Then he relinquished control to the master immediately when the ship failed. He said, 'I'm sorry, you'll have to take control until the ship is operating again.'

"When the ship got down to about ten knots I let go the port anchor hoping to sheer the ship to that side a little bit and had them put one shot at the water's edge. They got the anchor down and stopped but they had it stopped at about one shot in the hawse pipe. Somebody said, 'He said 'water's edge.' So they decided to open the brake and let a little more chain out. They never quite got the chain stopped again after that, but they had enough force on the brake trying to stop it that it slowed the ship down and it fetched up on the end. I think the Doppler log said about one and a half knots. We started making sternway. By that time they had managed to get steering control aft. I had them start heaving around on the anchor to get it a little shorter and just a few minutes later they called up and said they were done heaving on the anchor and they went on to explain that they were at eight shots and that was all because the chain had broken between the eighth and the seventh shot.

"So we were underway and now there's about thirty knots of wind on our port beam and we're floating down the river sideways at about three or four knots and there's an upbound vessel. So we have to back and fill two hundred seventy degrees because, obviously, with the wind on the port side, the ship isn't going to turn the hard way.

"We're kind of on a range and we're about to go around a forty-five degree bend in the river and I'm backing and filling with the pilot telling me I'm going to go aground at any time! I called the guy upbound. I asked him to slow down 'til I can get the ship around. I back and fill across this range trying to keep myself enough in the middle of the river to stay in deep water. We ended up pointing up the right direction heading down river and, shortly after, we got steering back up on the bridge and a couple of hours later picked up the bar pilot and we're out at sea.

"It was about midnight when we got out of the river and my adrenaline was still flowing so I didn't sleep a wink that night. But, with the exception of the loss of an anchor, which the Reserve Fleet gladly replaced, it was an interesting experience."

— Robert Stewart: "We were in American Samoa, and we had taken the ship to the dock but the dock was very close to the edge of the reef. We're taking a lot of surge and over the course of the first forty or fifty minutes we parted a back spring and we parted a breast line. It was decided that we would move the ship off the dock and move it out to anchor. By the time that this occurred, most of the midshipmen had gone ashore, so now we had three hundred midshipmen ashore and we took the ship with what people we had aboard and moved it out to anchor. So, imagine the concern from the first midshipmen coming back and the ship was gone.

"Once we got past that part of it, we had to run boats. The swell that was running in the harbor was even rougher outside and it was probably running eight feet. We had a gangway down and a float in the water. But we had to get these three hundred midshipmen back aboard. And because the ship was laying right to the wind, there was no lee, and we had this eight foot swell running down both sides. We put a line down. It was like a Tarzan movie where the line was down and it was knotted and the directions were, 'When the boat comes up to the top of its ride, you grab this line and as the boat drops away from you, you swing over (there was a gap of about three feet) and get on the bottom of the gangway and go.'

"One of our galley workers, one of the women, climbed up there, and didn't understand the directions or whatever and she went across as the boat was about halfway down and she couldn't get up onto the gangway. She was too low and she fell down on to the float and fell into the water. Here she was, in this gap, literally in the water between the ship and the float. Every time the sea came up the float hit against the ship. She had about six seconds to live before this thing squashed her. The third class midshipman standing at the bottom of the gangway jumped onto the float and into the water with her and pulled her down. And, of course, she was fighting for her life to get to the surface. She was scared to death being in that water. He pulled her down so that, above her, the float and the ship came together and then apart. They came back to the surface and we pulled them to the after end of the float and pulled both of them back.

"It could have been just tragic but for the reaction of the midshipman. I was really surprised that this guy actually had the wherewithal to get down off that gangway and get in the water and knew enough to pull down on this woman rather than try to help her up. Because I think that would have been the first reaction in a lot of people. And that would have caused a tragedy."

— Holly Fuerstenberg: "My first cruise we went to the South Pacific and the Philippines. We were in Fiji, and we hear this great reggae music. We're a bunch of teenagers and can't wait, let's go find the party. It was a demonstration. They were burning the American flags and we're standing there decked out in white, you couldn't miss us.

"When we were in the Philippines it was the fall of the Marcos regime. They were burning hotels that Americans were staying in. It really focused it. My horizons had broadened so quickly.

"After my first cruise I would get together with girl friends from high school and we were worlds apart. There was absolutely nothing that we had in common. They were very into their sororities, and oh, well, I belong to a fraternity? [Laugh] And they're interested more in their formals and colors for the spring dance. That's all well and good, but I was here [in the Far East] and I saw things happening and are you aware that this is going on in the world? Just totally worlds apart."

"Our pilot . . . had never been through that reef on anything other than a dugout canoe."

— Robert Stewart: "We went to one of the islands, around the west side of Fiji and we went up through the lagoon. Our pilot came aboard and he was going take the *Golden Bear* up through the reef. We find out in talking to this guy he had never been through that reef on anything other than a dugout canoe, but he was going to take the *Bear* up and lead us through there. He was successful but there was a lot of concern."

— John Keever: "That's one nice thing about being a training ship captain. As a commercial ship captain you generally drive from pilot station to pilot station. Because of the different kinds of places you go as a training ship captain and because of your public vessel status, a lot of times you're put in a position to do your own piloting, either by choice or by necessity. So you go into these ports that either don't have pilots or tugs or both and you have to do your own shiphandling. I always thought that's kind of a plus in being a training ship captain. And the interesting thing about that is when the conditions are nice and you're in a nice well-structured bay with piers that are built appropriately for docking and undocking and large tugboats are available, you have a pilot. When you go to some South Pacific port where the pier is only half as long as the ship and there's a lot of surge and a lot of onshore or offshore wind and no tugboats, then there are no pilots and the captain has to do it. I've been in that position several times and lived through it so I guess I must be OK."

In all the cruises and adventures in foreign ports, the students generally had a good time. But there was one terrible accident.

— John Keever: "The only student that's been killed was while on a training cruise in Guayaquil, Ecuador in 1977.[4] He was uptown in the afternoon with one of our early woman students and they were just walking across the street. He was talking to her and a bus turned the corner and the side mirror of the bus hit him in the head and knocked him down; the rear wheels ran over him.

"The young lady was thrust into shock because the traffic just kept right on going. She made her way back to the ship and I and a consular officer from the embassy went down

---

[4]   Actually, there were three others: the cadet lost at sea off the *Jamestown*, the menengitis incident in 1936 and just before World War II, while the ship was at Tiburon, a cadet fell from the mast top to the main deck and died. The effectiveness of CMA's safety program, which spans 120 years, is outstanding for a profession which is inherently dangerous.

to the intersection. Nothing was there so we started making the rounds of the emergency rooms in the hospitals.

"To approach a social public hospital from the emergency room entrance in Guayaquil, Ecuador is not a fun experience at all. The first two hospitals didn't know anything about it. When we got to the third hospital they immediately knew what we were looking for. Somebody had stopped and put him in the back of a pickup truck and taken him to the hospital. He was dead when he got there. We had to go through the process of arranging the repatriation of the body and we had to send a cadet with the body. That was a tragic experience.

"The bus driver disappeared. Drove the bus about a block down the street. Parked the bus full of people, got out and was never seen again. The risk of ending up in an Ecuadorian prison is so horrible that when something like that happens they just take off for the hills."

— Brandon Moser: "Pusan was very crowded. The captain decided we had to kill time because we were waiting for parts to our Inmarsat [satellite communication system] to arrive in Pusan. We went for a cruise in the Sea of Japan and had failed to tell the Japanese authorities we were coming. We passed by some pilot station at fifteen knots and the next thing you know we had a grey vessel behind us flying the Lima flag, meaning 'Stop Instantly.' They had a couple of guns trained on us. The Japanese Coast Guard pulled us over. We cleared it up with a couple of *Golden Bear* baseball hats.

"After Pusan came Vladivostok. That was kind of a special port for me. The Circle K Club, which is a college version of Kiwanis, had combined the efforts of all the service clubs in Vallejo and gathered up a twenty-foot container of food, toys, clothing and medicine for an orphanage in Vladivostok. I got to go along with the delivery of the container.

"First we had to get the container off the ship. We unloaded the container with the jumbo boom. The guards would not let the truck drive in to set the container on. We had to set the container on the dock, then use a portable crane to set it on the truck.

"Then Customs decided they wouldn't let the container in without a letter of approval. Ferguson [one of the ship's officers] went up to his room and wrote one out. Then they wanted the letter stamped, so he went back to his room and stuck a couple of Circle K foil stickers on it. They were happy with that. Then the Russian Mafia came aboard and wanted a payoff to get the container off the dock without opening it. So Ferguson paid them something like fifty dollars to make sure that didn't happen.

> *"Then the Russian Mafia came aboard and wanted a payoff . . ."*

"The orphanage put on a wonderful show for us, folk songs and dances. It was very touching. They have no sense of poverty. The people have little, but whatever they have they will share with you.

"We also toured the Russian Maritime Academy in Vladivostok. I was looking forward to seeing their electronic lab. When we got there it was all Furuno, Trimble, Sperry and Magnavox as far as the eye could see. I think I saw a Raytheon Radar in there, too.

"A surprising number of the students bought the typical fur hat for forty or fifty dollars from the scalpers on the streets. I was one of the few that found it was available for fifteen in the State store."

The 1978 training cruise included Noumea Harbor, New Caledonia and Suva, Fiji Islands. John Keever: "The ship had been stationed in the South Pacific most of the war. We made a port call in New Caledonia and it turned out that there were enough historians in New Caledonia that recognized that the ship had been there and they were certainly very pleased with the outcome of World War II and the U.S. involvement and so we had about a half a mile line of visitors trying to get on this

"To this day I can't look at Tabasco without thinking about the equator crossing ceremonies."

ship that had been in New Caledonia during the war."

Robert Stewart: "The *Golden Bear* had been in New Caledonia as the *Crescent City* in 1943 or '44 and one of the first people aboard was the mayor or the governor general or one of these people and he brought aboard a picture. He said, 'Here's a picture of the last time the *Golden Bear* was here': smoke in the sky, painted grey, guntubs on it. It was really pretty wild to think forty years later, here we are back again and these folks have pictures of this ship the last time we were here."

~~~

For the ship's officers and instructors the annual cruise involves far more than just traveling from port to port. They have to ensure that every aspect of the voyage is a learning experience. Often their methods are quite subtle. John Keever '70: "September first, 1982, I became captain. That had been

my goal working here at the school. Once I decided to stay in this field, I decided I wanted to be the master of the training ship. At this particular school that role had been a fairly significant one, it had been the number two administrator. And that helped keep the training ship very integrated with the program, professionally oriented. That position, besides requiring somebody with reasonably good mariner skills, shiphandling and navigation and seamanship, also requires somebody who has the ability to deal with people, both students and staff. What I had found over time, particularly with Captain Bowman and some of the others I've known, was their matter-of-fact, kind of gruff attitudes and the students' perception of the captain's position often caused a communications breakdown. The students were fearful of that position. So they would not learn anything from that person. Rather, they just tried to stay away and they were unable to observe very much what really went on.

"I tried to break down that barrier so the students felt comfortable about seeing what the master was doing, asking him questions, being involved in what was going on without breaking down the 'mystique' of the master. Of course, the more that you did, the harder that became to accomplish."

— Robert Stewart: "I think sometimes the hardest part is being trained as an officer and knowing that in certain situations there are certain things that need to be done. It's much like driving your car. When I see the red light I don't have to think about braking but I know I need to be stopped by this point and so I slow the car down and stop. And those responses are ingrained in your training and probably the hardest thing you have to do on the bridge with cadets is, don't do it, let them do it. When the lights come up and I see that I'm head-and-head with this guy, my immediate response is to lay out a new course and bring

As goodwill ambassador, the Golden Bear *finds itself constantly entertaining visitors. Here Capt. Keever explains the workings of the vessel to such a group. Courtesy California Maritime Academy.*

the ship right to meet it. No, no, NO, I can't do that. I have to wait for the midshipman. Some of them, you see the lights at eighteen miles and you suggest to the midshipman that a course change may be in order and what situation exists here with respect to the Rules of the Road.

"You ask questions, and at fourteen miles you ask questions, and at twelve miles you ask questions, and at eight miles you ask questions and at seven miles you begin to get very insistent in your questions and occasionally at four miles or three miles you finally have to give the order yourself. I think that's one of the hardest things for virtually any of the faculty members because we are all trained professionals and it's a reactive thing. You have to actually back off on your reactions and let the student do it whether it's on deck or on watch or whatever."

~~~

They didn't know it, but King Neptune's days on the *Golden Bear* were numbered. But, for a while at least, the tradition continued. Holly Fuerstenberg: "I thought it was fun. We hadn't crossed in two or three

years, so there weren't that many shellbacks on board. They'd start for three days out. It was just fun. We were wearing our clothes backwards. The day of the ceremony the tension was real high. It was really hot and they sprayed the fire hoses over the top of us so we were all nice and cool. They'd start us on the quarterdeck and trickle us down to the fantail and that's where they would hose us.

"You crawl up there onto the bow and they christen you with bunker C [fuel oil], they take a ladle and pour it over you. Then you'd see the royal barber and they'd clip something, either half your moustache or take a notch out of your bangs or something. From there they would put something in your mouth, I think it was Tabasco. To this day I can't look at Tabasco without thinking about the equator crossing ceremonies. Then you had to bow before the royal court. They had the sea baby and King Neptune and the sea hag. She had all this gunk and she was shoving her foot in my face so I kind of bit her toe. King Neptune gave me the blessing, and then the sea baby made me take the olive out of his belly button. But he took my face and just smeared it in the lard that's on his stomach. Then they send you off to the whale's asshole. That's a liferaft they have full of old garbage and seawater and God only knows what else. It's covered with a cargo net. You had to go under the cargo net to get out and if you were a special case they had a harness that they could put on you and keep pulling you back through. You really couldn't see when you got out of there 'cause of all the garbage. But then you get all cleaned up and we had a big barbecue and it was all in good fun. It was a rite of passage. It was a tradition.

"I have my certificate and I keep my card in my scrap book. I'm proud that I'm a shellback. But I don't think it's any different than any fraternity initiation or any sorority thing. It's just the way of the ancient mariner."

Lynn Korwatch: "My third year, it was the first time across the Equator in several years. The Neptune ceremony, I didn't want to go through it. My attitude was, this was silly, I don't want to go through it. An instructor who I respected pulled me aside and said, 'You should, it will build a sense of camaraderie.'

"And I didn't regret it. The night before there was some kind of general hazing activities. The upper classmen told us the women were going to be singled out, but I didn't get that sense. There wasn't anything sexually specific in the ceremony. It involved crawling on your hands and knees down the gauntlet while they swatted you with fire hoses. Then you had to kind of roll around in a lot of garbage. Then there was a little ceremony with the court and then you were washed down by a fire hose. And that was it. It wasn't nearly as humiliating as I thought it was going to be."

On one cruise in the late 1980s, however, some of the activities surrounding the Crossing the Line ceremonies got out of hand and some cadets crossed a line into inappropriate behavior. The ensuing brouhaha put an end to the tradition.

Brandon Moser: "The Neptune ceremony in question was in '89, maybe 1990. Although it was never said in so many words, that led to the downfall of the superintendent."

The captain was also relieved of his command and strict guidelines were laid down on all future ceremonies; in effect, there would never again be a Neptune ceremony on the *Golden Bear*.

Bob Black recalled the tepid observance which took place a year or two afterward: "There was no Crossing the Line ceremony and that was an offshoot of the earlier lawsuit by a student over some alleged improprieties in the way the ceremony was conducted. We were simply given our shellback cards. That was disappointing.

"Probably the biggest ceremony was everyone was waiting by the toilets, flushing them when we crossed the equator, to see if they would swirl the other way."

Holly Fuerstenberg: "I'm really sorry that the tradition's gone. It should have continued."

The times were changing in other ways, as well. For the first time in its history, and unique among maritime academies, CMA was headed by a woman, Dr. Mary Lyons, who guided the Academy into the California State University system as its 22nd campus. A major accomplishment in and of itself, it is also noteworthy because it put CMA under the protective umbrella of that system, eliminating the funding problems the college had as an individual entity.

Many of the older military traditions gradually faded out after CMA became a four-year school. Marching, drill and hazing diminished to the point of nonexistence. Lynn Korwatch: "There was a little hazing, but at the time the school was faced with the challenges of getting students to attend. There was some hazing during indoctrination week, a lot of marching around and fire drills in the middle of the night and that type of thing but it slacked off fairly quickly.

"We were somewhat regimented. We had to march once a week with the Marines but that lasted only the first year. I think the Marines gave up on us. At the time we had never really been exposed to that and then along came the marines and we couldn't understand them. It turned out to be kind of a

---

TUITION

In 1993 the tuition for California Residents was $7,868; for those out of state, $13,458.

joke. They'd shout something and we had no idea what they were saying."

By the 1990s the only semblance to militarism lay in the wearing of uniforms and a weakened tradition of giving demerits. Brandon Moser: "Every year they go through what they call Orientation Week, that's the more politically correct term for it. Previously it was known as Indoctrination Week. You get introduced to classmates, learn watch standing. But there was no organized hazing. Just silly little pranks. By my time even the nickname 'Gar' was no longer used for freshmen, gar being an unattractive fish."

Bob Black: "CMA seems to be notoriously free of hazing. There's no physical abuse like at other academies. None that I was aware of. If it existed it was more in the nature of personality conflicts and expressed by practical jokes like buckets of water leaning on doors and that sort of stuff."

As the old traditions waned, they were replaced with newer ones. A new jargon, indicative of the times, evolved. Holly Fuerstenberg: "There is a 'middie-ese,' a language that's spoken aboard the ship and the campus. 'Racking' is sleeping, 're-racking' is taking a nap. 'Rack burns' are the pillow marks on your face, you slept too hard. I was brought up that I was a middie. Girls are middie-chicks or midship-chicks.

"I wouldn't understand the kids from So-Cal — the surfer language. It took me a week to figure out what 'gnarly' was. Every division picks up one word. In 2-D and 3-D everything was just totally 'gnarly.' We had a guy from the East Coast and everything from our division was just totally 'wicked.' 'Wicked, twisted' and they always have a new term for how drunk they were. 'The box' was the old Res hall. Or 'in the condos,' the new Res hall. And then there's different parts on the ship like my division was 1-D, they had the main

berthing area and they also had 'the cage, the rat's nest, the Ritz' and 'the head's head.' And those are all little sections. 4-E had Casa Grande."

Walking through the second *Golden Bear* one finds murals in the passageways and common rooms painted by the cadets. They are bright, colorful histories of the ship's voyages. Brandon Moser: "The murals really do tell the stories of the cruises. From my first cruise to Alaska there was an eight-by-ten mural with a totem pole with characters. Each division did one mural per cruise."

. . . unique among maritime academies, CMA was headed by a woman.

"My senior year they introduced the hard hat rule, which made everybody angry. But the hard hat was a good platform for antlers for the antler dance. That started on Capt. Craig's [master from 1977-1982] last cruise. The students wanted to do something that would embarrass the captain in front of the pilot. They came up with the antler dance. The academy tried to stop it by announcing that the next year everyone would get fifty demerits if they did that. Well, the following year those that had too many demerits only watched from the flying bridge. But they were laughing so much that they jumped up and down and that's how <u>that</u> started. The idea is you run fore to aft, wearing a set of antlers, while going under the Golden Gate Bridge."

Bob Black: "The antler ceremony consists of seniors, solely, who are coming home on their last cruise. It takes place as the ship comes under the Golden Gate Bridge. Seniors try to outdo each other in making up large antlers which they wear and then they run around the deck screaming and wearing their antlers at precisely the time the ship crosses under the Gate."

Brandon Moser: "Then you go up to the flying bridge and jump up and down and make as much noise as possible. It died down the last cruise I made. It's probably not done any more.

"Another tradition is to wear a tie on watch. Someone started the idea that your last engine room or your last bridge watch on the *Golden Bear*, you wear a necktie. Most just wore a black tie, but I know of one middie who wore an Alcatraz ascot. It's for the last watch on the *Bear* and the last formal occasion."

One tradition that continued, however, was the role of cadets or midshipmen as ambassadors for the State of California and for the United States. Robert Stewart: "When we go places, people roll out the red carpet. We

went to Australia and we were invited to go down and play golf at the Royal Australian Golf Club in Sydney. The Australian-American Club turned out with a tremendous reception and everything for us. Bitong, Indonesia. We went there. It was just a little port. I guess we were the first American ship in there in thirty years. They turned out with bands, two or three bands on the dock, every dignitary they could round up, native dances. We had the same thing in Fiji. We got out there and there were gifts, clam shells and things like this, from the chief. And the dancers, the native dancers were aboard. They put on a show on the quarterdeck that was just amazing to me. And we had that kind of reception, you know. Even when we went to Alaska, in Juneau, besides the Southeast Alaska Pilots providing a pilot and tugs and a dock, Princess Cruises donated

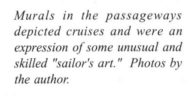

Murals in the passageways depicted cruises and were an expression of some unusual and skilled "sailor's art." Photos by the author.

The antler ceremony, one of the more unusual rites of passage of Cal Maritime seafarers. Courtesy California Maritime Academy.

the use of tour busses to the midshipmen for a day so that they could go to the Mendenhall glacier. There were receptions in Ketchican, there were receptions in Eureka. They rolled out the red carpet, put out a tremendous feast for us. And I don't know that we have been anywhere where we have not been really positively received. We've always been, really, really well-received no matter where we've gone."

Holly Fuerstenberg: "Being in uniform you stand out, especially being a girl. So you get a lot of attention and people want to know where you're from and why you're doing this. You have to be ready to not only explain yourself but explain your school and at times explain the merchant marine and what's drawn you to it. So the ship's an ambassador but then any time you're in a uniform or any time you come off that ship, you represent the ship and the school and the United States.

"A lot of them aren't used to seeing a woman in the role. I was CMA's first female student body president. I was the Corps admin officer. One time I was leaving the ship in Hong Kong, all ready to go for liberty and the commandant turned me around and told me to go get in my uniform 'cause George Schultz was

coming and I was serving lunch. Well, OK. A lot of times I felt like the CMA poster child. Here's a girl. There she is, we got one, see, there she is. Usually I didn't mind."

John Keever: "One cruise we were scheduled to go to Shanghai. This was early on in relations with the Chinese government. We were in Hong Kong prior to departing for Shanghai and just at that time the Chinese government finally figured out that they had invited us to come over the period of Chinese New Year. They decided they wouldn't be able to accommodate us during Chinese New Year because nobody worked. So they wanted us to change our schedule. That wasn't possible at that late date so we diverted to Manila. That was during the time that the hotels were all being burned down in Manila, an anti-Marcos move. So there was some parental concern and when we got there you couldn't even tell there was any problem.

"We were in Cairns, Australia just a few months before the big Coral Sea celebration was going on and they were going to send down some current navy ships for that celebration. In fact, the *Golden Bear* had been one of the ships in the battle of the Coral Sea, but it wasn't able to be there [at the celebration]."

Being a good guest also means reciprocating the hospitality. John Keever: "Because we were always trying to function in the public vessel light we generally had at least one event and sometimes several events in port, in addition to having public visiting, if it was a port where public visiting was allowed. So the embassy would usually prepare an invitation list and distribute invitations prior to our arrival, to the appropriate government officials and private officials who were contributing to the free or reduced port costs that the ship was enjoying. This was pretty common on a Navy ship and we'd have a luncheon or an evening reception or a dinner and generally there'd be

Taken in February 1994, these photographs show the Golden Bear *before her penultimate cruise. Although old and becoming obsolete, she still looks better than when put into service in 1971. Photos by George Bonawit.*

some kind of return social function or the master would be asked to speak at some function while you were there. So there was a fair amount of socializing. If there was a maritime or naval academy in the area we usually tried to have some kind of exchange with that academy so our students saw whatever was taking place in that country. So the in-port time as master was pretty much taken up with business during the days and early evenings."

By the late 1980s it was apparent the *Golden Bear* had served her time. She was old and increasingly costly and difficult to repair. Her steam turbine was outmoded as a training engine for future mariners; the industry was shifting to diesel engines. The search began for a replacement.

John Keever: "That ship [*Crescent City*] came out with twenty-five years in the Reserve Fleet. It served as a training ship and made twenty-plus cruises and may make a few more relatively seaworthy runs. It has gone to sea for its twenty cruises without a long list of outstanding 835's.[5] It took a lot of hard work

to get it there and a lot of pushing because there weren't dollars.

"I learned a lot about the ship. I've done everything on that ship from chipping out old decking to laying new decking, laying tile, putting in new overheads, pulling wire, patching holes in bulkheads. You name it, I've probably done it on there, in addition to being its captain and navigating it and taking charge of the people on board."

Robert Stewart, professor: "I think the attention that is paid to schoolship cadets is so far superior in certain areas. Our students, the schoolship students, get a tremendous amount of faculty interaction. You stand on the bridge with a faculty member who teaches you classes. So when you discuss Rules of the Road, the instructor is discussing that with you as you see lights on the horizon. In that aspect, in the interaction between students and faculty and the attention paid to students, I think the schoolship experience is far superior to any commercial experience you can get.

"But the limitation that I see on the schoolship concept is there are things you just

---

[5] When a U.S.-flag merchant ship is inspected by the Coast Guard and they find something that can't be repaired immediately, it is recorded on a form numbered "835." This puts the owner on notice to have the repair done and records the fact that there was a problem and what it was.

absolutely cannot get. Labor relations. There is nothing like going on a ship and finding out that the ship is MMP, MEBA, SUP, MFOW, MC&S and ROU.[6] There's six unions aboard and today's a holiday for four of them and tomorrow's a holiday for the other two and you know the management of that process, the settlement of conflicts within the labor relations structure. That's something that students don't get on the training ship. Another area is the cargo operations. We load some cargo, stores and boats and things like that on the training ship, but that is not indicative of the industry today. Containerization, eight-hour port calls, tankers, lightering, are things that the student cannot possibly see aboard the training ship and I think those are important.

"Then there's all the business, because shipping is a business. Payroll, overtime, budgeting, ordering, requisitions, all of these things that chief mates do, second mates do, masters do, on a daily basis, that the ship's officers on the training ship do, but that students never become involved with. So, I think those are big areas where the commercial cruise experience that the Kings Point cadets have gotten for a long time is important to give our cadets. Because if they did three cruises on the *Bear* they would never get that. That's why just recently the deck department has gone to a two and one scenario. Our students will do what we will call freshman cruise on the training ship. They will do a sophomore cruise on a commercial ship. And they will come back to the training ship in their junior year. And I think that's a good mix."

Lynn Korwatch: "The thing that strikes me was really the camaraderie. I think one of the advantages of the training ship situation versus the Kings Point-type training[7] is you're all in that together. You go through the storms and the watches and you're tired and you go through all that together and you develop a sense of family."

Brandon Moser: "It was kind of sad for me when I read that they finally actually had retired the *Golden Bear*. If you want to get really poignant about the matter, it kind of really represented the passing of the American merchant marine. The last representative of that era retired. World War II being more or less the heyday of the merchant marine, and she was the next-to-last representative of that era, the last being the *Jeremiah O'Brien*."

The *Golden Bear* ex-*Crescent City* made her last cruise on May 5, 1995. Her swan song included: Nawilliwilli, Hawaii; Hilo, Hawaii; San Francisco, Mazatlan, Mexico; Cabo San Lucas, Mexico; San Diego, Coos Bay, Oregon and Vallejo.

On September 16, 1994 the *USNS Maury* was officially transferred to the California Maritime Academy as the third *Golden Bear*.

On July 1, 1995 the California Maritime Academy joined the California State University system as the 22nd campus.

---

[6] Masters, Mates and Pilots; Marine Engineers Beneficial Association; Sailor's Union of the Pacific; Marine Firemen, Oilers and Watertenders; Marine Cooks and Stewards; and Radio Officer's Union.

[7] The U.S. Merchant Marine Academy at Kings Point, New York does not have a training ship. Kings Point students spend a year at sea on commercial vessels.

PART III

THE TWENTY-FIRST CENTURY

CHAPTER 7

THE *GOLDEN BEAR* III

The *Golden Bear* III comes into service in relatively new condition after operating six years for the Military Sealift Command. Laid down as the USNS *Maury* (T-AGS 39) in 1988 she was the first Navy oceanographic deep survey ship built from the keel up for that purpose. Her duties were limited to deep-sea charting. One of the peculiarities of the concept was that when under way the ship required 7,339 tons of ballast water to ride and operate effectively. Her normal payload was only a few tons in the form of the AS/SQN-17 Bottom Topography Survey System (BOTOSS).[1] The design was criticized by the Navy as being inefficient and the ship was deactivated in September 1994.

The *Maury* was transferred to CMA in that same month. There followed several months during which the ship underwent the by-now-familiar task of conversion to a training vessel. Midshipmen and instructors went eagerly aboard, using the renovation as an opportunity to learn ship modification procedures while actually doing them. Needed equipment was transferred from the old *Golden Bear*. Machinery, piping, electrical circuits and dozens of other internal systems were modified for training ship use. Classrooms were created, dormitories constructed, meeting rooms fabricated.

The student body was quick to adopt, and adapt to, the new ship. Whether the passageway murals will continue remains to be seen, but the vessel has already acquired a nickname. Brandon Moser '95: "The new *Golden Bear*, the 'Square Bear.' Aka two boxes on a barge."

The *Golden Bear* III successfully completed her sea trials during the weekend of April 27-28, 1996 and departed on May 14 for her first cruise as a training ship. Ports of call were: San Diego, Long Beach, Cabo San Lucas, Seattle and Vallejo.

~~~

The third *Golden Bear* will carry the legacy of the school into the twenty-first century. It is a proud heritage that reflects the ever-more-rapidly-changing demands of a modern world. The school has always mirrored both the state of the art in the maritime

---

[1] *Proceedings*, April 1996. p. 109.

Underway, the Maury *cuts a fine wake while still under MSC colors. It seems odd to see a training ship without booms or cargo handling gear. But the newest* Golden Bear *accurately mirrors the state of the maritime industry in the 1990s. Modern ships have no cargo handling gear on board. All dry cargo is containerized and loaded and discharged with shore-based cranes. Courtesy California Maritime Academy.*

industry and the state of the society in which she operated. Sail gave way to steam which gave way to diesel; the sextant and pelorus were replaced by doppler logs and satellites. The first students were the children of the Gold Rush, then came the children of the Depression and World War II, then the children of the turbulent '60s and '70s and, finally, the casual, questing generation of today. The Nautical School/Maritime Academy matured beyond her trade school beginnings to achieve academic accreditation and then acceptance into the State University system.

In a voyage that began in the 19th century, expanded in the 20th, and now looks toward the 21st century, the California Maritime Academy and its training ships have stayed on course. Both carry with them the hope and the responsibility of the future. And as the class of '00 (2000) enters the Academy, they carry on the vision the Mechanics' Deliberative Assembly of San Francisco first set forth in 1875:

> To train officers for a career in
> the merchant naval service.

~~~

Taken in June of 1995, the Maury *is in drydock for conversion to the* Golden Bear. *Photo by George Bonawit.*

From past to present and into the future. The Golden Bear *caught at the moment of transition — "US Naval Ship" remains from the* Maury *while "Golden Bear" has just been welded in. Photo by George Bonawit.*

Appendix A
Swab Rules
of the
California Nautical School

We, the cadet corps of the California Nautical School, being united by divine providence into a social, economic and spiritual unity and believing that:

Whereas-

All third classmen entering this institution with the avowed intention of advancing Nation, State, School and self in the maritime industries, are of lamentable necessity lacking in that integral quality of mental manipulation necessary to success, and:

Whereas-

Said third classmen, being weak of mind, but willing, might prosper by prodigious effort and industrious emulation of noteworthy example, and:

Whereas-

The second classmen, being endowed with ability and a great kindness of heart, having in mind the eventual positions of said third classmen in the maritime industries as representatives of American Youth and the products of a noble institution,

Therefore-

Be it resolved, by the cadet corps assembled, that a system of "Swab Rules" for the proper conduct of third classmen, be created, and be it further resolved that each and every third classman entering the California Nautical School be equipped and acquainted with said "Swab Rules" and be it further resolved that each and every hereinbefore mentioned third classman at all times conduct himself in a manner befitting his station in life, and ever remember the motto he represents —"Servility-Simplicity-Chastity".

Rules.

1. This set of rules and the preamble shall be memorized immediately by each third classman, and he must be able to repeat any or all, by number upon the request of an upper classman.

2. Third classmen shall be termed "Swabs", they must never, at any time, fraternize with upper classmen.

3. They shall use "Sir," and "Mister" when addressing upper classmen; and shall render the

193

hand salute when meeting them off the reservation.

4. The after ladder into the berth deck shall not be trespassed upon by swabs.

5. They shall choose mess table seats at the outboard extremity of the benches, and must refrain from unnecessary conversation during meals.

6. The school's recreational equipment may be used only when not in use by upper classmen.

7. They shall uncover in the mess deck at all times, except when marching to mess, under arms, or actually on watch.

8. When necessary for use by upper classmen, chairs in the recreation room aboard ship shall be relinquished promptly.

9. Neckerchiefs shall be worn with a small, neat knot, tied through the becket on the jumpers.

10. They shall always, when at the base, go around the outer stanchion of the gantry, opposite the gangway, when coming aboard or leaving the ship.

11. Hats and caps must be worn squared at all times.

12. Attempting the creation of musical expression with anything other than an approved musical instrument is prohibited at all times.

13. The possession and use of any device for the creation of artificial light shall not be tolerated at any time.

14. Their representation in the engine room shall never ring the bell.

15. They shall conduct themselves in a gentlemanly manner at all times, avoid the use of profane and bawdy language, and refrain from reading obscene literature.

16. They shall speak coherently without gum, cigarettes, or any other foreign matter in their mouths, when addressing others.

17. Polar jackets and raincoats must be worn "collar down".

18. They shall clear passageways upon perceiving the approach of an upper classman by the use of the phrase "make way".

19. They shall carry at all times a regulation box of matches, reasonably full, for the use of upper classmen.

20. They shall not polish the apple with any of the upper classmen in any manner whatsoever.

21. They shall cheerfully respect the unwritten swab rules.

22. They shall attend all social and athletic functions when invited.

23. They shall cooperate with the second class in making the education program for swabs a success.

24. They shall willingly volunteer to show visitors about the ship, and shall equip themselves to do so intelligently.

25. They shall learn immediately the definitions of "cadet" and "swab".

APPENDIX B
CRUISES OF THE TRAINING SHIPS

—

SUPERINTENDENTS

Jamestown:

1876 — H. Glass, master.
San Francisco, California
Honolulu, Sandwich Islands
San Francisco, California

1877 — H. Glass, master
San Francisco, California
Hilo, Sandwich Islands
Lahaina, Sandwich Islands
Honolulu, Sandwich Islands
San Francisco, California

California State:

1931-32 — E. Topp, master.
Tiburon, California
Balboa, Canal Zone
St. Elmo's Bay, Panama
Callao, Peru

Valparaiso, Chile
Buenos Aires, Argentina
Montevideo, Uruguay
Rio de Janeiro, Brazil
Port of Spain, Trinidad
Hampton Roads, Virginia
Washington, D.C.
New York, New York
Cristobal, Canal Zone
San Diego, California
Los Angeles, California
Santa Barbara, California
Tiburon, California

1932-33 — E. Topp, master.
Tiburon, California
Honolulu, Territory of
  Hawaii
Apra, Guam
Manila, Philippines
Singapore, Malaysia

Colombo, Ceylon
Suez, Egypt
Alexandria, Egypt
Naples, Italy
Capri, Italy
Villefranche, France
Barcelona, Spain
Gibraltar
Funchal, Madeira
Curaçao, Dutch West
  Indies
Cristobal, Canal Zone
San Diego, California
Los Angeles, California
Santa Barbara, California
Tiburon, California

1934 — R.C. Dwyer, master.[1]
Tiburon, California
Crescent City, California
Eureka, California

---

[1] Newspaper and magazine accounts of the era show Richard Dwyer as master of the ship. However, as an engineer he did not have a master's license. George Barkley, as a licensed master, was the technical captain of the ship with Richard Dwyer acting as staff captain.

Monterey, California
Port San Luis, California
San Pedro, California
San Diego, California
Tiburon, California

1935 — R.C. Dwyer, master.
Tiburon, California
Hilo, Territory of Hawaii
Lahaina, T.H.
Honolulu, T.H.
San Diego, California
Long Beach, California
Santa Barbara, California
Stockton, California
Tiburon, California

1936 — R.C. Dwyer, master.
Tiburon, California
San Pedro, California
San Diego, California
Acapulco, Mexico
Balboa, Canal Zone
Cartagena, Colombia
Vera Cruz, Mexico
Houston, Texas
Cristobal, Canal Zone
San Diego, California
Long Beach, California
Santa Barbara, California
Tiburon, California

1937 — R.C. Dwyer, master.
Tiburon, California
Papeete, Tahiti
Auckland, New Zealand
Melbourne, Australia
Sydney, Australia
Suva, Fiji Islands
Pago Pago, American
  Samoa
Honolulu, Territory of
  Hawaii
San Diego, California

Long Beach, California
Tiburon, California

1938 — N.E. Nichols, master.
Tiburon, California
Honolulu, Territory of
  Hawaii
Hilo, T.H.
Acapulco, Mexico
Mazatlan, Mexico
San Diego, California
Long Beach, California
Santa Barbara, California
Tiburon, California

1939 — N.E. Nichols, master.
Tiburon, California
Long Beach, California
San Diego, California
La Union, Salvador
Balboa, Canal Zone
Callao, Peru
Balboa, Canal Zone
San Diego, California
Long Beach, California
Santa Barbara, California
Tiburon, California

1940 — N.E. Nichols, master.
Tiburon, California
San Diego, California
Acapulco, Mexico
Balboa, Canal Zone
Havana, Cuba
San Juan, Puerto Rico
Miami, Florida
Newport News, Virginia
Washington, D.C.
Cristobal, Canal Zone
San Diego, California
Long Beach, California
Santa Barbara, California
Tiburon, California

1941 — N.E. Nichols, master.
Tiburon, California
Long Beach, California
San Diego, California
Balboa, Canal Zone
Callao, Peru
Stockton, California.
Tiburon, California

1942-45. The training ship
confined her cruises to the San
Francisco Bay Area due to
World War II. During that time
her master was C.B. Mayo.

Golden State:

1946 — L. Martin, master
Vallejo, California
San Pedro, California
San Diego, California
Acapulco, Mexico
Balboa, Canal Zone
Callao, Peru
Valparaiso, Chile
Balboa, Canal Zone
Long Beach, California
Santa Barbara, California
Vallejo, California

Golden Bear I:

1947 — R. Swany, master
Vallejo, California
Long Beach, California
San Diego, California
Balboa, Canal Zone
Vera Cruz, Mexico
New Orleans, Lousiana
Kingston, Jamaica
Cristobal, Canal Zone
San Diego, California
Long Beach, California
Santa Barbara, California

Monterey, California
San Francisco, California
Oakland, California
Stockton, California
Vallejo, California

1948 — R. Swany, master
Vallejo, California
Stockton, California
Oakland, California
San Francisco, California
Long Beach, California
San Diego, California
Balboa, Canal Zone
Gibraltar
Marseilles, France
Genoa, Italy
Naples, Italy
Piraeus, Greece
Algiers, Algeria
Funchal, Madeira
Cristobal, Canal Zone
San Diego, California
Long Beach, California
Santa Barbara, California
Oakland, California
Vallejo, California

1949 — R. Swany, master
Vallejo, California
Callao, Peru
Valparaiso, Chile
Balboa, Canal Zone
Acapulco, Mexico
San Diego, California
Long Beach, California
Santa Barbara, California
Oakland, California
Vallejo, California

1950 — R. Swany, master
Vallejo, California
Oakland, California
Long Beach, California

Balboa, Canal Zone
Houston, Texas
New Orleans, Louisiana
St. Thomas, Virgin Islands
Curaçao, Dutch West Indies
Cristobal, Canal Zone
Balboa, Canal Zone
Acapulco, Mexico
San Diego, California
Long Beach, California
Santa Barbara, California
Oakland, California
Vallejo, California

1951 — R. Swany, master
Vallejo, California
Portland, Oregon
Seattle, Washington
Vancouver, British Columbia
Honolulu, Territory of
  Hawaii
Hilo, T.H.
Acapulco, Mexico
San Diego, California
Long Beach, California
Santa Barbara, California
Oakland, California
Vallejo, California

1952 — R. Swany, master
Vallejo, California
Manzanillo, Mexico
Callao, Peru
San José, Guatemala
Acapulco, Mexico
San Diego, California
Long Beach, California
Santa Barbara, California
Vallejo, California

1953 — R. Swany, master
Vallejo, California
Hilo, Territory of Hawaii

Pago Pago, American Samoa
Lahaina, T.H.
Honolulu, T.H.
San Diego, California
Long Beach, California
Santa Barbara, California
Oakland, California
Vallejo, California

1954 — R. Swany, master
Vallejo, California
Los Angeles, California
Callao, Peru
Valparaiso, Chile
Balboa, Canal Zone
Acapulco, Mexico
San Diego, California
Long Beach, California
Oakland, California
Vallejo, California

1955 — R. Swany, master
Vallejo, California
Honolulu, Territory of
  Hawaii
Papeete, Tahiti
Acapulco, Mexico
San Diego, California
Long Beach California
Santa Barbara, California
Vallejo, California

1956 — R. Swany, master.
Vallejo, California
San Francisco, California
San Pedro, California
Balboa, Canal Zone
Acapulco, Mexico
San Diego, California
Long Beach, California
Santa Barbara, California
Vallejo, California

1957 — R. Swany, master
Vallejo, California

Acapulco, Mexico
Balboa, Canal Zone
Manzanillo, Mexico
San Diego, California
Long Beach, California
Santa Barbara, California
Monterey, California
Vallejo, California

1958 — J. Anderson, master
Vallejo, California
Richmond, California
Galapagos Islands, Ecuador
Callao, Peru
Balboa, Canal Zone
San Diego, California
Long Beach, California
Santa Barbara, California
Vallejo, California

1959 — E. Turpin
Vallejo, California
Martinez, California
Portland, Oregon
Seattle, Washington
Vancouver, British Columbia
Santa Catalina, California
San Diego, California
Long Beach, California
Santa Barbara, California
Vallejo, California

1960 — E. Turpin, master.
Vallejo, California
Richmond, California
San Francisco, California
Balboa, Canal Zone
Kingston, Jamaica
Cristobal, Canal Zone
San Diego, California
Long Beach, California
Santa Barbara, California
Vallejo, California

1961 — C. Bowman, master
Vallejo, California
Richmond, California
Papeete, Tahiti
Pago Pago, American Samoa
Hilo, Hawaii
Pearl Harbor, Hawaii
Honolulu, Hawaii
San Diego, California
Long Beach, California
Port Hueneme, California
Vallejo, California

1962 — C. Bowman, master
Vallejo, California
San Francisco, California
Galapagos Islands, Ecuador
Callao, Peru
Buenaventura, Colombia
Acapulco, Mexico
San Diego, California
Long Beach, California
Monterey, California
Vallejo, California

1963 — C. Bowman, master
Vallejo, California
Balboa, Canal Zone
Port of Spain, Trinidad
Rio de Janeiro, Brazil
Curaçao, Dutch West Indies
Cristobal, Canal Zone
Acapulco, Mexico
San Diego, California
San Pedro, California
Long Beach, California
Vallejo, California

1964 — C. Bowman, master
Vallejo, California
Galapagos Islands, Ecuador
Callao, Peru
Papeete, Tahiti
Galapagos Islands, Ecuador

Guayaquil, Ecuador
Cocos Island, Costa Rica
San Diego, California
Long Beach, California
Vallejo, California

1965 — C. Bowman, master
Vallejo, California
Honolulu, Hawaii
Manila, Philippines
Hong Kong
Yokohama, Japan
Vallejo, California

1966 — C. Bowman, master
Vallejo, California
Balboa, Canal Zone
Carenage Bay, Trinidad
Rio de Janeiro, Brazil
Curaçao, Dutch West Indies
Cristobal, Canal Zone
Acapulco, Mexico
San Diego, California
Vallejo, California

1967 — C. Bowman, master
Vallejo, California
San Pedro, California
Galapagos Islands, Ecuador
Valparaiso, Chile
Callao, Peru
Balboa, Canal Zone
Acapulco, Mexico
San Diego, California
Long Beach, California
Vallejo, California

1968 — C. Bowman, master
Vallejo, California
Honolulu, Hawaii
Papeete, Tahiti
Acapulco, Mexico
San Diego, California

Long Beach, California
Vallejo, California

1969 — C. Bowman, master
Vallejo, California
Balboa, Canal Zone
Cristobal, Canal Zone
Port of Spain, Trinidad
Rio de Janeiro, Brazil
Curaçao, Dutch West Indies
Cristobal, Canal Zone
Acapulco, Mexico
San Diego, California
Vallejo, California

1970 — C. Bowman, master
Vallejo, California
Long Beach, California
Papeete, Tahiti
Auckland, New Zealand
Sydney, Australia
Suva, Fiji Islands
Hilo, Hawaii
Vallejo, California

Golden Bear **II**:

1971 — C. Bowman, master
Vallejo, California
San Diego, California
Honolulu, Hawaii
Seattle Washington
Vallejo, California

1972 — W.H. Aguilar, master.
Vallejo, California
Long Beach, California
Balboa, Canal Zone
St. Thomas, Virgin Islands
New Orleans, Lousiana
Curaçao, Dutch West Indies
Cristobal, Canal Zone
Balboa, Canal Zone

Galapagos Islands, Ecuador
Acapulco, Mexico
San Diego, California
Vallejo, California

1973 — W.H. Aguilar, master.
Vallejo, California
San Diego, California
Papeete, Tahiti
Auckland, New Zealand
Sydney, Australia
Suva, Fiji Islands
Hilo, Hawaii
Long Beach, California
Vallejo, California

1974 — W.H. Aguilar, master.
Vallejo, California
Long Beach, California
San Diego, California
Acapulco, Mexico
Mazatlan, Mexico
Kahului, Hawaii
Honolulu, Hawaii
Seattle, Washington
Portland, Oregon
Vallejo, California

1975 — W.H. Aguilar, master.
Vallejo, California
Long Beach, California
Amapala, Honduras
Balboa, Canal Zone
Cristobal, Canal Zone
Curaçao, Dutch West Indies
Port of Spain, Trinidad
Cristobal, Canal Zone
Balboa, Canal Zone
Acapulco, Mexico
San Diego, California
Vallejo, California

1976 — W.H. Aguilar, master
Vallejo, California
San Clemente Island,
 California
Long Beach, California
Papeete, Tahiti
Auckland, New Zealand
Honolulu, Hawaii
San Diego, California
Vallejo, California

1977 — W.D. Craig, master
Vallejo, California
San Clemente Island, California
Los Angeles, California
Ajacutla, El Salvador
Guayaquil, Ecuador
Callao, Peru
Acapulco, Mexico
Puerto Vallarta, Mexico
San Diego, California
Vallejo, California

1978 — W.D. Craig, master
Vallejo, California
San Clemente Island, California
Los Angeles, California
Honolulu, Hawaii
Lahaina, Hawaii
Noumea, New Caledonia
Suva, Fiji Islands
Hilo, Hawaii
San Diego, California
Los Angeles, California
Vallejo, California

1979 — W.D. Craig, master
Vallejo, California
Sacramento, California
San Diego, California
Balboa, Canal Zone
Cristobal, Canal Zone

New Orleans, Lousiana
Cristobal, Canal Zone
Balboa, Canal Zone
Mazatlan, Mexico
Seattle, Washington
Portland, Oregon
Vallejo, California

1980 — W.D. Craig, master
Vallejo, California
San Diego, California
Isla Chechos, Mexico
Manzanillo, Mexico
Callao, Peru
Puntarenas, Costa Rica
Acapulco, Mexico
San Diego, California
Vallejo, California

1981 — W.D. Craig, master.
Vallejo, California
Lahaina, Hawaii
Honolulu, Hawaii
Nukúalofa, Tonga Islands
Auckland, New Zealand
Pago Pago, American Samoa
Honolulu, Hawaii
Vallejo, California

1982 — W.D. Craig, master.
Vallejo, California
Sacramento, California
Isla Cedros, Mexico
San Diego, California
Ensenada, Mexico
Balboa, Canal Zone
Lazaro Cardenás, Mexico
San Diego, California
Seattle, Washington
Vallejo, California

1983 — J.M. Keever, master
Vallejo, California
Long Beach, California
Cabo San Lucas, Mexico

Papeete, Tahiti
Hilo, Hawaii
Lahaina, Hawaii
Vallejo, California

1984 — J.M. Keever, master
Vallejo, California
Los Angeles, California
Zihuatenejo, Mexico
Balboa, Canal Zone
Puerto Vallarta, Mexico
Los Angeles, California
Vancouver, British Columbia
Portland, Oregon
Vallejo, California

1985 — J.M. Keever, master
Vallejo, California
Long Beach, California
Lahaina, Hawaii
Guam, Marianas Islands
Hong Kong
Manila, Philippines
Naha, Okinawa
Honolulu, Hawaii
Vallejo, California

1986 — J.M. Keever, master
Vallejo, California
Lahaina, Hawaii
Tonga Islands
Sydney, Australia
Brisbane, Australia
Suva, Fiji Islands
Lautoka, Fiji Islands
Apia, Western Samoa
San Diego, California
Santa Barbara, California
Vallejo, California

1987 — J.M. Keever, master
Vallejo, California
Honolulu, Hawaii
Cebu, Philippines
Singapore

Hong Kong
Kobe, Japan
Yokohama, Japan
Vallejo, California

1988 — J.M. Keever, master
Vallejo, California
Long Beach, California
San Jose, Guatemala
Balboa, Canal Zone
Curaçao, Dutch West Indies
Cartegena, Colombia
Callao, Peru
Valparaiso, Chile
Mazatlan, Mexico
Guaymas, Mexico
Cabo San Lucas, Mexico
San Diego, California
Long Beach, California
Vallejo, California

1989 — J.M. Keever, master
Vallejo, California
Lahaina, Hawaii
Suva, Fiji Islands
Sydney, Australia
Noumea, New Caledonia
Honolulu, Hawaii
Seattle, Washington
Vallejo, California

1990 — J.M. Keever, master
Vallejo, California
Long Beach, California
Lahaina, Hawaii
Saipan, Marshall Islands
Bitung, Indonesia
Hong Kong
Guam, Marianas Islands
Kona-Kailua, Hawaii
Vallejo, California

1991 — J.M. Keever, master
Vallejo, California
Zihuatenejo, Mexico

Valparaiso, Chile
Punta Arenas, Chile
Buenos Aires, Argentina
Montevideo, Uruguay
Puerto Angel, Mexico
Mazatlan, Mexico
San Diego, California
Vallejo, California

1992 — J.M. Keever, master
Vallejo, California
Honolulu, Hawaii
Tonga Islands
Sydney, Australia
Cairns, Australia
Majuro, Marshall Islands
Honolulu, Hawaii
Seattle, Washington
Astoria, Oregon
Vallejo, California

1993 — J. Johnson, master
Vallejo, California
Long Beach, California
Lahaina, Hawaii
Cabo San Lucas, Mexico
Long Beach, California
Sitka, Alaska
Glacier Bay, Alaska
Prince William Sound,
  Alaska
Juneau, Alaska
Ketchikan, Alaska
Eureka, California
Vallejo, California

1994 — B. Butterfield,
  master
Vallejo, California
Honolulu, Hawaii
Pusan, Korea
Vladivostok, Russia
Kodiak, Alaska
Seattle, Washington

Vallejo, California
1995 — P. Bonebakker,
  master
Vallejo, California
Nawiliwili, Hawaii
Hilo, Hawaii
San Francisco, California
Mazatlan, Mexico
Cabo San Lucas, Mexico
San Diego, California
Coos Bay, Oregon
Vallejo, California

1996 — J.M. Keever, master
Vallejo, California
San Diego, California
Long Beach, California
Cabo San Lucas, Mexico
Seattle, Washington
Vallejo, California

SUPERINTENDENTS:

1930-34 — Emile Topp
1934-37 — R.C. Dwyer
1937-40 — N. Nichols
1940-47 — C.B. Mayo
1947-55 — R.M. Ihrig
1955-65 — H.E. Reighter
1965-71 — F.T. Williamson
1971-72 — E.C. Miller
1972-83 — J.P. Rizza
1983-90 — J.J. Ekelund
1990-96 — M.E. Lyons
1996   J.A. Aspland

Appendix C
Statistical Data

JAMESTOWN

Type	Sloop
Gross Tonnage	1,150
Length (overall)	163' 6"
LBP	157' 6"
Beam	35' 0"
Depth	16' 2"
Complement	186
Armament	4 8"
	18 32-pounders
Masts	3
Rig	Ship

GOLDEN STATE
(ex-*California State*, ex-*Henry County*, ex-*Lake Fellowship*)

Length Overall	261 feet
LBP	251 feet
Beam	43' 6"
Depth	28' 2"
Gross Tonnage	2,592
Net Tonnage	1,613
Disp. Tonnage	4,000
at 17 ft. draft	3,985
Normal draft	17 feet

Range	10,000 miles at 9 knots
Speed	9.5 knots at 72 rpm
	(max 81)
Fuel capacity	1,107 tons
Pitch	13 ft. 7 1/2 in.
Engine type	Triple Expansion
Cylinder and stroke	21-35-59x42
Horsepower	1,500
Boilers	2
Type	Scotch
Crew:	12 officers
	132 cadets
	16 crew
Equipment:	4 24-foot whaleboats
	2 28-foot whaleboats
	2 26-foot motor whaleboats
	2 16-foot wherrys
	1 20-foot dinghy
	1 36-foot motor launch

GOLDEN BEAR I [1]
(ex-*USS Mellena* AKA-32).

Mar. Comm. Design	S4-SE2-BE1
Gross Tonnage	6200 tons
Net Tonnage	2742

---

[1]   These characteristics are as of August 14, 1961, after several modifications had been made to accommodate the vessel to service as a training ship.

Displacement, full	7080 tons
Displacement, light	4029
Ballast in ship	474 tons
Length overall	424' 2-1/8"
Length on waterline	400 feet
LBP	399' 0-15/16"
Beam	58' 0-1/8"
Depth, molded	37' 4-3/4"
Draft	15 feet, 6 inches (loaded).
Designed by	Joslyn & Ryan, Naval Architects of San Francisco.
Built by	Walsh Kaiser, Inc., Providence, Rhode Island.
Propulsion	Turboelectric.
Boilers	Wickes, two.
Horsepower	6,000
Propellers	Two.
Maximum speed	17.5 knots.
Maximum sea speed	17.5 knots.
Economical speed	15 knots
Cruising speed	12 knots.
Fuel capacity	9,500 barrels.
Range	12,000 miles.
Range at max. speed	10,070 miles.
Fuel Consumption	7 barrel/nautical mile.
Water consumption	10,000 gallons/day (domestic).
	7,000 gallons/day (boiler).
Water capacity	70,000 gallons.
Evaporator capacity	20,000 gallons per day.
Crew	25 officers.
	28 cooks and stewards.
	215 students.
Radio Call Letters:	KIYG

GOLDEN BEAR II
(ex-*Crescent City*, ex-*Del Orleans*)

LOA	492 feet
LBP	465
Beam	65' 6"
Depth	39' 6"
Load Draft	25' 6"
Displacement	14,210 tons
Deadweight	8,710
Gross Tonnage	8,300
Net Tonnage	5,100
Speed (maximum)	18.7 knots
Service speed	16.5 knots
Maximum H.P.	8,600
Normal H.P	7,800
Main Engines	General Electric turbine, single screw.
Boilers (2)	Babcock and Wilcox

GOLDEN BEAR III
(ex-USNS *Maury*)

Builders:	Bethelehem, Sparrows Point, Baltimore, Md.
Displacement:	8,810 tons light 15,821 ton full load
Length:	449 5/6 feet (152.4 m) oa
Beam:	72 feet (22.0 m)
Draft:	30 1/2 feet (9.3 m)
Propulsion:	2 diesels (Transamerica Delaural Enterprise R5-V16); 25,000 bhp; 1 shaft
Speed:	21 knots
Range	18,000 n. miles at 20 knots
Crew (*Maury*)	56 civilian + 32 Navy (3 officers + 29 enlisted) + 20 scientists

APPENDIX D
THE SHIPS AFTER TRAINING

JAMESTOWN

The Sloop of War *Jamestown* had a long career after her service as a California State training ship. It seemed that each time the Navy decommissioned the ship a new use for her was discovered and she was recommissioned. Following her decommissioning on October 7, 1879 she remained idle at Mare Island until May 8 of the following year. Then she was recommissioned and sent to Sitka, Alaska for the combined purpose of surveying the harbor and protecting American interests. In 1881 she sailed the Pacific, again providing an American presence until September 21 when she was decommissioned in San Francisco.

Her days as a school ship were not over. She was once more fitted out as an apprentice training ship for the Navy and recommissioned on February 14, 1882, proceeding to the Atlantic seaboard via Cape Horn. In this capacity she sailed the Atlantic, with voyages to the West Indies and Spain. On August 31, 1888 she was decommissioned at Norfolk.

It was to be a short respite. On April 13, 1889 the *Jamestown* was recommissioned and cruised to France and the West Indies with apprentices. After three years of similar voyages she was decommissioned at Norfolk on September 6, 1892. On September 9 of that year she was transferred to the Treasury Department for Marine Hospital Service and quarantine purposes in Hampton Roads. There she served until she was returned to the Navy Department. She was destroyed by fire on January 3, 1913 at the Norfolk Navy Yard. She was 69 years old.

GOLDEN STATE

The *Golden State*, ex-*California State*, ex-*Henry County,* ex-*Lake Fellowship* languished in the Reserve Fleet at Suisun Bay until 1948. Sold to Panormetis, a Greek steamship company, she was renamed *Isle of Patmos*. She operated under the flag of that nation until 1952 when Navebras S.A. (Comercio de Petrolo) of Rio de Janeiro bought

Circa 1949, this photo shows the former Golden State *as the* Isle of Patmos. *Credit Institute for Great Lakes Research, Bowling Green State University.*

the ship, renamed her *Santa Rosa* and placed her under Brazilian registry. The ship was then sold to Transmaritima and remained under the Brazilian flag and with that owner until 1963 when she no longer appears in the standard references (Lloyds and American Bureau of Shipping Registers). One can only guess at the final fate of the ship, sometime after 1963, when at the age of 43 she was no longer usable.

GOLDEN BEAR I

The ex-*Mellena*, was sold for scrap shortly after returning to the Suisun Bay Reserve Fleet.

GOLDEN BEAR II

The ex-*Crescent City*, ex-*Del Orleans*, is in the Suisun Bay Reserve Fleet. At the time of this writing (1996), there are inquiries from a group in Oakland, California who are interested in converting her into a museum to be berthed at Jack London Square in that city.

BIBLIOGRAPHY

Bunker, John Gorley. *Liberty Ships, The Ugly Ducklings of World War II.* The United States Naval Institute, Annapolis, Maryland: 1972.

"Carries 'Bids' to World Fair," *Oakland Tribune*, Nov. 23, 1936.

Chapelle, Howard I. *The History of American Sailing Ships.* W.W. Norton & Company, Inc. New York: 1935.

"Destroyer Nears S. F. Plague Ship," *San Francisco Examiner*, February 13, 1936.

Dictionary of American Naval Fighting Ships. Vol. III. U.S. Government Printing Office. Washington, D.C.: 1968

Dodson, Bennett M., Lt. (j.g.). "The California Nautical School." *U.S. Naval Institute Proceedings*, May, 1940.

Fuerstenberg, Holly E. "A Study on the Privatization of the California Maritime Academy." May 22, 1993. Submitted to Dr. John Bray, PA 396 Graduate Project, Golden Gate University.

Goldberg, Mark H. *Caviar & Cargo.* The American Merchant Museum Foundation, Kings Point, New York: 1992.

"The 'Jamestown'." *Daily Alta California* 29 Nov 1875.

"The 'Jamestown'." *Daily Alta California* 11 Apr 1877.

"The 'Jamestown'." *Daily Alta California* 28 Nov 1877.

"The 'Jamestown' in Port — Commander Glass Reports to the Supervisors." *Daily Alta California* 24 Sep 1876

"The Last of the 'Jamestown'." *Daily Alta California* 2 Mar 1879.

Moser, Brandon. *Fifty Years at Morrow Cove.* Panic! Productions. Vallejo: 1993.

"Our Training Ship, 'Jamestown'." *Daily Alta California* 15 Feb 1877.

Perlman, David. *The San Francisco Chronicle.* "At Sea With the Pollywogs." Thursday, Jan. 30, 1964.

"Plague Ship Quarantined After Arrival," Panama-American, February 16, 1936. p. 1, 14

Robberson, E.L. "Merchant Marine Cadets." *Our Navy, 1940.*

"Serum Reaches Death Ship." *San Francisco Chronicle.* February 13, 1936, p.1.

Smith, Susan. *NOAA's Fishery Research Laboratory at Tiburon: History of the Site and Present Activities.* August 1982, National Marime Fisheries Service.

"Success of the First Experiment of the Training Ship." *Daily Alta California* 27 Aug 1876.

"The Training Ship." *Daily Alta California* 12 Nov 1875.

"The Training Ship." *Daily Alta California* 28 Nov 1875.

"The Training Ship." *Daily Alta California* 11 Feb 1876.

"The Training Ship." *Daily Alta California* 7 Mar 1876.

"The Training Ship." *Daily Alta California* 9 Apr 1876.

"The Training Ship." *Daily Alta California* 16 Apr 1877.

"The Training Ship Abolished." *Daily Alta California* 2 Feb 1879.

"Training Ship Cadets Obtain Shore Leave," *Panama-American*, February 22, 1936.

"The Training Ship Fees to Be Abolished." *Daily Alta California* 21 Nov 1876.

"Union Group Protests Schoolship Appointment," *San Francisco Examiner*, May 6, 1937.

Index

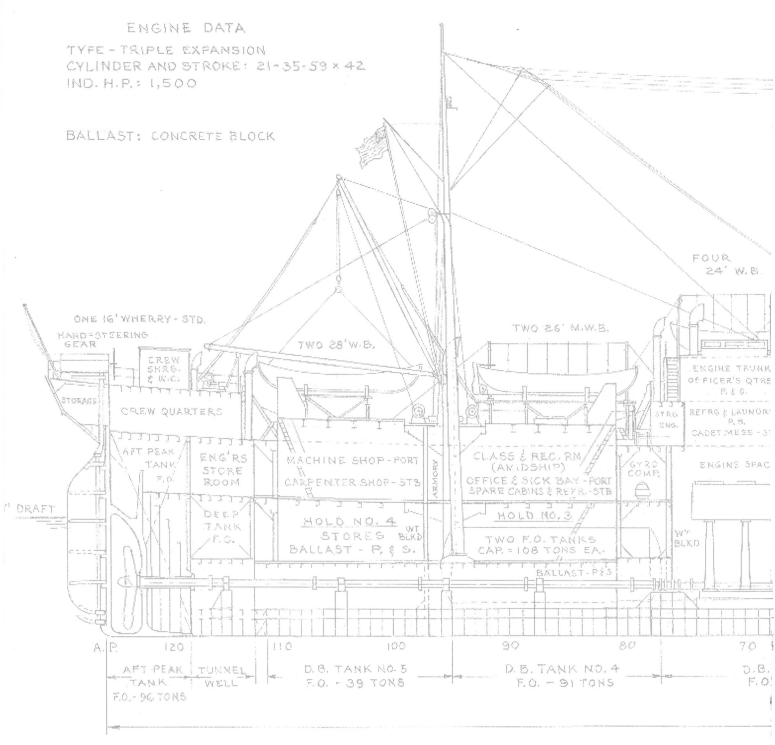

ENGINE DATA

TYPE - TRIPLE EXPANSION
CYLINDER AND STROKE: 21-35-59 × 42
IND. H.P.: 1,500

BALLAST: CONCRETE BLOCK

ONE 16' WHERRY - STD.
HAND-STEERING GEAR

FOUR 24' W.B.

TWO 28' W.B.

TWO 26' M.W.B.

CREW SHRS. & W.C.

ENGINE TRUNK
OFFICER'S QTRS.
P. & S.

STORAGE

CREW QUARTERS

REFRG & LAUNDRY
P. S.
CADET MESS - 3'

STRG
ENG.

AFT PEAK TANK F.O.

ENG'RS STORE ROOM

MACHINE SHOP - PORT

CARPENTER SHOP - STB

CLASS & REC. RM.
(AMIDSHIP)
OFFICE & SICK BAY - PORT
SPARE CABINS & REFR. - STB

GYRO COMP.

ENGINE SPACE

ARMORY

" DRAFT

DEEP TANK F.O.

HOLD NO. 4
STORES
BALLAST - P. & S.

WT BLKD

HOLD NO. 3

TWO F.O. TANKS
CAP = 108 TONS EA.

W° BLKD

BALLAST - P.&S.

A.P.   120   110   100   90   80   70

AFT PEAK TANK
F.O. - 96 TONS

TUNNEL WELL

D.B. TANK NO. 5
F.O. - 39 TONS

D.B. TANK NO. 4
F.O. - 91 TONS

D.B.
F.O.

IN